WOMEN AND CHILDREN FIRST
The Fiction of Two World Wars

WOMEN AND CHILDREN FIRST

The Fiction of Two World Wars

by

MARY CADOGAN AND
PATRICIA CRAIG

LONDON
VICTOR GOLLANCZ LTD
1978

© Mary Cadogan and Patricia Craig 1978

ISBN 0 575 02418 6

Printed in Great Britain at
The Camelot Press Ltd, Southampton

ACKNOWLEDGEMENTS

The authors and publishers would like to thank the following for permission to reproduce the extracts and illustrations indicated below:

Faber and Faber Ltd for the quotations on pages 111 and 159 from *Collected Poems of Louis MacNeice*.

David Higham Associates for John Pudney's 'For Johnny' on page 186.

The Executors of the Estate of C. Day Lewis, Jonathan Cape Ltd, and the Hogarth Press for the quotation on page 188 from *Collected Poems of C. Day Lewis* (1954).

George Allen & Unwin Ltd, for the quotation from 'Autumn 1939' by Alun Lewis on page 273.

IPC Magazines Ltd for illustrations from *The Gem, The Union Jack Library, Woman's World Library, The Magnet* and *The Schoolgirls' Own Library* and *Home Chat* on pages 28, 30, 43, 84, 69 and 163.

Hodder & Stoughton Ltd for the illustration from W. E. Johns's *Biggles—The Rescue Flight* on page 86.

Oxford University Press for the illustration on page 118 by Victor Ambrus to *Flambards* by K. M. Peyton (1966).

Macmillan Ltd for the illustration on page 121 by Alexy Pendle to *Mademoiselle* by Geraldine Symons (1973).

Mirror Group Newspapers for the 'Jane' illustration on page 172 by Norman Pett (1940).

The Hamlyn Group for the illustration on page 219 by Thomas Henry for *William Does His Bit* by Richmal Crompton (1941).

Routledge & Kegan Paul Ltd for the illustration on page 224 by Irene Williamson to *Mary Plain Lends a Paw* by Gwynedd Rae (1949).

William Collins Ltd for the illustration on page 249 by Marjorie Gill to *When the Siren Wailed* by Noel Streatfeild (1974).

Victor Gollancz Ltd for the illustration on page 266 by Faith Jacques to *Carrie's War* by Nina Bawden (1973).

CONTENTS

ILLUSTRATIONS

INTRODUCTION

Women and Children First is concerned with the experiences of British women and children in the two major wars of the twentieth century, as presented in contemporary and retrospective fiction. We have occasionally digressed from this theme in order to give a fuller picture of the social background, and to indicate how various literary forms were developed.

In wartime, of course, society tends to be divided into two groups: those who fight and those who do not. Women and children, although generally classed as non-combatants, were forced into a degree of participation in the wars of 1914 and 1939. Their rôles have been accurately described or bizarrely fantasized in a variety of fiction from magazine stories to serious literature. We have given some emphasis to popular and ephemeral writing, as this illustrates what most people felt, or were expected to feel, at the time. For instance, in romantic novels and women's-magazine fiction, successful authors rarely lost sight of their perennial theme of love, ultimately requited, after complications arising from temporary emotional frustration. Naturally this motif took on a new intensity in the conditions of wartime.

The first world war, at any rate in England, dramatically advanced the interests of women by extending the possibilities for employment, particularly for those of the previously sheltered middle classes. (Nevertheless, when the war ended women were subjected to propaganda urging them to return to the domestic environment.) The lives of young girls changed more slowly. They were not encouraged to take an active part in the war, apart from the proverbial sock-knitting and shirt-sewing for soldiers. However, women's new independence sometimes resulted in an easing of restrictions in home life for girls, and eventually led to better educational opportunities between the wars.

For boys, of course, the first world war brought about not so much a change in status as in conditions and environment.

They had already been conditioned by unrealistic, high-flown adventure fiction written before 1914 to volunteer themselves as soldiers prepared to die for their country and the empire. Maturity, for many boys just out of school, came rapidly, with the end of idealism after their precipitation into the nightmare of the trenches.

Several chapters on children's fiction provide an interesting parallel to attitudes and developments in wartime writing for adults. These stories also give a view of war that is simplified but not necessarily distorted. When the second world war began in 1939, younger children expected to participate than in 1914. At first through lively, mass-media propaganda, and then through air-raids, the war had a radical effect on the lives of children of both sexes. Young girls as well as boys helped vigorously with the work of civil defence, the junior services, civic restaurants, etc.

As far as women were concerned the fiction of the second world war largely reflected the pattern of 1914–1918. Official propagandists and popular novelists joined forces to urge housewives out of their homes into war work of incredible diversity and challenge. Then, when the war ended, the media began once again to harp on traditional concepts to encourage women to give up ideas of independence and ambitions unrelated to the domestic sphere. The settings in factories, service camps and government ministries had been merely topical; in light fiction they did not persist for long after the second world war, when, of course, with the demobilization of the army, many women workers were made redundant. Romantic writers were especially responsive to the pressures of social conformism. As a popular figure, the little man of the 1940s, a character who embodied British tolerance, good nature and independence of spirit, was succeeded in the 1950s by the little woman whose sole function was to make the home happy.

In the course of the last twenty years much of the standard imagery of both wars has been re-evaluated in the light of current attitudes, and presented in a way that directly relates it to the present. As a subject for fiction and poetry (as well as film and television) the world wars have acquired an extraordinary persistence and vitality. In the chapters dealing with retrospective fiction we have tried to show how past and present can interact to good effect.

From the vast body of literature connected with the wars, it has been necessary to concentrate, more or less, on books especially relevant to our theme. There are many novels in which the wars are used to account for an absence, a death, a twist of fortune or the existence of a set of circumstances crucial to the author's purpose; but in several of these cases we have decided that war, as a theme, is too tenuous to justify their inclusion in *Women and Children First*. This book is about British women and children but it has occasionally been necessary to mention stories set in the occupied countries in order to draw parallels or point contrasts. In occupied Europe, of course, the war reduced many women and children to the status of victims. In England their counterparts experienced the effects of enemy action, but escaped the extreme forms of repression and persecution; 'atrocity' themes, therefore, are outside the scope of this study.

Two other important groups of fiction have fallen outside our range: the 'social-realist' novels of the 1930s and the novels of straight action—the hard-hitting, raw or thundering accounts of the more dramatic aspects of army life. The former has little connection with the actual conditions of wartime; and the latter, though its treatment of women characters would bear examination, is largely concerned with technical issues.

We should like to thank Alex and Teresa Cadogan and Jeffrey Morgan for their help and encouragement; also Mrs Dorothy Harrison, Mr Norman Wright and Mr William Thurbon for information and advice; and the Librarian and staff of the Beckenham Public Library, the Librarians of the London Old Boys' Book Club and Miss M. McKenna.

MARY CADOGAN
PATRICIA CRAIG

WOMEN AND CHILDREN FIRST
The Fiction of Two World Wars

I

THE TREACHEROUS YEARS

Tension and Transition from 1900 to 1914

. . . to take it all now for what the treacherous years were all
the while really making for and *meaning* is too tragic for any
words.

Henry James, *Letters*

ALTHOUGH THE EDWARDIAN era is no longer regarded as
a lost golden age, a remote and tarnished glamour still attaches
to the years that preceded the first world war. There was an
apparent social stability which the shake-ups of the Boer war
and the challenges of radical scientific and political thought
had not dispelled. Victorian ideas of worth and respectability
were in the process of being played out; the fashionable tone
was knowing, glossy and sophisticated. With the beginning of
the new century had come an expansive sense of modernity
and progress.

Many women, however, found that for them conditions and
standards were slow to change. Those from the working class
still had no alternative but to accept appallingly paid menial
work while middle- and upper-class women were discouraged
from undertaking professional jobs. Some openings existed for
voluntary work; intelligent women campaigned for the vote,
and for better educational and career opportunities. On the
whole, however, they were expected to centre their lives on the
home and they were still restricted by rigid social conventions.

In *A College Girl* (1913) and *The Independence of Claire* (1914)
and several other novels Mrs George de Horne Vaizey endorsed
the popular view that economic and spiritual independence for
women was illusory, and that fulfilment could come only
through marriage. Her lively, ambitious heroines are presented
sympathetically but the point is always eventually made that
careers and feminine respectability are almost mutually
exclusive. There is a persuasive elegance about Mrs de Horne

Vaizey's stories, as well as a kind of fatalistic innocence that was largely to disappear from popular fiction by the end of the first world war. Then, of course, many young women realized that they were ill-equipped to support themselves but that their prospective husbands and providers had been killed off in the war.

Other writers tackled more lightheartedly the theme of women who wanted to work, but their conclusions were usually similar to those of Mrs Vaizey. As early as 1899 Mrs C. N. Williamson produced *The Newspaper Girl*; this is a brisk, perceptive account of an American heiress's attempt to live incognito in London and to maintain herself on her earnings as a journalist. Lucille Chandler's success is only partial, and mainly due to the support that she is given by the enamoured Sir Griffith Knight, an MP who is also the editor of a prominent newspaper. And of course when Lucille tires of being 'a penny-a-liner journalist girl' she is immediately able to become Lady Knight. In effect, if not in tone, Mrs Williamson is echoing one of Mrs Vaizey's typical story endings: 'Yes, she will be happy—she has found a good man to take care of her!'

An extraordinary number of pre-1914 novels explore the question of feminine struggles for independence. In *Where Angels Fear to Tread*, which at first appears to be a comedy of morals and manners, E. M. Forster relates the disappointing results of one woman's escape from a repressive environment. The story develops into a fascinating complex of challenge and response. There is an unusual awareness of hidden feelings and relationships which is expressed occasionally through images that remain in the mind of the reader long after the plot has unfolded. Lilia Herriton has neither the innocence nor the intelligence that characterize many fictional heroines who want to break away from restricting circumstances. 'Her one qualification for life was rather blousy high spirits.' She is an embarrassment to the in-laws with whom she lives in respectable Sawston and at the age of 33, after being a widow for some years, is on the point of contracting an unsuitable engagement with a man who has 'the knack of being absurd in public'. To avoid this Lilia is shipped off to Italy for a year by her husband's family. It is there that she decides to change the meaningless pattern of her life by marrying an Italian, twelve years her junior, whom she hardly knows. Gino Carella has no profession and the Herritons are convinced he is after her money. Worse still, perhaps, in the eyes of the Sawston relations, he is the son of a dentist. Rejected by her in-laws because of this impulsive marriage, Lilia at first rejoices in severing her connections with the restraints and social pressures that they represent.

However, realization soon sets in that her new state, instead of bringing freedom, has become narrower than the life she has abandoned. (Gino is not consciously cruel: there is 'his infidelity' but Lilia's isolation results from his acceptance of the Italian tradition of husbands having separate interests and activities from their wives. He enjoys the male society of the cafés; *she* has no friends, and few inner resources.) Ironically Sawston with its bourgeois associations becomes a symbol of liberality.

Lilia's insufficiency is only too credible against the social background of 1905, when *Where Angels Fear to Tread* first appeared. Realism, however, is conspicuously lacking in Warwick Deeping's *The Pride of Eve* (1913). The overt theme of the book is sociological, but Eve Carfax's efforts to achieve independence through an artistic career are elaborated merely in order to demonstrate their futility. The author's main preoccupation is with what he calls 'wonder' and 'nature'; but only his leading characters are in touch with these, and their sensitivity is thrown into sharp relief by the materialism of the 'over-sensed and under-bodied neurotics' who form the supporting cast. James Canterton, the hero, is characterized as progressive but he is in fact nothing more than a quirky reactionary with frustrated élitist desires. His passion is for gardens and appropriately the book is full of overblown flowery images. (Even his head gardener is called Lavender.) James's first meeting with the youthful Eve takes place in his 'rosery' where she has come to sketch. Of course she is a 'flowerlike' figure, and the dilations of her nose, throat and bosom in response to the beauty of James's roses mark her down immediately as his spiritual mate. (Spiritual is the operative word because James already has a wife who is a grotesque caricature of the well-to-do committee woman who at least tries to make a constructive contribution to society.)

Gertrude Canterton is abused in a series of narrative clichés. Just as the reader begins to wonder how 'a big man with big views' like James ever became involved with 'this fussy, sallow-faced, fidgeting egotist' it is pointed out that he was trapped into marriage by his own idealism. Words like 'magic' and 'mystic' that James misuses so liberally do not apply, at any rate in his estimation, to the general run of women, as he confides to Eve:

'What I mean is that the average woman seems a cad when she is compared to the average man. . . . They haven't the bigness of men—the love of fair-play.'
    Her eyes brightened to his. 'I know what you mean. If I described a girls' school to you——'
    'I should have the feminine world in miniature.'
    'Yes. The snobbery, the cult of convention, the little sneaking jealousies, all the middle-class nastiness.'

Despite this black-legging against her own sex and class Eve does try to strike out on her own in London. Here she meets with more lurid versions of the difficulties that H. G. Wells's Ann Veronica encountered. (*The Pride of Eve* contains several echoes of Wells's much more convincing story.) Associations with suffragettes who appear mentally unbalanced, the sexual attentions of vulgar men and her inability to scrape a living by selling her drawings force Eve back on James's protection. At this point Warwick Deeping begs the question that Wells pursues to its logical realization in *Ann Veronica*: in the context of *The Pride of Eve* it is impossible for a married man and a young girl to live together without offending the society whose conventional values they are supposed to have rejected. Of course James and Eve are *not* inwardly free, so the author resolves the difficulty by making it clear that they are simply going to be 'big children' together. James is always eulogizing about the human body, because it is after all closely related to the animals, flowers and fairies that he admires so much. But 'the god in him was master of the beast'; he has no physical desire for Eve although he is supposed to be in love with her. Fortunately for him Eve's eyes alone 'could quench all the thirsts of his manhood'. Eve's womanhood is thus of course effectively negated. The basic dismissal of her right to sexual fulfilment and motherhood highlights the bogus nature of the quasi-liberal tone which the text frequently assumes. The acceptance, however convoluted, of a double standard of morality for men and women is still there.

At least the unnatural relationship of James and Eve *did* keep the book from suffering the fate of *Ann Veronica*. When Wells's novel was published in 1909 it was considered sufficiently shocking to be banned from many circulating libraries. Ann's departures from convention include suffragist activities for which she is imprisoned, and her serious and lasting relationship with a man who is not at first able to marry her. These are the logical outcome of her particular search for independence. Wells's development of this theme is naturally rational rather than romantic; for the modern reader there are no offensive excesses and *Ann Veronica* avoids the vulgarity of an ostensibly moral story like *The Pride of Eve* which is actually shot through with suppressed sexuality.

Ann Veronica conveys more potently than most Edwardian heroines the aspirations and frustrations of an intelligent and reasonable young woman who is at odds with the society in which she lives. Despite her more clearly defined capacities, however, Ann was no more able to support herself than Warwick Deeping's uninspiring Eve or Mrs Vaizey's thwarted career girls.

Dorothy Richardson's novels underline the association of feminine independence with a squalid, boarding-house type of existence. Young girls, living around 1900, provide their visitors with soup at 'twopence a packet' and deprecate 'the sheltered life' that they have given up. The central character of the twelve volumes of *Pilgrimage* (1915–38) begins as a governess but later becomes a dentist's receptionist. *Pilgrimage* has been criticized on many counts, chiefly for its unrelenting subjectiveness, its lack of form, its persistent transcription of undoctored experience. ('It is just life going on and on,' wrote May Sinclair, in a contemporary review of *Painted Roofs*, 1915.) But there is no more precise or comprehensive evocation of the London of the 1900s. Miriam Henderson, the novelist's intelligent protagonist, is critically aware of current ideologies and general preoccupations. She develops an incisive, stringent faculty of appraisal that makes her intolerant of dissembling and frivolity. She is influenced by the forces of socialism and feminism. Inevitably her expression of the latter takes sometimes a stern and didactic form, but many of her pronouncements have retained their original clarity and relevance: 'The wonders of science for women are nothing but gynaecology'; 'Religion in the world had nothing but insults for women.'

Alongside the business girls in their tight-waisted suits and pancake hats, another type of independent woman was beginning to emerge. The little Chelsea models with their straight fringes and joss sticks and studio flats are a common feature of novels set in the period just before the war. Usually their function is to provide the hero with a form of gratuitous sexual amusement; typically, however, they have an attractive honesty and lack of delusion that give them at least a semblance of equality.

Where feminism and sexual morality overlap in the fiction of this period there is usually an endorsement of the latter. Freedom to experiment with one's erotic leanings was rarely advocated. Custom and the most obvious kind of realistic caution are at work here, of course; the ethical standards of the Victorians had not been seriously undermined, and contraception afforded only rudimentary protection. Where the 'double standard' was denounced, therefore, the onus to reform was put on men. The sexual nature of women was hardly allowed; in this respect the myth of their moral superiority persisted. It seems clear, too, that novelists like Dorothy Richardson were not imaginatively concerned with sex as a motivating force. Of the Edwardians, only Henry James in his later novels acknowledges its power: in Kate Croy and Charlotte Stant he created a prototype for the modern, complex, sexually discriminating heroine. Henry James, in fact, in his novels *The Awkward Age* and *What Maisie Knew*—both written before the death of Victoria—comes near to exemplifying the Edwardian ideal: the circumlocution, the emotional delicacy and gradations of meaning, the confrontation, in one situation after another, of a tainted sensibility with one that is incorruptible.

At quite a different level some contemporary girls' magazines expressed the tensions and contradictory attitudes of the pre-

war years. At this time girls' books tended to be simply pallid
reflections of women's novels; girls were still often regarded as
domesticated and decorous 'little women', though of course
their brothers were allowed to be exuberant, and were given a
completely different kind of fiction. The tone of the *Girl's
Realm* magazine manages to be both progressive and extremely
lady-like. It indicates the type of readership that it endeavoured
to attract: as early as 1903 it is urging readers to consider
'elementary school-teaching as a Profession for Girls. . . . Have
any real ladies—using the term for want of a better one—
attempted the work? The answer is Yes, and with encouraging
success.' This magazine stimulated girls' interest in careers and
better education and never shirked discussion of social
problems. At the same time it urged readers not to neglect
'fresh air, fragrance, flowerlike neatness . . . and the associations
that we like to weave about girls . . .'.

The cheaper 'mill-girl' papers like Lord Northcliffe's *Girls'
Friend*, *Girls' Home* and *Girls' Reader* were more concerned with
entertainment than serious social issues. However, in an attrac-
tively anarchic way their stories conveyed a responsiveness to
new ideas, and a challenge of accepted authority. The constant
debunking of pompous adults, for instance, was bound to
appeal to girl readers who were likely to have just moved on
from elementary school to factory. In the *Girls' Friend*
headmistresses are never allowed to retain their rather tatty
dignity for long. There is a Miss Bellchamber who regularly
falls in love with casual visitors to her school. Made kittenish by
infatuation she confides to one of her prefects: ' "Oh Maudie
dear . . . I declare I feel quite a foolish girl".' This particular
headmistress eventually comes to grief when she tries 'with all
the pent up passion of 39 years—at least' to vamp a bizarre
Japanese prince who comes to see the school, and turns out to
be one of Miss Bellchamber's pupils in disguise. Schoolgirls in
these papers seem to equate feminist progress with the right to
indulge in flirtations. In a series of stories in 1909 Lillie, Millie
and Tillie, 'the three maddest romps of Riddleby School',
never get near the classroom. They are enterprising enough to
go out and about a lot, attending such functions as flower shows
and suffragette meetings, but their main interest is in the male
sex.

There were other lively trends in girls' fiction of the decade before the first world war. Angela Brazil produced *The Third Class at Miss Kaye's* in 1908 and a new exhilaration came into girls' stories: schoolgirl characters were permitted to be more natural and vigorous: 'Let them fizz, poor dears!' And of course the creation of the Girl Guide movement led to a spate of books for girls in which the keynote was enterprise and adventure. In spite of their attractiveness as a fictional subject, however, the Girl Guides had to wait until after the outbreak of war to become accepted by the community. It was only then that girls in uniform suddenly became respectable—even admired—rather than objects of suspicion.

Although many pre-war novelists were concerned with working girls and women, none could have predicted the actual extent of their participation in the first world war. 1914 has been regarded rightly as a point of hiatus in social development in the twentieth century. It is possible to isolate, in the literature of the era immediately before the war, certain indications of changing mores and a gradual adjustment to progressive ideas; but it is only with hindsight, of course, that a moment of transition may be identified.

From the beginning of the twentieth century stories began to appear which predicted hostilities between Britain and Germany. An interesting example which gives prominence to a woman character is *The Coming Conquest of England* by August Niemann. J. H. Freese's English translation was published in 1904 and, because of the book's German origins, it must have been especially disquieting, underlining English fears of German aggressiveness. Britain is berated as the common enemy of Germany, Russia and France, but the exact nature of British perniciousness is not explained beyond the fact that her commercial supremacy cuts across German trading interests. With four million men Germany and Russia strike first through Afghanistan into British India, which they quickly annexe. Hermann Heideck is a German agent in India who hates the British, but inconveniently falls in love with Edith Irwin. She is the wife of a British officer who is shown as an embodiment of decadence: having gambled away his money and possessions he offers to give Edith to a lustful maharajah in settlement of his debts. When Heideck meets Edith she has fled from her husband to the protection of the British commanding officer. Her troubles, however, are not over. The maharajah has been persuaded to put his troops at the disposal of the British and the colonel feels that Edith may have to be handed to him as a goodwill offering: '"Oh, Mr Heideck, you have no idea what regard for so-called good form means for us English people".'

Edith and Heideck plan a future together when her husband obligingly gets killed in the fighting in India and, in an attempt to shorten the war and to help her lover, the Englishwoman betrays her own country and gives Heideck an Admiralty report about the navy's plans of attack. This brings about an interesting conflict of loyalties. Heideck obeys his patriotic impulses and passes the report to the German High Command; but he is so horrified by the fact that Edith has acted like a spy that he renounces her and rushes off to seek honourable death in battle. Edith, apparently having no place in either Germany or England, is driven to suicide. The narrative tone, which had been sympathetic towards the heroine so long as she was cast in the rôle of victim, now becomes extremely condemning. Edith had certainly not been particularly well treated by the British establishment, of course, and there is always something distasteful about the actions of a person who spies, or turns traitor to his own country. *The Coming Conquest of England* makes the point that it is especially dishonourable—in fact disgusting—when the person in question is a woman. Ironically, when the reality of the first world war eventually took over from this kind of fantasy, the two women who achieved lasting fame, or notoriety, in connection with it were indicted as spies. Time and myth have made them into opposite symbols of the traditional rôles of women in time of war: Mata Hari represents seductive betrayal and Nurse Edith Cavell epitomizes resolute loyalty.

Boys, of course, unlike girls and women, were permitted to engage in espionage in fiction published in the decade before the war. For them spying activities could in many instances be associated with pluck and chivalry of the kind that had been celebrated in the epics of Ballantyne and Henty, and in stories with Boer war settings. From the end of the nineteenth century 'better quality' magazines like *Boy's Own Paper*, *Chums* and *The Captain* had been producing fictional heroes of unusual courage and intelligence; but in fact few of the stories are memorable in terms of their characterizations. Occasionally the *BOP* writers were rather maudlin about brave lads whose sense of honour did not evaporate when their lives were threatened. 'His Word His Bond' reports the execution in Paris of 'many communist fighters . . . the wall still bore marks of shot, and fragments of the skin and hair of the victims who were matted to the masonry'. One boy who is about to be shot appeals to the officer commanding the firing squad for permission to go to his mother in order to give her a locket that has been taken from the body of his slaughtered father. Granting the request the officer hopes that the youth will take the opportunity of escaping. But soon '. . . the boy returned and with hasty steps stood against the wall, and faced the soldiers. The first volley tore out his brave little heart . . .'.

In another group of boys' papers attitudes were less intense, though patriotism was just as vigorous. Alfred Harmsworth (later Lord Northcliffe) brought out the *Marvel*, *Boys' Friend* and *Boys' Herald* in the 1890s. These were exciting but wholesome derivatives of the 'blood and thunder' penny dreadfuls that he deplored for their corrupting effect on youthful minds; the new magazines also began to reflect the tension between receptivity to new ideas and fear of change that was prevalent in Edwardian England. Whatever their themes, Northcliffe's authors presented young characters with whom boy readers could find a means for self-identification. These fictional teenagers participated in an exhilarating range of exploits, working as assistants to super sleuths like Sexton Blake, for instance, or simply flourishing as alert and patriotic schoolboys and Boy Scouts.

After the publication in 1903 of Erskine Childers's *The Riddle of the Sands* a recurrent theme in Northcliffe's Amalgamated Press papers was that of Britain's vulnerability to attack. Although it was a work of fiction, Childers's impressive story of espionage and political intrigue was presented as an authentic account of a sequence of factual events which suggested that Britain might at any moment become the victim of German aggression. Worse still, according to Childers, the British government was singularly reluctant to take preventive action. In the preface to *The Riddle of the Sands* it is stated that thanks to the decisive action of Carruthers and Davies (the leading characters), German plans for a lightning invasion of Britain had in this instance been foiled. Childers leaves his readers in a state of acute unease in relation to the British defence authorities' capacity and willingness to counter future attacks: '. . . the information wrought with such peril and labour from the German government, and transmitted so promptly to our own had none but the most transitory effect, if any, on our own policy. On the contrary, some poisonous influence, whose origin still baffled all but a very few, was persistently at work. . . .'

As early as 1897 and 1898 the *Boys' Friend* had published some realistic war stories by Hamilton Edwards, with France and Russia as the enemy nations. (Chesney's 1871 *Battle of Dorking* might have inspired these.) Other stories followed; at first France was cast in the enemy rôle but after the *Entente* the boys'-paper writers settled on Germany as the aggressor. The model for several of these stories was William Le Queux's *The Invasion of 1910*. Before its publication in book form it had been serialized in 1906 in Northcliffe's *Daily Mail*. Field Marshal Lord Roberts collaborated with Le Queux to work out the military possibilities of the German invasion. However, his strategy was modified by Northcliffe, whose aims were not only patriotic but political and commercial: he insisted on alterations that sent the German army through all the main towns of England, in order to boost the sale of the *Daily Mail* in these areas. The invasion almost succeeds: 'London—the proud capital of the world . . . was at last ground beneath the iron heel of Germany! And all, alas! due to one cause alone!— the careless insular apathy of the Englishman himself.' The British army is unready (many units exist only on paper); German ships scuttle themselves at Chatham and the entrances to other naval depots so that the British navy is temporarily rendered ineffective; spies blow bridges all over the country and the invaders are soon looting the banks and grabbing art treasures from the museums. Britain is saved only after desperate resistance on the part of her people, the navy's recovery and colonial intervention. But she is beggared and humiliated.

The tone of Le Queux's adventure is sombrely appropriate to the warnings that it issues. Prophecies of war which appeared in boys' magazines were equally dramatic, but ended with positive victory because, for a juvenile readership, Britain *had* to win. Invasion stories appeared between 1906 and 1914 in

24   THE BEST 3ᴰ· LIBRARY ☞ THE "BOYS' FRIEND" 3ᴰ· LIBRARY. ᴺᴼᵂ ᴼᴺ ˢᴬᴸᴱ·

Please tell your Friends about this Story.

A Powerful War Story — ᴮʸ JOHN TREGELLIS.

BRITAIN'S REVENGE

Illustration to a serial in *The Gem*, 1909

the *Boys' Friend*, *Boys' Herald*, *Marvel*, *Magnet* and *Gem*. Some of the most popular were those written by Sidney Gowing under the pen-name of John Tregellis. His 'Britain Invaded', 'Britain at Bay' and 'Britain's Revenge' appeared first in the *Boys' Friend*; Northcliffe kept up the pressure by reprinting them in the *Gem* and *Marvel* a year or two later. Tregellis produced a second series in 1912 and began a third just before the outbreak of the first world war. Some of his characters were of course boys: 'Sam and Stephen Viliers, two cadets of Greyfriars

School, by a combination of luck and pluck render valuable service to the British army during the great invasion'. Sam and Stephen are active on land, on sea and in the air. Their flying exploits might well have been stimulated by the publication in 1908 of H. G. Wells's world catastrophe story, *War in the Air*, but Wells's conclusions about the British government's attitude towards defence were then certainly not in accord with those of Erskine Childers, William Le Queux and Lord Northcliffe:

... Her rulers could have kept the whole population learning and exercising up to the age of eighteen, and made a broad-chested and intelligent man of every British subject in the islands, had they given the resources they spent in war material to the making of men. Instead of which they waggled flags at him until he was fourteen, incited him to cheer and then turned him out of school. ...

As well as fiction centred on catastrophe the Amalgamated Press boys' magazines produced accounts of conflicts of will between German and British partisans. Kaiser Wilhelm has to contend with Sexton Blake, who is called in from time to time to help out British Intelligence. Though shrewd and resourceful the German emperor is no match for the detective. One of their most interesting encounters is related in the *Union Jack* of 15 August 1908: 'The Case of the Naval Manœuvres'. Blake is surprised to see that the kaiser is watching British naval manœuvres in the North Sea, from a German airship. (British unpreparedness again.) He discovers that Germany plans, in the event of war, to overrun the Shetland Isles as a base for the invasion of Britain. Realizing that the emperor's presence in the area of the manœuvres could spark off hostilities between the two countries, Blake takes him prisoner and conveys him to London. A sequence of exciting incidents follows: on the train journey from Liverpool to London the kaiser tries to escape and the detective discovers him in an undignified position on top of the moving train. (' "Hardly a comfortable way of travelling, sire!" ' calls out Sexton Blake, nonchalant as ever.) They are soon locked in combat on the train roof. Some time later, the kaiser is rescued by German patriots, then kidnapped

by anarchists who leave him tied up in a burning building—
from which the detective rescues him. By the end of the story
the kaiser is distinctly subdued: 'I have been too ambitious
and I have paid the price . . .'. However, Blake still has to
take him to task for declaring that 'War is a good thing for a
nation. It makes her self-reliant, it keeps her on her guard, so
that she does not get slack . . .'. Blake tersely points out that it
also means that men have to die. The kaiser is so impressed by

EVERY FRIDAY.   Vol. XI. No. 271. New Series.

The 'Union Jack Library.' 1ᴰ·

SEXTON BLAKE'S WEEKLY FOR READERS OF ALL AGES.

A Powerful Novel, Specially Written to Appeal to Readers of all Ages.

·The KAISER'S MISTAKE·

A Stirring Story of Sexton Blake
and a Great Political Crisis.

*Specially written for Readers
of all Ages.*

From the title page of a 1908 *Union Jack*

Blake's reasoning that he decides to operate less aggressively, in
the international sense, in future. He also offers Blake, not for
the first time, a position as head of the German secret service
which the detective categorically declines. (With equal vigour
he rejects the peerage which the prime minister tries to arrange
for him: '. . . the name of Sexton Blake is all that I want'.)
Unfortunately the kaiser is unable to keep his good resolutions
and Blake has to intervene to keep the peace of Europe on other
occasions.

Generally speaking, the inexhaustible resourcefulness and

patriotism of Sexton Blake and other boys'-paper heroes were as inspiriting as they were unlikely. If by 1914 the boys of Britain and the empire were not rearing to go and have a crack at the kaiser it was certainly not the fault of Lord Northcliffe or his authors.

II

'SHE ALSO SERVES WHO SITS AND KNITS'

The Women's View of the First World War

... His blood is in the rose's veins,
  His hair is in the yellow corn.
My grief is in the weeping rains
  And in the keening wind forlorn.
...

The spring will come by Meuse and Marne,
  The birds be blithesome in the tree.
I heap the stones to make his cairn
  Where many sleep as sound as he.
                    Katherine Tynan, 'A Girl's Song'

WOMEN'S PATRIOTIC INSTINCTS were appealed to initially on two levels: they were asked to keep calm and to encourage their menfolk to enlist. The country was not ready at once to take advantage of their offers of practical help. In the early weeks of the war the Voluntary Aid Detachments were told by the War Office that the provision of nursing facilities was already adequate. Fourteen units, however, left at once to take service with the armies of Belgium, France, Russia and Serbia. In Britain, in 1915, women doctors were employed to run hospitals in London (without official status); but the War Office's prejudice against the widespread use of VADs persisted until 1917.

By June 1915, 78,000 women had volunteered for war service in the fields of clerical and shop work, manufacture of armaments, agriculture and transport. Of those who had registered, 1,800 had been given employment. Even encouragement from *The Engineer* (August 1915) failed to allay the nation's fears about women's traditional incompetence. Girls might be able to solder government tins at an 'astonishing rate', and even turn out work 'of which any skilled artisan might feel proud'; but employers were still reluctant to use women in jobs for which they had received no training, and male trade unionists remained hostile for economic reasons. Even when the women's efforts were praised the tone was often grudging. Mr W. T. Massey, speaking at Birmingham in 1915, remarked that much was expected from the men in a time of crisis: 'It is the women who surprise us.'

He might have found their conduct less surprising if he had been able to dissociate the patriotic impulse from the straight-forward desire for paid employment: for the first time, for many women, this had become a practical possibility. By 1918 the number of working women in this country had risen to one-and-a-third million, with 700,000 directly replacing men. (Vera Brittain, *Lady into Woman*, 1953.)

As the propaganda got under way in 1914 women were addressed specifically in their own periodicals and in posters designed to support the recruitment drive. The 'young women of London' were asked:

Is your 'Best Boy' wearing Khaki? If not, don't you think he should be? If he does not think that you and your country are worth fighting for—do you think he is WORTHY of you? Don't pity the girl who is alone—her young man is probably a soldier—fighting for her and her country—and for YOU. If your young man neglects his duty to his King and Country, the time may come when he will neglect you. Think it over—then ask him to JOIN THE ARMY TO-DAY.

Printed in bold letterpress, this was one of the posters that appeared on hoardings in the capital. Its simplified arguments and its use of emotional blackmail are typical of the crude but effective fusion of personal and idealistic motives that formed the basis of the appeal to women. Naturally, 'Women of Britain say—GO'; the famous caption to E. V. Kealey's recruitment poster puts the message at its most terse. Even in Ireland, men's cowardice was condemned indirectly through the use of women as patriotic images. In one Irish poster a wild-haired girl is shown indicating a group of burning buildings, labelled 'Belgium'; the caption is 'Will you go or must I?'

The alleged behaviour of German soldiers in Belgium gave rise to expressions of outrage in the British press. Even *The*

Englishwoman, a sober periodical, was emotionally aroused to the point of joining in the general outcry against the 'unspeakable barbarities of German soldiers'. In October 1914 its editorial spoke of 'the sensuality of male animals who have thrown all restraint to the winds'. Erich Maria Remarque, in his post-war German novel *All Quiet on the Western Front,* mentions the reaction of ordinary German soldiers to one piece of current libel: ' "But there are more lies told by the other side than by us," say I; "just think of those pamphlets the prisoners have on them, where it says that we eat Belgian children. The fellows who write that ought to go and hang themselves. They are the real culprits." '

This kind of realism would hardly have been acceptable in Britain before 1929, when *All Quiet* was published. In the first year of war the horror stories proliferated. 'Atrocity' posters began to appear: in one, a German 'sister' is pouring a glass of water on the ground while a wounded prisoner gasps with thirst. 'There is no woman in Britain who would do it', the capital letters state. 'There is no woman in Britain who will forget it.' The English, of course, treated their prisoners with kindness. 'The German prisoners simply worship the Tommies, and the Tommies are delightful to them,' *The Times* of 9 October 1914 assured its readers.

The cheering, singing and flag-waving that had greeted the declaration of war in August 1914 soon gave way to another impulsive activity: the distribution of white feathers to men who were not in uniform. This was an hysterical gesture that has aroused universal disgust; but for some women apparently it was a natural response to the propagandist exhortations. One of Berta Ruck's more vacuous characters gets the right note of spite and smugness: '. . . "One comfort about being only a woman these days is that one *can* walk about the streets without needing to feel sick with shame that one isn't carrying a rifle or wearing khaki!" ' Another uses righteous indignation to administer a topical rebuff: ' "The idea of *you* having the Face to speak to a lady—*and you not in khaki!*" ' (*Khaki and Kisses,* 1915.)

By November 1914 *The Englishwoman's* own brand of chauvinism is beginning to evolve. 'War is brutal, barbarous, materialistic, whereas women's influence in the world is of the spirit,' it states with complacency. But 'this war is really a war on our part for the maintenance of moral principle as against brute force'—and therefore not essentially opposed to women's spirituality. The journal was enlightened enough, however, to remark on the moral impasse that results when 'whole nations [are] convinced that they are slaying each other upon the highest principles'. On a practical level it endorsed the sensible view of Sydney Webb, who advised unoccupied young women to put themselves through a systematic course of training for social work. (*War and the Workers*, 1914.) For those girls who had managed to find employment, there was advice about clothes: *The Englishwoman* was pleased to note that

> Boot shops, despite the shortage of leather, have managed during these last few months to provide watertight, strong boots for postwomen and 'bus girls because their employers saw the necessity for something better than the high-heeled, brown-paper soled slippers which used to be the only shoes within the means of working girls who could not wear men's heavy boots. . . .

Rules about the appearance of girl workers were laid down quickly. 'If she wears an overall . . . the frock under it must still be neat.' All frivolous tendencies were discouraged: *The Englishwoman* spoke severely of 'gay, flimsy, showy-looking garments, which call forth the censure of their [the workers'] newspaper critics'.

Plainly, a girl's moral standards could be deduced from her taste in dress. This was the crux of the matter especially for strait-laced periodicals like *The Girl's Own Paper and Woman's Magazine*; in February 1917 the author of its leading article spoke out against 'the craze for extravagant and even ridiculous underwear'. Later in the same issue the garments' exotic details are enumerated:

> As an example of the sort of thing that can only be called a national disgrace when indulged in at a time like this, I recently saw knickers, chemises, nightdresses and combinations of pale blue georgette, exquisitely hand-embroidered

with violets and leaves in their natural colouring; wide heliotrope ribbon of superfine quality being run in at the waist and elsewhere, and finished off with huge rosettes, while narrow bands of ermine trimmed neck, sleeves and knee bands.

The tone is that of an outraged headmistress, and certainly the paper's objective was to lay down firm moral guidelines for its readers. The desire to wear flimsy underwear was invested with unethical connotations: 'The blame for the present-time reckless orgy in expensive and unsuitable under-garments lies at the door of that section of womankind that is the least use to the country—the parasite who spends all her time, and a great deal of money (chiefly other people's) in self-indulgence'. It is possible, however, that a secret longing for unpatriotic frilly knickers and petticoats was fostered in the less staunch type of reader by alluring descriptions like the one above.

The 'glorification of under-clothing' was carried on in magazines less sanctimonious than *The Girl's Own Paper*. The line quoted with disgust and exasperation by the anonymous author of 'Publicity in Underwear'—'Nighties to Wear when Zeppelins are Coming'—could only have come from *Vogue*, launched in England in 1916, and quickly displaying the discernment and élan of its American counterpart which had first appeared in 1892. The sales in Britain of American *Vogue* had been affected by the wartime paper shortage and the cuts in non-essential shipping, and this led to the decision to produce an English edition.

Vogue's wartime function was not to promote austerity and self-restraint (that was left to the more overtly Christian publications), but simply to provide an antidote to the general depression and the impoverishment of living standards. (In 1914 American *Vogue*'s circulation in the trenches was second only to that of the *Saturday Evening Post*.) In its more serious moments the magazine took a mildly feminist standpoint: 'In the greatest crisis the world has ever faced woman has more than established her claim to be regarded as a vital part of the machinery outside the domestic sphere'. It was quick to state the only social advance effected by wartime conditions, though its language here is rather sententious: 'War Enlarges the

Horizon for the Educated Girl and The Woman of Ideas and
Modifies Man's Point of View'. But it was the tone of
sophisticated coyness that marked the journal's originality. In
a voice as suggestive as Aubrey Beardsley's in *Under the Hill* it
remarks: 'Nervous people do well to avoid this number; it is
full of thrilling surprises in costumes and hair-raising adventures
in millinery, and its short stories about lingerie are apt to be
just the least bit risqué.' Later, this approach becomes
audacious and irreverent: '*Vogue* is a great believer in the
strengthening of our coast artillery—that's why we are going
to have a page of the best constructed bathing suits we could
find, and during the season they will appear prominently
around the coast'.

It is the artfully ingenuous pose taken to an extreme—as
whimsy, however, it is acceptable because it is completely
knowing: it has astringent undertones. On the surface, it is
simply amusing—and amusement was at a premium. *Vogue*
could mock nationalistic excesses and get away with it: 'a long
row of buttons, which trims the entire front of the costume,
emphasizes the general idea of straight and narrow lines
which is characteristic of the spring silhouette in its patriotic
endeavour.'

Vogue had its own way of encouraging resilience: 'There are
little dances, and rumours—apologetic—of more little dances.
Not all the bishops and county councils in the world can make
us go to bed at twelve-thirty if we wish otherwise.' However, in
November 1916 it did remark somewhat ominously that
'Becoming mourning is a fine art'; and war news became more
prominent as hostilities drew to a close. There were purely
informative articles on 'Fany' (First Aid Nursing Yeomanry),
Voluntary Aid Detachments in France, and the Women's
Land Army (beaming girls in smocks and breeches). Steinlen's
war lithographs were reproduced in the magazine; and in the
issue for late May 1918 a Red Cross nurse, drawn by Porter
Woodruff, appeared on the cover. But *Vogue*'s irrepressible and
therapeutic frivolity was always in evidence. 'There the war
bride is, wondering what on earth she's going to do with her
evenings until the victorious Allies declare a closed season on
the Huns. Till then, she will be one of those things you used to
read about in all the asterisk-illustrated asbestos-bound

novels—A Wife in Name Only!' The point was elaborated a little later: 'It Takes Two to Play a War Wedding March— one plays "Here Comes the Bride", the other, "There Goes the Groom".'

In November 1918 *Vogue*'s editor was realistic enough to concede that 'for many the end of the war must necessarily imply the closing of a stimulating chapter of experiences. . . . Many a chauffeuse in navy blue or military khaki will regret the Mercédès in which she came to have almost a proprietary interest.' And more seriously: 'To many—especially women— the war has brought responsibility and conspicuous service of which peace must necessarily deprive them'. But the magazine was sufficiently affected by current pressures to shirk effective consideration of the issue. 'There are few who would not rather have the men than the men's jobs,' it declared, abandoning principle in favour of a succinct phrase. This little remark in fact is an extremely subtle piece of propaganda—far more subtle than the anti-feminist enthusiasm for 'dear housewife-liness' that was to follow. 'The men's jobs' implies a kind of inborn right; and women's sexuality, femininity and so on are posited covertly as an alternative to usurpation. Then there were the questions of gratitude to the men who had fought, emotional ties, proper renunciation of selfish aims, and all that.

Women on the whole had shown up well in the course of the war; now they were thanked, suitably rewarded with the vote (if they were over 30) and packed off home. (The whole process of encouragement, organization and redundancy was to recur on an even wider scale in the years between 1939 and 1950.) Of course even the most radical feminists didn't expect, or even want, a complete reversal of sex rôles. Naturally those returning soldiers who were fit for work expected to resume the occupations they had left. But pre-war ideas about women's limited capacities had been forcibly modified—and this might have led to adjustments in the national approach to job distribution and training schemes. It didn't. Instead, every known psychological trick was used to persuade the women war workers to relinquish ideas of independence and sexual equality. The magazines took up the chorus: 'The tide of progress which leaves woman with the vote in her hand and scarcely any clothes on her back is ebbing, and the sex is returning to the deep, very deep sea of femininity from which her newly-acquired power can be more effectively wielded.' (*Woman's Life*, February 1920.)

The same magazine stated unequivocally, 'Miss Fluffy Femininity carries off the prizes'. Unlike *Vogue*'s, this type of coyness is merely cloying: it isn't sharp, and it evokes a horrible image of silly and simpering behaviour. Coyness ostensibly in the service of commonsense is the tone adopted most frequently by the popular author Berta Ruck ('whose novels are a challenge to the cult of gloom,' her publishers claimed). Miss Ruck (Mrs Oliver Onions) wrote several stories about the war as it affected the marriage prospects of her leading characters. In *The Bridge of Kisses* (1917) it is the heroine's mother who goes off to work in a soldiers' canteen in France; she leaves her daughter to run the household, look after two small cousins and sort out the romantic complications that arise from wilful innocence.

Berta Ruck is a skilled sentimentalist who uses humour and ruefulness to put across the most conventional ideas of domestic happiness, romantic entanglement and women's innate docility. Her heroines are usually nineteen, high-spirited, moderately frivolous, and deluded in an endearing way about their appearances (they are prettier than they think) and dignity (they have less than they imagine). They are always wistful, charming and divertingly candid. The author's style is effervescent and technically competent.

Berta Ruck is especially good on period details of clothing and idiom and social behaviour. The 'nightie of black-silk voile, patterned with lemon-yellow nasturtiums' that appears in *The Bridge of Kisses* is reminiscent of the garments disparaged by the editor of *The Girl's Own Paper* ('one has met with them in orange georgette'), but Berta Ruck is unequivocally on the side of fashion. When Joey Dale goes shopping with her aunt she is horrified by the idea of 'Aunt Montague's Early Victorian patterns! Couldn't I see them? Prim collars fastened right up to the chin with linen-covered buttons and button-holes. Sleeves down, down to the wrist. I thought of Mollie's shoulder-straps; made of four pink ribbons and a rosette! "And now we will look at some nice thick woollen vests for winter wear," said Aunt Montague.'

The time is the summer of 1916, 'with war-time industry going on all round us, and "quite nice" girls in khaki coats driving Ministry-of-Munitions motor-cars through the thick of the City traffic without turning a hair'. A white banner with scarlet lettering announces that 'England Must Be Fed'. Girls

Friend: 'But I thought Jack was pleased that you were learning to cook for the wounded soldiers?'

She: 'So he was; but last night at dinner he said he hoped—I'd only cook—for the w-wounded G-G-Germans.'

From *The Girl's Own Paper and Woman's Magazine*, August 1915

are being recruited to the Land Army, and this is central to another of Berta Ruck's romances. When Joan Matthews becomes a farmworker (*The Land-Girl's Love Story*; 1918) she discovers a number of fundamental truths about herself and others. Cleaning out a stable is hard work; the city girl is about to give up when she is taken in hand by a supercilious, competent young man who shows her how to do it. Exasperation soon turns to infatuation. With a little help from her friends, Joan makes good: ' "When you're on a man's job you've got to dress the part—you never find a man wearing pink crêpe-de-Chine all day . . .".' The uniform of a land-worker is actually rather becoming:

'I thought you admired pretty frocks.'
'Those suited you too. But in this you're a young Ceres.'
'I'm afraid I've forgotten what those were.'

Berta Ruck's interest in the war is confined largely to appearances: 'I could not help noticing what a tremendous difference there is in every inch between a man who has done any drill at all and a man who has never even learnt to stand to attention'. In *The Bridge of Kisses* Joey's pacifist fiancé Hilary Sykes is treated with would-be subtle contempt; although it should be added that one conscientious objector is presented sympathetically (the story as usual is written in the first person). Hilary calls Joey his 'child-sweetheart' and he wears an 'artistically baggy grey Norfolk jacket'. When he is ordered to appear before a military tribunal he breaks into a diatribe against 'impertinence . . . petty official tyranny. Insidious militarism!' Joey is one of those innocently dense heroines whose feelings, from the first page on, are apparent to everyone but herself. She misinterprets the nature of her regard for the young military bridge-builder even when she is prattling to him about the problems of being engaged:

'. . . What is this man Sykes thinking of? [the bridge-builder asks]. Does he imagine you are in love with him?'
'Oh, no, I told him I wasn't. And he said a child of my age couldn't be expected to know anything about love,' I explained, 'and that he would teach me——'
'Oh, he would, would he?' said the bridge-builder in the most curious voice. 'He hasn't been strikingly successful so far it seems.'
'Oh, but he hasn't started yet,' I explained, thinking how awful it would be when he did. 'You see, he very kindly promised not to bother me with any love-making while father's wound was bad. He did see that I couldn't put up with two kinds of worry at once.'

The heroines of this type of fiction have to remain winsomely asexual, of course: they arouse protectiveness in men but never lust. 'Love' is rarely evoked in terms other than those of the utmost banality:

'It was like living in a world without sunshine.'
. . . 'A world without sunshine, was it? And has her Billy been a little ray of sunshine to her——?'

There is no kissing until the final pages and then it is surrounded with fatuous expressions of bliss: ' "Isn't it wonderful to think we are 'us' at last?" ' Berta Ruck is at her worst when she can't keep her characters physically apart any longer, when humour and gaiety have to give way to an embarrassing note of rapture. But she had left herself no other way to suggest intensity.

Berta Ruck's objective was to provide cosy reassurance and wholesome entertainment. Her fantasy has a homely, cutie-pie basis. She doesn't deal in romantic inflation or suggest lurid passions. She acts as a spokesman for youth in its revolt against stuffiness—but her characters' gestures of defiance are often both covert and superficial in the extreme. One heroine screws herself up to act in a way that doesn't accord with social expectations: she takes it upon herself to *propose*. Spirit and honesty can be directed to no more worthwhile end. Berta Ruck's little women were the forerunners of those that are still flourishing, in one guise or another, in current magazine fiction.

'Helen Zenna Smith' (Evadne Price) was a popular author whose objective, in one trilogy at least, was to shock her readers and disabuse them of complacent, romantic illusions about the first world war. *Not So Quiet* . . . and its sequels, *Women of the Aftermath* and *Shadow Women*, were written in the early 1930s, when interest in the war had assumed a nostalgic or factual-historical bent. The first-person narrator is 'Helen Smith', an ambulance driver in France, who is out to ram home the discrepancy between the cant and the conditions of active service. The method is blunt, brutal, and ferociously expository. Subjective indignation has a corrosive effect, however, and the pile-up of disasters tends towards farce. The end of the war brings no improvement: before the series is finished the middle-class heroine at 31 has become a beggar and a down-

and-out sleeping on the embankment. Social realism, the impulse to tell the truth about war service and its aftermath, has given way to emotional melodrama and a crude bid for the reader's attention.

A typical illustration from a wartime *Woman's World Library*

Nevertheless the details at the beginning of *Not So Quiet . . .* have an ironic validity in relation to the euphemisms they destroy:

'Our ambulance women take entire control of their cars, doing all running repairs and all cleaning.' This appeared in a signed article by one of our head officials in London, forwarded to me by Mother last week. It was entitled 'Our Splendid Women'. I wondered then how many people comfortably reading it over the breakfast table realized what that 'all cleaning' entailed.

The reader's sensibilities are not spared: it entails the removal of pools of vomit, faeces, blood, mud and vermin. 'How we dread the morning cleanout of the insides of our cars, we gently-bred, educated women they insist on so rigidly for this work that apparently cannot be done by women incapable of speaking English with a public-school accent.'

Each aspect of the physical discomfort endured by the drivers is listed ruthlessly. The girls suffer from perpetual cold, they have to eat food that looks like shit and causes vomiting and boils, they are infested with lice, they are stupid from lack of sleep and emotionally shocked from constant exposure to the horrors of death and mutilation. They have to take orders from a sadistic commandant who fills their free time with punishment duties.

Evadne Price's characterization is rudimentary: it works best when it is not inflated with uncontrolled sarcasm. Outspoken, bawdy Tosh, the strapping niece of an earl, is one of the few characters who can be accepted on the author's terms. The lines are heavy but recognizable. With 'The BF', however, and Helen Smith's appalling relatives, the method is akin to caricature. The BF (the girl's name is Bertina Farmer, but the reader knows without being told that the initials stand for Bloody Fool) is refined, gushing and snobbish. So are the elder Smiths of Wimbledon Common and their peer Mrs Evans-Mawnington, whose son Roy gets engaged to Helen (Nell). The author keeps up a constant outcry against hypocrisy, mis-representation, culpable stupidity, one-upmanship and self-delusion. Usually it is the older generation that exhibits the most wanton forms of callousness and self-glorification. (The pattern is repeated in her *Jane* series—see Chapter X—but here the viciousness is modified by an undertone of humour and the effective use of juvenile slang.)

There is no subtlety of emotion or imagery in the trilogy. Its punchball effects are gained from the repeated juxtaposition of angry realism and wartime jargon:

'. . . Once women buckled on their men's swords. Once they believed in that "death-or-glory boys" jingo. But this time they're in it themselves. They're seeing for themselves. . . .
And the pretty romance has gone. War is dirty. There's no

glory in it. Vomit and blood. Look at us. We came out here
puffed out with patriotism. There isn't one of us who
wouldn't go back to-morrow. The glory of the War . . . my
God! . . .'

'Oh, darling, we are doing our bit,' says the BF.

Occasionally, however, a plain statement of protest or disillusion is presented without emotional aggression or self-pity:
'I am 21 years of age, yet I know nothing of life but death,
fear, blood, and the sentimentality that glorifies these things in
the name of patriotism.'

Evadne Price takes a brisk and sensible attitude to changes in
sexual behaviour: '. . . "The biggest harlot or the biggest
saint . . . what the hell does it matter as long as they put up a
decent performance behind the steering-wheel and can keep
their engines clean? You can't get up to much immorality with
dying men, can you?" ' The speaker is Tosh, but the sentiments
accord with the narrative tone. Nell's suburban conditioning is
undermined without difficulty:

'Baynton kissed me on the way back. It was not a platonic
kiss, either. When I ticked him off he said: "Have a heart,
old dear, I'm going up the line to-morrow. I'll probably
be dead mutton before I get a chance to kiss another girl."

'So I let him kiss me again. I have never looked at it in that
light before. . . . How one's outlook changes!'

Promiscuity, however, isn't so much a positive gesture as the
result of lethargy and moral numbness. Casual sex is by no
means condoned: on a practical level it can lead to disease or
abortion; physically it is unsatisfying (at least to the heroine,
now known as Nello) and morally it causes bitterness and self-
denigration. The narrative outrage is simply directed against
the view that can be bothered with concepts like chastity and
monogamy in the face of the more urgent pressures of slaughter
and social disintegration. Sex is a last resort, an illusory
antidote to purposelessness and chronic shock—and even that
may be denied to war heroes like Roy Evans-Mawnington
(now married to Nello), blinded, crippled and castrated, who
tells his mother: '". . . here's your MC—shove it down the
lavatory for me"'.

Roy commits suicide and Nello 'drifts'. The author has attempted to dramatize the effects of war on a generation by the simple device of heaping on to her protagonist as much misery as her deadened sensibility can stand. Nello's misfortunes begin when Tosh dies in her arms, wiped out by a piece of shrapnel. Her beloved younger sister Trix is torpedoed in the Channel. She is persecuted by her relatives. She becomes an assistant cook in France and sees ten of her work-mates killed by a bomb. Her fiancé is mutilated. After their marriage he becomes morose and violent. When he kills himself Nello is censured publicly at the inquest for having driven him to suicide (she hasn't). She lives with a number of arrogant or petulant young men but she is a graceless and resentful courtesan and knows it. She is not equipped to earn a living and this is a further cause for bitterness. 'My parents, being of the independent class, considered it lowering to their social position to have me taught anything useful, such as typing or shorthand.'

At this point the author digresses to define the predicament of ex-war workers, jolted out of their pre-1914 apathy or submissiveness and now a glut on the market. Her remarks are worth quoting at length, since they present clearly an aspect of the current self-assertive, aggressive but ultimately ineffective feminist stance:

... The women refuse to go back to their country villages and towns and their uneventful pre-war existence. They want to keep their jobs or else steal the jobs that rightfully belong to the men who cheated the German guns, and they are determined to get them if they can, by fair means or foul.

... We responded to the call, sentimental, noble, sloppy, doing-our-bit, all uplifted, patriotic and unpowdered, that's how we went into the war—but we emerged a bit different to [sic] what people expected. The glory of war. Bottoms. Don't talk to us women of the glory of war unless you want the bird.

Watch us grab our chance. Grab, grab, grab! You killed sentimentality in us. You can't blame us because we are too selfish to feel pathetic at the sight of an unemployed hero.

What do we care about disabled men out of jobs? Let the government look after them. It promised to. It's not our affair. We refuse to sink into oblivion. . . .

And so on. As a manifesto, this is strangely crude and offensive in tone. It makes no statement that isn't realistic or plausible: but it constitutes a violent, unconsidered reaction to an extreme social condition. In the context of the novel, it appears as a piece of ranting that bursts in from the outside. It is a furious rebuttal of the propagandist appeals to 'dear housewifeliness' (see above) that began as soon as the war ended: as such, its forthrightness has a momentary validity, but it is far from being an objective assessment of the situation, and it doesn't provide a basis for action. It was bound to peter out. In effect, the narrator is behaving like a child who is going to make her parents sorry for being nasty to her. Later in the same novel (*Women of the Aftermath*) the women's failure to 'grab' the 'men's jobs' is explained in the following terms:

Generally speaking, we war women are a failure. Directly the war was over, we had a chance to make ourselves solid in the working market that no other generation has ever had. And what have we done with it? Used it to make things easy for the next generation—our small sisters who were still at school while we were paying so dearly for their freedom. About one in fifty of us has succeeded in securing a permanent future. The truth is, the war made us too restless. We were discontented, disorganized, and unbalanced. A trifle abnormal, too, and lacking a sense of proportionate values. Things moved so swiftly for us during those hectic years from 1914 to 1918, we were left breathless and incapable of plodding amiably along in an amiable groove. Difficult to realize we were babies at the wage-earning business and must crawl before we could walk, and walk before we could run. We started off at a hell of a pace, and came a hell of a cropper in most cases.

The tone is muted, but still embittered. Almost by accident, Evadne Price has caught the sense of isolation that characterized the war generation and the aggression that had to be directed towards some object: first the 'old men' who had caused the war, then the youngsters who had missed it.

The intimations of feminine solidarity, however, are curiously at odds with the method of survival adopted by the heroine: the passive character she assumes in relation to her male 'protectors' is hardly made more palatable by her furious awareness of it. (She pays for her keep by pretending to enjoy the status of a pampered house-pet.) The reader's feelings towards her are bound to remain ambivalent. The elements of her nature are in no sense integrated. Passages like those quoted above have little connection with the image of a kind-hearted, conventional girl presented elsewhere. The poor girl has suffered unmercifully, of course; and each time she attempts to get up she is punched in the face by an author carried away by her own impulse to shock. Nello is allowed one moment of optimism, when she imagines that she might become a flying instructress (in the 1920s and 1930s, flying was a persistent metaphor for liberation); but she crashes her machine, is dragged out barely alive, and left with permanently damaged health and a badly scarred face.

Nello is apparently the victim of circumstances, but in fact the downward trend is predetermined by commercial requirements. The heart-wringing antitheses of destitution and affluence are posited with all the sentimentality of the Victorian pot-boiler. The novels move towards a contrived and mawkish resolution. As a literary starting-off point, the determination to call a spade a bloody shovel has imposed a fundamental limitation. The novels' value lies in their initial outspokenness—but this kind of honesty, like patriotism, is simply not enough.

The *Not So Quiet* . . . trilogy doesn't claim to be anything other than fiction, but it is perhaps significant that it isn't based on actual experience: the author never was an ambulance driver in France. (It is possible that inside knowledge might have modified the narrative vehemence.) This need not detract from its authenticity, of course: the facts were available for assessment by the competent researcher. The experiences of the war workers had been thoroughly documented. The non-fictional accounts of the women's services that appeared during the war were usually factually accurate but extraordinarily biased and reverential in tone. The average Voluntary Aid Detachment, according to Thekla Bowser (*The Story of British V.A.D. Work in The Great War*, 1917), for example, is 'a wonderfully happy little community of workers, who take the trials and the emergencies which come along, in philosophical fashion, as part of the daily routine'. The wounded men are invariably optimistic, 'courageous under their sufferings, unselfish in the extreme'. The women workers are motivated only by 'the love which lies in the hearts of all true women for their dear fighting men'.

It was inevitable that this type of bland propaganda should have provoked ridicule and anger in the post-war years. The women's achievement might have been appraised in more vigorous and realistic terms: in fact the quality of hospital service—the tedium and the unavoidable tensions—is adumbrated by Enid Bagnold in *A Diary Without Dates* (1918). On the curious bureaucratic tendency to confuse efficiency with self-effacement, for instance, the author remarks:

Here I see for the first time grown women trying with all the concentration of their fuller years to be as like one another as it is possible to be.

There is a certain dreadful innocence about them too, as though each would protest, 'In spite of our tasks, our often immodest tasks, our minds are as white as snow.'

And, as far as I can see, their conception of a white female mind is the silliest, most mulish, uncurious, unresponsive, condemning kind of an ideal that a human creature could set before it.

The protagonist apparently stands outside the silliness, recording: 'The ranklings, the heart-burnings, the gross injustices.... Who is to make the only poultice?' But her low-key, sardonic attitude is in keeping with the book's objective: to correct the inflated image of stern, dutiful and selfless hospital volunteers. The VADs were not any less admirable because their members were susceptible to ordinary petty resentments and personal discontent.

A book of pseudo war memoirs, adapted to the paper-back market, was published by Newnes in 1930. The title of this

6d (2½p) novel is simply *W.A.A.C.: The Woman's Story of the War*; and for dramatic effect its author remained anonymous. It is written in the usual drab, unquickened prose of the commercial story, and it contains the requisite quota of spies, shirkers, profiteers, seducers, heroes and victims. It is the curious ambiguity of its feeling that makes this book worth noting: its underlying moral orthodoxy is forcibly reconciled with the surface theme of consummated sexual passion. Quite simply, this is achieved through the author's reiterated statement of the moral deterioration wrought by war. '. . . it seems to me that . . . most of us . . . must in some sort of way have taken leave of our senses—though we afterwards regained them,' the narrator claims. And again: 'Of course the war was to blame. It made some men sexually mad.' Some women, too:

> I got a shock one day.
> Gwen came into my room when I was alone—we were in huts just then—put her arms round my neck, kissed me, and whispered in my ear: 'Connie, I want a man most frightfully.'
> Though I no longer called myself a moral woman . . . I was horrified. Gwen had seemed to me to be so different from other girls I had been meeting, and so clean-minded. She had high ideals too, and was the last girl I should have expected to say a thing like that—or feel like that. So the war atmosphere—that atmosphere which destroyed the souls of so many of us, as it destroyed the bodies of others—had engulfed her too.

In a seriously intended piece of fiction this evasiveness would have been inadmissible. There is no attempt to define or even specify this aspect of the war atmosphere, though it is essential to the novelist's purpose: it is merely presented as an extenuating circumstance and left at that. In an oddly literal way it is equated with actual infection: the closer one gets to the front line, the more one's morals will be put at risk. Yet experience of combat can also be beneficial: 'The war had not broadened these girls' outlook. That was obvious. Yet not very surprising, for I gathered that . . . they had not been near the danger zone. . . . I was forcibly struck by the difference that existed between the women—and the men too—who had seen something of the actual war, and those who had all the time remained in safety. It was rather remarkable.'

Of course the black-and-white terms, the simplifications of cause and effect, the take-it-or-leave-it inconsistencies, are typical of popular fiction. The authors' business is to make statements that needn't be disputed. There is no attempt to follow even the most rudimentary kind of narrative logic. At the level of moralizing, a facile appeasement of conservative opinion will usually be found to underlie the most apparently unconventional or forthright episodes. In *W.A.A.C.*, concupiscent Gwen (see above) finds sexual relief with the man whom she is to marry; and the chastity of Connie, the narrator, is sacrificed only in the cause of romantic 'love'. There is no need for these girls to be promiscuous, since they find instant satisfaction. Connie can still be outraged by exhibitions of sexual laxity: 'In the forest of Rouray, some miles above Rouen and close to the hospitals, also in the Forêt Verte (through stretches of which I often had to drive), I came several times upon spectacles which before the war would have upset me very much.'

The prurient aspects of this novel are wholly distasteful. It reduces a complex pattern of social currents and shifts of emphasis to a simple outbreak of sexual immorality—and elaborates it on the plane of titillation. This is bad enough, but the author lacks the courage to be openly pornographic: apparent lustfulness is allied to a sanctimonious repudiation of 'animal behaviour'. The result is a curious and reprehensible exploitation of the wartime background.

Nothing in the books and papers discussed above was intended to be of permanent literary value. At best, popular fiction expresses in the most obvious terms social attitudes currently in vogue; there is no need to assess these or to place them within a wider context. Of course the war provided merely a topical background in the fiction of authors like Berta Ruck whose sole objective was to entertain. At this level, there is no question of radical change in the lives of women land-workers and munitionettes: these are called upon to do nothing more than look decorative in uniform and embody patriotism in its most unthinking form. Later retrospective novelists found that the war offered plenty of scope for adventure and emotional drama —strong 'plot' elements for the commercial writer whose approach is always blatant.

Serious fiction is naturally more authoritative and illuminating in the long-term sense. In 1915, St John Ervine ('The War and Literature', *The Englishwoman*, Vol. XXVIII) estimated that the war would continue to determine the content of all forms of imaginative literature for the next 50 years. 'Books will begin in all sorts of ways, romantically and realistically, but somewhere in the middle of them, the war will relentlessly thrust itself, diverting the characters from the normal course of their lives.' Twenty years would have been nearer the mark, and in fact the war's effect on literature in the 1920s and 1930s is in many cases oblique or subliminal, a question merely of the authors' response to the social changes engendered by war. His prognosis was right, however, in relation to the family chronicle and other traditional literary modes. In the years between 1914 and 1918 there was no one in England who was not 'touched in some way, in most cases very closely, by the war'.

Rebecca West's first novel *The Return of the Soldier* was published in 1918. This is a rather complex little parable with clinical overtones: both moral and psycho-analytical issues are at the centre of its theme. The effect of shell-shock on Chris Baldry is to obliterate all memory of his wife: this is very plain symbolism, and it acts to determine the reader's view of Kitty. The soldier is important only in his relation to three women: his wife and cousin, homemakers and guardians of the illusion of gracious living; and his lost sweetheart Margaret Allington, a plain woman coarsened in appearance by poverty and years of marriage to a dull husband.

The narrator is the cousin, Jenny, the unmarried relative who reveals in the course of the story the rather obsessive, distorted quality in her devotion to Chris. Uneasily allied with Kitty at the beginning (for Chris's sake), she struggles to transfer her allegiance to the shabby housewife whom Chris has come to idealize. Margaret's defects and deprivations have been stressed from the start: the squeamish, privileged women are revolted by her clumsy gestures, her muddy boots and cheap umbrella. Even while the reversal in Jenny's attitude is occurring, when she is beginning to see in Margaret an 'inner' beauty, she can't overcome the instinctive habit of snobbery. Margaret remains 'that sort of woman'; but she is too humble or too noble to resent condescension. 'Against the clear colours of the bright bare wood her yellow raincoat made a muddy patch, and as a dead bough dropped near her she made a squalid dodging movement like a hen. She was not so much a person as an implication of dreary poverty. . . .'

She is satisfactory to Chris, however; he doesn't notice her shortcomings. But Chris has regressed into a kind of romantic trance. This is the pivot on which the moral question turns: should he be left in this happy state, or cured and returned to the trenches? Margaret has the strength of mind to make the right decision.

The basic point about the deceptiveness or unimportance of appearances is modified by the meticulous, almost sensuous evocations of mood and scene. On a vague ethical plane, Kitty may embody falsity and Margaret, goodness; but the author retains sufficient detachment to charge each quality with a sense of the other. We are reminded that the handle of Margaret's umbrella is a fake, just as Chris's contentment is based on delusion: his behaviour will soon become unseemly, less than human. Kitty's chintzes and roses at least are *real*. External order and beauty have their own virtue, as much as self-sacrifice or self-indulgent charity. The novel is at times quite beautifully composed, at others deformed with an overflow of emotion.

It suits the author's purpose to concentrate the effects of war in one significant casualty: Chris. In other respects the fighting and propaganda have been kept out of the heroines' lives. Only 'the heavy blue blinds, which shroud the nine windows' of the drawing-room at Baldry Court, denote the adjustments in day-to-day living required of civilians. A lost Zeppelin clanking across the sky doesn't arouse much apprehension. In fact, the prospect of air raids on London and other cities was treated seriously: German bombs had killed citizens of Yarmouth and King's Lynn as early as January 1915. The overall damage was negligible, of course, in comparison with the destruction wrought by the bombers of the second world war; but the random quality of the raids and the novel character of the weapon gave rise in 1915 to a special panic.

In Pamela Hinkson's *The Ladies' Road* (1932) there is only one emotion and one mood: nostalgia. The mellow richness of Stella Mannering's childhood is broken short by the war; afterwards, her memories are encompassed by a dreamy haze that surrounds the two great houses, Winds and Cappagh, one English, the other Irish, representing between them a whole lost world of custom and happiness. Nostalgia infuses an absolute quality of perfection into each doomed relationship and social phase. The details of security and graciousness and natural beauty and emotional warmth are savoured most poignantly in retrospect.

The languorous sweetness and charm of the narrative are at once tempered and compounded by a sense of hopelessness; but there are occasional lapses into the idiom of romantic fallacy. Of Edward Urquhart we are told that he 'looked rather beautiful in uniform, so beautiful that anyone seeing him must have known that he was going to be killed'. This observation is sentimental; it is valid only with hindsight. The general tone is rhapsodic; even sadness is sleeked over with the glamour of entranced reverie. The style has a lovely, melancholy flow.

The qualities that the novel lacks are stringency and humour; but the school episodes at least have an admirable briskness and realism. At Maythorpe, Stella suffers from 'the terror of being left behind'. She knows that her brother David

> must go alone eventually, but if she knew enough she could go too, not shut out, although her body would be back at Maythorpe learning things that did not matter at all. She learnt quickly, patiently, things that did matter, building the road for herself.
>
> ... The road was familiar to her, a part of her life like the names of towns she had never seen, which were yet more familiar than any towns she knew. Bapaume, Ypres, Menin, Loos. People one knew had been killed in these places. They stamped themselves on her childhood, being part of it, to be remembered afterwards when many closer memories would be forgotten. They were part of life, of the making of life in those important, ineffaceable years. She accepted them in

common with all her generation, not realizing their importance. The road belonged to all of them.

The school is badly heated and the girls are always hungry. Maythorpe has come to resemble a convent; the young teachers have gone off to do war work and those who remain are 'nun-like'. In class the pupils are absent-minded. The appearance of a telegraph boy causes the colour to leave the faces of half-a-dozen seniors. There is the awkward business of knowing whether or not to say one is sorry when a relative is killed. Consolation is well-meant but usually misfires: 'Brigid took a chocolate with agonized politeness and ate it with great difficulty'. The schoolgirls are all knitting strange garments for men they do not know. One dormitory is infested with mice. Stella longs to leave: 'Would she ever get to France, like some of those girls who had left Maythorpe, drive an ambulance near the line?'

Though it is expressed here in an adult novel, the sentiment is especially familiar to readers of girls' school stories of the period. As long as France remained inaccessible it represented involvement, excitement and freedom; to express a wish to go there was merely to assert one's spirit. The actual life of ambulance drivers was not enviable, as Evadne Price and others have pointed out (see above). But only timid or worthless schoolgirls could fail to respond to the idea of service and adventure.

Pamela Hinkson's title has a double meaning. David is killed in 1918 on the Chemin des Dames; but the book explores the ladies' way in a more general sense. The ladies become more wistful and stoical; they expect disaster and behave well when it occurs. Inbred, upper-class reticence and poise are positive qualities in this novel; not a sham like the personal virtues of Kitty in *The Return of the Soldier* or a shambles like the bogus gentility of Evadne Price's ladies. Stella, with each successive death, accepts a diminishment in the possibilities that life offers. Retreat to Ireland is merely a prolongation of war's disruption; Ireland has its own vicious disorder. Like Elizabeth Bowen's remarkable *The Last September* (1929), the book ends with the wanton burning of a great house. 'The flames leaping up, when it was too late to save anything more . . . spread through the long corridors into the room where Edmund Urquhart had stood before the war trying to define the smell of Irish country houses faintly sad, as though they waited for this.'

The Ladies' Road is one of the books that look back with unequivocal regret. In others the war is treated as a crisis but also as a break in some deadly social pattern or a test of character in which the author's protagonist may win through to a kind of moral enlargement or a healthy adjustment of values. In these cases the war is a catalyst, important only in its side-effects. The horror and squalor are not ignored, but these are not the central issue. Winifred Holtby's *The Crowded Street* (1924) is an odd, uneven, slightly melodramatic novel with a dreary heroine whose final gesture of self-assertion is preceded by too much effacement to be effective. (It seems only fair to point out that this is not Winifred Holtby's best novel; but the others fall outside the scope of this discussion.) The point about social repressions and delusions is laboured until its expression becomes irksome. Muriel Hammond's timidity and pessimism are tedious, for all the scorn and aversion to social niceties that lie underneath. She isn't an impressive character. It is only the negative aspects of failure and purposelessness in the author's conception of Muriel that give her at least a documentary validity. She is typical of a certain type of middle-class provincial young woman, intelligent but inarticulate and resentful. Her seductive friend Clare, on the other hand, tempestuous and temperamental (these adjectives are unfortunately apt), is merely a figment of commercial fiction.

Clare is the most blatant example, but other subsidiary figures in *The Crowded Street* are lacking in verisimilitude. Probably it was the author's intention to indicate the plight of a usual young woman whose only merit is an ability to see through the posturing and prinking of her marriageable contemporaries and their mothers. The plight is real enough, but Muriel's ultimate independence hardly seems adequate to its implied cost. Changes in attitude, increased freedom resulting from war, her sister's misfortunes and a friend's tragedy have all been necessary to shove her along the road to personal liberty. At this point it hardly seems to matter whether she marries Godfrey Neale or not. It *is* possible to write about a dull, humourless or stodgy character without being in the least dull or humourless, as other writers have shown (Dorothy Richardson, for example). But there is nothing *in* Muriel to hold the reader's interest; and the author has opted for the easiest way of showing her in relation to her background. Something more than an undemanding narrative would have been needed to make *The Crowded Street* successful.

The heroine of Vera Brittain's *Honourable Estate* (1936) has more courage and vigour; but this novel too has technical failings. To begin with, it is really three novels: the typical Victorian 'three-decker' in post-war clothing. The feminist principles of Janet Rutherston are vindicated in the life of her daughter-in-law Ruth Alleyndene, whom she never meets (or meets only briefly, as an inconsiderable child). Janet is the central character of the first section; in the second, Ruth's fortunes are traced from 1906 to 1919. The third part of the book is concerned with Ruth's marriage to Denis Rutherston.

Ruth, at Oxford, prays that her 'nightmares' about her brothers' safety may be ended as soon as she is brought 'within range of their experience'. But her favourite, Richard, is killed before she gets to Wimereux as a VAD nurse. When she falls in love with an American soldier Ruth is not inhibited by her childhood conditioning; she simply considers the alternatives and decides what she is going to do. She is not deluded about Eugene Meury's 'intentions': he won't abandon his American fiancée. When he is killed Ruth regrets nothing about her lost virginity but the fact that she was careful about contraception.

She is rational, but she doesn't expect her views to be shared. When Denis Rutherston proposes marriage, in 1921, Ruth has to tell him that she isn't a virgin. As a reply, Denis is given the wittiest line in the book: '"I was asking you to be my wife," said Denis's gentle, precise voice. "I'm not exclusively interested in one part of your anatomy."'

One can sympathize totally with the feminist standpoint of Vera Brittain and still feel that the novel's drift is forced to accommodate an ideological preconception. The author's admirable convictions get in the way of artistic necessity. The narrative is cumbersome and often unrestrained. Crucial motivations are sometimes presented with a lack of complexity.

In fact the book's chief merits are sociological: it places the war in relation to the social conditions in England before and after, and comes down on the side of sanity and progressiveness.

In a great deal of pulp fiction the war was used merely as a means of effecting extraordinary reconciliations between villainous husbands and wives, softening their natures and generally bringing out the best in all kinds of reprobates. War was topical and had to be brought into stories in the cheap periodicals: one pot-boiler has an angry colonel sock in the jaw an apparently cowardly young farm-worker who won't enlist, only to discover that he has knocked down a *woman*. Her short hair is simply a convenience. To make up for his loss of temper he marries her. Vera Brittain and Winifred Holtby were among the radical social critics whose fiction is geared to promote change. In a serious literary context the internal state of corruption and injustice in England is examined by D. H. Lawrence (chiefly in *Kangaroo*) and others; in fact few novelists of the period attempted to bypass the major event of contemporary history. Only the fantasy or historical writer could avoid, with justice, all mention of the current crisis. For the generation that was just too young to fight, whose memories of 1914–1918 were complicated by the emotions of boredom and guilt, the war provided a special image of horror, as the following lines from *Autumn Journal*, XV, 1938, by Louis MacNeice (born 1907) suggest:

> Was it the murderer on the nursery ceiling
> Or Judas Iscariot in the Field of Blood
> Or someone at Gallipoli or in Flanders
> Caught in the end-all mud?

But the inter-war years were to bring decisive shifts in attitudes to war and its presentation in literature at all levels.

III

GRITTY BUT GIRLISH

Schoolgirls to Munitionettes

'We did rag her, rather,' said Deirdre half-apologetically. 'Serve her jolly well right for talking German!' snapped Dulcie.

Angela Brazil, *The School by the Sea*

BRENDA GIRVIN, Christine Chaundler, Bessie Marchant, Angela Brazil and one or two other writers managed to make participation in the war seem colourful and inviting to girl readers. Generally speaking, however, in spite of the inspiration of women doctors in Serbia, plucky Belgian refugees and British children who remained undaunted during Zeppelin raids, girls' wartime fiction was not particularly impressive. Story-openings like the following—'. . . at Ashfield we were awfully keen about the war, right from the beginning, ages before other schools took in that there was much girls could do . . .'—usually meant that girls were simply encouraged to worship the male heroes at the front, and to knit comforts for them.

Although it had a female editor (Flora Klickmann), the *Girl's Own Paper and Woman's Magazine* was anxious that young girls should not regard increased wartime career opportunities as a means of advancing the feminist cause. Soon after war was declared an article on 'Women and the War' ('Help they can Render, Follies they can Avoid') suggests that girls as well as their mothers should steer clear of 'comic-opera-like efforts that involve horses, tents or a pseudo-military uniform'. The *GOP* is apt to imply that the war has come about to enable girls to straighten out their values: 'we have been taking many unimportant things too seriously during the past few years; the worship of money, feminism, the latest fashion'. Feminism is equated with 'fripperies' like transparent stockings and cotton gloves: the latter 'cheap rubbish of Austria and Germany which has entered into the very soul of commonplace taste' is seen as part of the craze for newness which the *GOP* frequently condemned. There were stern warnings to working girls. In 1915 readers were told that '. . . what we call the independence of woman is a thing that comes and goes. . . . But although the independence of woman may change or fluctuate . . . the dependence of woman, is, I believe, desirable at all times: and I mean by that the dependence of womanhood on manhood.'

Girls and women on the whole were expected to follow the advice of the Duchess of Albany: 'We must learn to be heroic, to be calm, and of good courage and to remain in the place where God has placed us, and to do our duty there'. The *Girl's Own Paper* condoned the type of patriotism that 'blossomed in [feminine] souls . . . as naturally as the old-fashioned rose grows in the old family garden'. In other words, girls were expected to send their menfolk to the trenches—'Woman will forgive almost anything in a man except cowardice'—but to channel their own energies into crochet work and sewing for Queen Mary's Needlework Guild.

Girls who had envisaged more exciting war work were catered for, to some extent, in Brenda Girvin's books. In these the heroines are continually on the defensive, forced to prove their efficiency in jobs taken over from men. *Jenny Wren* (1920), for example, is the story of a WRNS decoder, and throughout there is a tone of cautious narrative commendation for the girl cipher clerk who *can* keep secret information to herself. This is not flattering to girls in general, since it is based on the clichéd assumption that women are too frivolous to be trusted. Jenny has to make tremendous efforts to overcome her own tendency to blurt things out. One is reminded of Oscar Wilde's remark that *he* never gave away secrets: the fault lay with the people to whom he had gossiped.

Jenny's naval base is surrounded by parasitic civilians (women, of course) craving for information about the comings and goings of ships and high-ranking officers; somehow they find out what they want to know. Jenny, though conscientious, is rather stupid. She throws the drafts of her decoded messages into a wastepaper basket which is easily accessible to spies and nosy-parkers. She mistakes loyal sailors for spies and vice versa. Superficially *Jenny Wren* is a plea for the approval of girls' employment in positions of responsibility. It could have achieved the reverse effect, however, because of Jenny's unsuitability for her particular job: 'Quick and impulsive, on the spur of the moment, she would burst out with some remark and regret it the second after she had said it'. But there is a happy ending when Jenny eventually leaves off her 'jolly nice' three-cornered hat to become the wife of the naval officer who has most deeply resented her.

Masculine prejudice against working girls is expressed more strongly in Brenda Girvin's other wartime book, *Munition Mary* (1918). Armaments-factory owner Sir William Harrison is even reluctant to enter a lift operated by a woman, climbing up many flights of stairs in preference: 'He would ruin himself rather than let one of them set foot inside his workshop'. Mary who is 'sweet-faced . . . with long golden hair falling below her waist', has an uphill task in demolishing Sir William's prejudice against girl employees. The efforts of the first intake of workers are undermined by saboteurs, and Mary is driven to the expedient of unmasking no less than four enemy agents (the hostel-matron, factory-canteen manageress, a bench-hand and one of Sir William's maids) before he changes his views. Even then it is womanly weakness rather than the efficiency of his new workers that impresses the factory owner. When Mary has outwitted the spies 'all her pluck went. Suddenly she felt she was just a weak girl with no self-control or courage left. She sank down into a chair and burst into a flood of tears.' Sir William is delighted to find that this modern miss is in fact just a 'dear sweet girl with all the gentleness of our grandmothers'; in what is presented as a moment of deep insight he realizes that it is all right for girls to make shells so long as they still busy themselves in the kitchen in their off-duty times 'making chutney'.

The achievements of girl factory workers also formed the substance of at least one novel by Bessie Marchant, an author who had been writing adventure stories for nearly two decades before the war began. Her books with wartime settings include *A Girl Munition Worker* (1916), *A V.A.D. in Salonika* (1916) and *A Transport Girl in France* (1918). In the last-named, heroine Gwen Lovell finds release from domestic drudgery in war work. Orphaned and living in her aunt's home, Gwen 'could not even knit for the soldiers, for every spare minute of her time had to be spent in making and mending for the children. . . . How bleak the future looked! The years stretched before her in a perspective of greyness . . .'.

All this is altered when Gwen becomes a WAAC. First she helps on a farm, enthusiastically 'droving' pigs and pulping turnips for animal feeds; then she is transferred to France as driver to a dashing flight commander. The tone of Bessie Marchant's stories is robust—'Steady there! England expects that every WAAC this day will do her duty!'—but her wartime heroines are remarkably subservient in some respects: 'My word, I'd be grateful for the privilege of blacking his boots! But to drive his car would be a foretaste of heaven! Oh, I know it sounds silly, but girls are made that way! Hero-worship is a first necessity to us . . .'. It was often too the motivating force in Angela Brazil's patriotic schoolgirls, who idolized their brothers and cousins in khaki. Active service of course was not possible for the youthful Deirdres, Marjories and Winonas who were aching to get into the war. Even ambitious home-front projects like spy-catching proved abortive. Fervent 'planning and scheming for King George' was likely to lead to nothing more exciting than cheering up wounded Tommies in hospital or making toys for the Soldiers' and Sailors' Orphanage. Frustration flared into indignant outbursts of Teutophobia: 'I wouldn't consciously speak to a German for ten thousand pounds, and if I happened by mistake to shake hands with one —well I'd go and disinfect my hands afterwards.'

The wartime fantasies of little girls were usually not so high-flown as those of Angela Brazil's adolescent characters. Contemporary magazines of course encouraged daughters to concentrate on 'being a comfort' to their parents; and at school —while their brothers chanted songs about 'captaining mighty armies'—small girls were still forced to sing 'Dolly is so Dainty' and other ditties of this type. In *Little Folks* magazine, girls' interest in dolls was turned to propaganda purposes. A 1917 article entitled 'Christine—and All British' ('How They Make the Dolls in England Now') emphasizes the superiority of these new British products over the German dolls which had dominated the pre-war market. '"Darling," said mother, "poor Bess Bumper is dead, so we must buy another doll for you." After a few minutes a very joyful Peggy walked out of the

shop carrying the box in which Christine was packed. "I shall
never want a *German* doll again," she exclaimed.'

Little Folks believed that growing potatoes was not out of
keeping with the 'little girl mother's' rôle. The July 1917 issue
includes a poem and a story on this theme. There is a
modernized version of 'Mary, Mary Quite Contrary' by
Harry Hamlyn, in which Mary has become impatient with
the Silver Bells and Cockleshells: 'And I do not waste my
garden upon silly things like those./I have planted War
Potatoes, all good seed and Up-to-daters,/And I'm very proud
and happy, for they're coming up in rows!' The potato-
growers in Dorothea Moore's 'Penelope Patriot' are less
efficient. The girls of the first form at the Manor School have
some difficulty in overcoming their distaste for mud and its
inhabitants. 'Jasmine Herrick felt [a worm] wriggle in her
fingers, and gave a shriek which sounded as though she were
half killed. Penelope repressed her sternly. "In time of national
crisis you shouldn't think of worms!" she said. "Think
imperially—then they won't matter." ' Far and away the most
successful of Penelope's patriotic schemes was—of course—
one which allowed her and other first-formers to help the
senior girls in sewing shirts for soldiers.

On the whole, girls' fiction of the first world war gives an
impression that the British Tommy may have suffered quite a
lot from the misapplied zeal of schoolgirls who were determined
to keep up the morale of the men at the front. Christine
Chaundler's *Little Folks* story 'Our Lonely Soldier' highlights
the complications that might arise for young girls who write
innocent letters to Tommies. A sentimental newspaper article
inspires 'Bobbie' and her brothers and sister to 'adopt' Private
Horace Smith. For this purpose they concoct the imaginary
personality of 'Alice Greene', whose lively letters appeal so
much to Horace that he asks for her photograph. Bobbie's
response is to send him a shop postcard—'you know, one of
those ladies with nice teeth . . . and curly hair'. The tone of
Horace's letters changes from grateful acceptance of patronage—
'Dear and Honoured Miss, Hoping this finds you as it leaves
me'—to intimacy. He begins to make suggestions about sharing
a little cottage in the country. (One of Angela Brazil's heroines
finds herself in a similar situation when her soldier correspondent

**" ' Please, are you
Private Smith ? ' "**

Drawing by E. P. Kinsella for 'Our Lonely Soldier'
Little Folks, April 1919

wants to 'keep company' with her: his letter is intercepted
by the headmistress and Marjorie Anderson faces expulsion.)
The dénouement of Christine Chaundler's story occurs when
Private Smith breaks off his engagement to a hard-working
girl who is devoted to him. (She is Jane Brown, kitchen maid
to Bobbie's family.) Bobbie had no idea that Horace and Jane
even knew each other. She puts things right, but not until

everyone has suffered a great deal of embarrassment. For well-intentioned and patriotic Bobbie the cruellest cut of all is Horace's disgusted, '"Well—I wouldn't have believed as how English children could have acted like that. . . . If you'd been little Huns, now——".'

Girl Guides, of course, made useful contributions to the war effort and these were elaborated in innumerable stories. Ethel Talbot's *Peggy's Last Term* (1920) shows how the fortitude of the troops can provide an example at a very simple level. As the improvised bracken-filled mattresses of the camping Girl Guides become more and more lumpy during the night Patrol Leader Peggy gives this rather confused reassurance: '"There's plenty of men sleeping on nothing but mud out in the trenches, and wet mud at that, and probably no sleep either"'. Peggy is a pupil at an east-coast school: predictably it is Guide pluck and practicality that save the girls from being seriously hurt when the school building is shattered in a German bombardment. E. L. Haverfield's *The Girls of St Olave's* (1918) deals with a rather less courageous juvenile victim of an enemy raid. Margaret MacDonald gets off to a bad start on her first day at an English school. 'Scotch and proud of it', she condemns English pronunciation as 'ugly, and silly, and mincing'. Her unpopularity is confirmed when she nearly faints with fright at the beginning of an air-raid. Her dorm-mates are contemptuously amused, but anxious that her fear should not be communicated to the younger girls. '"Look here, Margaret," said Rosalind . . . "don't let the kids see you in this funk. We always tell them there's nothing to be scared about, and if they see you pea-green it will upset everything."' Of course, in the tradition of this type of fiction, Margaret eventually 'redeems herself'. But there is no serious enquiry into her predicament—one which might have been shared by at least a few real-life schoolgirls.

The pert leading character of *Freda's Great Adventure* (Alice Massie 1917) is a twelve-year-old English girl. Freda is stranded in France when war is declared, having improbably arrived there in search of adventure. She feels that the war has been tailor-made for the fulfilment of her naïve ambitions: ' "Uncle, let me stay. Don't send me home . . . *I have never seen a battle in my life*."' Freda gets her wish, becoming involved in violence

C

when she encounters some marauding Uhlans 40 miles outside
Paris. (Uhlans scouted with singular viciousness all over France
and Belgium in a great deal of boys' and girls' fiction.) In
spite of its wartime atmosphere the story is unexciting, often
dreary. At the point when Freda is shipped back to England she
is still prattling about 'Life's big adventures' and an English
lady who accompanies her is inclined to be sympathetic. Her
husband, however, is more caustic, telling Freda with some
relish that 'death's the biggest adventure of the lot'. In fact
he is voicing the irritation that Freda must have engendered in
many readers.

The heroines of *The British Girl's Annuals* of the war years
were more dignified than Freda—but at times no less infuri-
ating. Their dauntlessness was belied by the complacent
gentility of the stories' narrative tone. *British Girl's*—the
Cassells annual associated with *Little Folks* magazine—liked
to present its heroic themes in the context of an acceptably
distant or historical background; but sandwiched between
epics of the French Revolution (on the side of the aristocrats)
and the Civil War (from the Cavaliers' viewpoint) were
stories of the current conflict. The liveliest of these were created
by popular schoolgirls' writers like Ethel Talbot; the dullest
were produced by women better known as the authors of
respectably romantic novels. As soon as the war ended *The
British Girl's Annual* was able to revert to its old policy, channel-
ling its tales of adventure completely into remote domains.
The India of the British Raj and post-revolutionary Russia
offered splendidly up-to-date and escapist settings for girls'
fiction. However, before the Teuton butchers were superseded
by the Bolshevist bogey (in stories intended as solemn warnings
to socialists at home) *British Girl's* produced one memorable
first world war episode. This was 'A Passage Perilous' by
Helen H. Watson. Like several real-life middle-class English
girls in the immediate pre-war period, Geraldine Fitzgerald and
Bettina Fairbrother are studying in Germany. The declaration
of war and confiscation of passports make it impossible for them
to return to Britain. (But they are not seriously harassed by the
Germans although there *is* the threat of possible future internment.) In spite of Geraldine's condemnation of the 'people that
toasted *Der Tag* in peace time and who sing their vile Hymn of

Hate now!' the Germans are represented as ordinary, reasonable human beings. In fact when Geraldine, in the guise of an American citizen, escapes penniless to Holland it is a German who helps her to get a boat to England.

The editorial policy of Lord Northcliffe's Amalgamated Press, unlike that of several other publishers, was to involve its girl characters and readers unreservedly in the war. However, girls' war dramas were often reminiscent of the weepy stories of home life that were featured in Northcliffe's pre-war women's magazines. The heyday of his papers for girls—as distinct from women—did not come until after the war with the advent of the *Schoolgirl* and the *Girls' Crystal*; but the *Girls' Friend, Girls' Reader* and *Heartsease Library* were extremely popular during the first decade of the century. These were weeklies with prices ranging from $\frac{1}{2}$d to $1\frac{1}{2}$d. Between 1914 and 1918, several of their leading characters—including Mary Latimer, Nun—were transferred from genteel English settings to battle-scarred Belgium. Mary Latimer in fact plays only a small part in 'Girlish Dreams' (*Heartsease Library*, 28 November 1914). Its real heroine is eighteen-year-old 'little flower' Nora Carver; the daughter of the village postmaster, she is in love with Jack Latham, son of the lord of the manor. When Jack throws her over for Elsie Motteux-Turner, a glamorous gold-digger of the most blatant type, Nora rushes off to nurse wounded soldiers in Mary Latimer's front-line Flanders hospital. Jack of course soon joins her there—temporarily blinded and disabled. He recovers to rejoice that 'I might have lost my little girl for ever, save for that ever-blessed German bullet that sent me here'. Both Nora and impossibly serene Mary Latimer continue to emanate 'sweet radiance'. Some of the stories in Northcliffe's girls' papers at this time were written by men; if their fictional characters represented contemporary ideals of womanhood the future for feminism looked pretty bleak. Nora, though alert and industrious, defers to every male she meets—even ferocious Uhlans—whom she addresses always in dreadfully serious 'quiet and brave' tones. Even in the final paragraphs of 'Girlish Dreams', when Mary Latimer is tenderly fastening the orange-blossom-trimmed veil on Nora's head, the bride-to-be is still protesting (in a whisper, of course): 'Reverend Mother— I am so frightened—I am not really good enough for him!'

Amalgamated Press author John Wheway was responsible for two of the most lurid girls' stories of the first world war: 'Maisie's Battlefield Search' (see Chapter VI) and 'War Maid of Flanders'. He wrote these under the pen-name of Gladys Cotterill; they appeared in the *Schoolgirls' Own Library* series, but their episodic, cliff-hanging structure indicates that they were issued originally as serials in one of Northcliffe's weekly girls' papers. By the mid-1930s John Wheway had become an exceptionally competent author for boys and girls. (As Hilda Richards he produced the lively stories of Cliff House School in the *Schoolgirl* throughout the 1930s.) But in his early post-war efforts Wheway's story-telling skill was undeveloped. As a very young man he had spent some time in the trenches where he managed to bring out a rough-and-ready magazine for his fellow soldiers. 'War Maid of Flanders' has some authentic touches including references to the Tommies' own versions (suitably censored for schoolgirl readers) of popular wartime songs; vivid descriptions of different sectors of Ypres under fire and 'the dull glazed look' of the tired, retreating infantrymen. But the author fails completely to give a credible personality to his teenage heroine; and his efforts to describe youthful femininity have a coy effect. Readers must have guessed what they were in for when they learned Patricia Pearson's nickname: '"Well, now, cheer up," she enjoined, "for your little Sunshine is here, and I'm never going to leave you any more."' At least Patricia, an English schoolgirl stranded in Belgium, does have a novel method of cheering up the troops; she puts on improvised circus shows for them. Patricia is lumbered with two elderly Belgian refugees who faint or reach the point of death a number of times in the course of the story. Somehow without money or travel papers she has to get them, herself and fourteen performing dogs safely to England. Every building in which they take refuge is bombed or shelled as soon as they get into it. But Patricia perseveres; and thanks to the unfailingly helpful Tommies—'Bong jewer, mamysal! Are we downhearted—No!'—and a powerful English woman impresario, she does eventually manage to reach England safely with her bizarre entourage.

The first world war continued to provide a stimulus for boys' writers until the beginning of Hitler's war in 1939. However it inspired very little retrospective girls' fiction, possibly because the idea of girls' participation in the war had been more exciting than the actuality. Many writers eagerly awaited the

SHE KEPT THE HOME FIRES BURNING!
4D. By Gladys Cotterill
A Story of the Great War 1914–18
The Schoolgirls' Own Library Nº 257

A cover from *The Schoolgirls' Own Library*, 1930

return of women and girls to 'normal' situations. As early as 1915 the *Girl's Own Paper* warned that the war would not open up a lasting 'Feminist Millennium'. In one of its dispiriting articles headed 'When the Troops Come Home: New Factors that will Influence the Employment of Women', it predicted that a job as a shop assistant was still the best that most post-war girls could hope for. The *GOP* clearly expected that reasonably well-educated girls would prefer to become full-time wives and mothers, and during the 1920s its fiction writers tended to concentrate on the impedimenta of domesticity. Fortunately other magazines and books provided themes that largely catered for the sense of adventure and enquiry in young girls. Before 1913 Angela Brazil had made the hockey stick and the gymslip into symbols of a certain kind of freedom. The school story was adapted and enlivened for post-war readers, who could also find a means of self-identification in stories of adolescent aviators, speed stars, explorers and so on. There was an abundance of career opportunities for girls in fiction—if not in fact—and readers were no longer likely to be excited by looking back at the exploits of VADs and girl munition workers.

IV

'ALL GLORY AND ALL STORY'

Wartime Boys' Fiction

'. . . we've got the measure of the old Boche now, and it's dogged as does it.'

John Buchan, *Greenmantle*

BEFORE 1914 THE atmosphere of *Chums, Boy's Own Paper* and *The Captain* had been firmly established. Whether lighting beacons for Nelson, tackling foreigners in 'fetiche-holes' or simply drilling with the OTC at their public schools, the heroes of these parentally-approved papers embodied high ideals of chivalry and patriotism. Sporting prowess and the team spirit were equally important. The war, of course, provided a ready-made heroic setting for authors to exploit: Flanders quickly became the new and bizarre playing field for the Great Game. In fiction, as in real life, young boys lied about their ages in order to get into the trenches as soon as possible; in most cases they had little idea of what awaited them there.

Biggles—The Rescue Flight by W. E. Johns was published during the 1930s. However, it is set at the time of the first world war and accurately expresses the mood. Seventeen-year-old Peter Fortymore learns that his brother is missing believed dead behind enemy lines. He wastes no time in blubbing. With only tenpence (in old currency) between them, he and another sixth-former set out for France where they enlist. (Usually there were no difficulties in getting into the services as a private, though application for a commission involved investigation into the recruit's personal background and exact age.) In Richard Bird's 'The Schoolboy Ranker' (*The Captain*, 1915) another public-school pupil bolts and enlists: 'who wants to swot at exams when our chaps are fighting over there?' Charles Errington 'knew that his OTC training fitted him for the field. He had been in the Dipcote OTC for five years, held the rank of sergeant, was a marksman and a trained scout.' Certainly Errington's OTC experience made him better equipped for service life than many fictional schoolboys. Vera Brittain, however, in her autobiographical *Testament of Youth* indicts the OTC as 'the exploitation of youth by its elders'. Her assessment is extreme but understandable. In the war she lost her brother, her fiancé and a close friend—all fresh from the sixth form at Uppingham. Thousands of young men of that generation went straight from school into the army believing that there was 'no better end' than a soldier's death. But it was not only the OTC —or public-school traditions—that encouraged aggressively nationalist attitudes. These were engendered by the popular press's lurid accounts of German 'butchery' in Belgium, by music-hall entertainers and even in the songs that were taught to boys at elementary schools:

> Daddy's dressed in khaki
> He's gone away to fight
> For King and home and country
> For honour and for right.
> We do not want the Germans
> To come all over here
> So Dad must go and fight them
> He'll beat them never fear. . . .

In contemporary boys' fiction, resistance to the Teuton Braggart comes across at one level as an extension of the old empire-building spirit; at another as a gigantic spree. (This word is actually used by F. S. Brereton's schoolboy recruit when he knocks out his first German sniper in *Under Haig in Flanders*.) Many of the stories were written by men with military rank—like Captain Brereton and Major Charles Gilson—and young readers generally believed them to be authentic. In fact these accounts of 1914–1918 battles were often based on Boer war experiences and on ideas of wish-fulfilment rather than on the actuality of the Somme, the Marne and Passchendaele. They were sufficiently exhilarating to entertain, and to satisfy a boy's heroic fantasies; but there is little doubt that such stories were also intended to encourage recruitment. (Conscription was not introduced until 10 February 1916.) 'The Old

Fag' in the October 1914 issue of *The Captain* mentions the regular procession of its authors and editorial staff who hurried to enlist as soon as war was declared: 'the chance of getting at close grips with the enemy was meat and drink' to them. Further editorials were written 'to the stirring sound of the marching song of soldiers swinging down the Strand'. The magazine devoted eight or nine pages each month to pictures of artillery guns in action, charging cavalry, battle ships, Zeppelins and so on.

The Amalgamated Press produced war stories for boys which were less pretentious than those of *The Captain* and *Boy's Own Paper*, but its recruiting drive was more blatant. Lord Northcliffe, of course, had been preparing his readers for war with Germany for some time (see Chapter I). Once this was formally declared the writers of editorials lost no opportunity of chivvying readers into uniform. 'A Word from the Skipper' in *The Union Jack* of 24 October 1914 begins by explaining that the paper's office is now 'curiously silent on account of my depleted staff ...'. It takes the editor well over a thousand words to ask 'how many of my readers have gone ... to take their part in making history, gone to take their part in drubbing the German bullies, gone to fight in the war for freedom, liberty and honour?' Of the laggards he says, 'I will not reprimand them, I will not censure them. I do not know what prevents them responding to the Call.' (His own lack of response is not referred to.) He goes on to suggest that 'Mr Begbie's fine [*Daily Chronicle*] recruiting poem ... puts the matter in a nutshell'. In fact Mr Begbie's sentimental doggerel is even less acceptable than the Skipper's rhetoric:

> How will you fare, sonny, how will you fare,
> In the far-off winter night,
> When you sit by the fire in an old man's chair,
> And your neighbours talk of the fight?
> Will you slink away as it were from a blow,
> Your old head shamed and bent?
> Or say—I was not with the first to go,
> But I went, thank God, I went.

In 1916 the *Boy's Own Paper* ran a series of poems by Lillian

Gard; pieces like 'Preparation' and 'Hero-Worship' were about
the 'little lads who were England's Heart'. They were not so
little actually, but adolescents who admired senior boys and
followed them to Flanders in a ritual manner reminiscent of
the central character in *Journey's End* (see Chapter V). Like
many women at the time Lillian Gard felt that without being
involved in the fighting herself she had every right to encourage
boys to play 'the soldier's part' with 'clean lips—straight life—
and daily duty done'.

Unquestioning patriotism—'Hold on! Heed not the croak-
ings of the cranks, of the Pacifists . . .'—is also the underlying
theme in Captain Brereton's wartime stories, a series that
includes *With The Allies to the Rhine* (1919) and *Under Haig in
Flanders* (1917). (Significantly an expression of exhilaration
used by his heroes is 'Jingo!') Brereton, a veteran of the Boer
war, was related to Henty whose stories he tried to emulate.
His epics of high adventure were extremely popular—but
this of course could simply mean that their tone was attractive
to the parents, aunts and uncles who bought the books for
children. Boy readers might well have been irritated by the
potted history lessons and propaganda which frequently slow
down the pace of Brereton's stories. The hero of *Under Haig in
Flanders* appears first as a schoolboy. Roger Norman believes
that he has killed a man in a street brawl (he hasn't, of course);
he assumes a false name, puts up his age and enlists as a private.
His initial training soon makes 'a real man of him . . . three
inches on round the chest'. Roger bursts out of his private's
uniform mentally as well as physically; public-school confidence
and leadership ensure that he is soon commissioned. Once in
Flanders he marvels at the nonchalance of the Tommies under
fire. Contrasts between British phlegm and German panic are
constantly spelt out. Roger and his men merely laugh when
trapped by the Germans in an enemy dugout; the Teutons,
however, are quickly reduced to trembling submission when
attacked by the British with fists and canes.

The strength and efficiency of the British howitzers and
heavies come in for a share of eulogizing. The tone alternates
between heroic inflation (guns 'thundering without cessation,
pouring a tornado of bursting steel upon those elaborate
. . . defences') and breeziness: 'Our chaps bowl their bombs

over as if they were cricket balls, and the beggars there hate 'em'. (It was not only the Germans who hated them, of course. Many men from both sides who were shell-shocked never fully recovered.) In terms of winning battles, the value of the relentless barrage which Brereton found so magnificent was doubtful. It was certainly costly. The three bombardments before the battles of Messines, Arras and Passchendaele cost the British government an estimated £52,000,000. (Figures like these were quoted with bitterness in the post-war years when the country could not afford a national maternity service at a cost of approximately £2,750,000 per annum. This was in spite of the fact that maternal mortality figures at that time were described by Arthur Greenwood, the Minister of Health, as 'a nightmare'.)

It is salutary to compare Brereton's fictional account of the Battle of the Somme with the actuality. In *Under Haig in Flanders* 'Britain's new armies . . . her bakers' and her tailors' sons' triumphantly avenged the earlier allied setbacks. 'Tingling with keenness' they charged over the top cheering, 'On the ball chaps. Forward!', and trounced the enemy. In fact, at the end of the first day's fighting 20,000 men of Kitchener's army had been killed, 35,000 wounded and 600 taken prisoner. During the five months of carnage that followed almost every family in Britain lost a relative on the Somme. The majority of the 500,000 British soldiers who died there were volunteers, receiving about a shilling a day.

It was this battle more than any other that took 'the cream of a generation'. Men at home from the front cut short their leaves to return believing that the Somme was indeed the decisive battle of the war. It became their only reality. In Brereton's story the mood of confidence is sustained to the end. His 1917 readers are given the impression that the Battle of the Somme *did* lead the way to final victory for the allies. But actually despite tremendous heroism and sacrifice its most positive achievement seems to have been that it produced serious questioning of outdated generalship and military tactics.

Misleading prophecies of early victory were a commonplace of boys' fiction. Authors rallied readers to the colours by suggesting that if they didn't hurry they would be too late to enjoy 'this daisy of a fight'. As early as 28 November 1914 one of Lord Northcliffe's papers implied that the war was all over bar the shouting. The crack troops of the German army were already completely demoralized: 'Ragged, unwashed, haggard and half-starved, they began to look more like a mob of scarecrows than soldiers'. The chief cause of their discomfiture was a young recruit, one of 'Sir John French's gallant boys', whose exploits were related each week in the *Gem* in 'From the Firing Line'. The stories ('My German Prisoners', 'German Funk', etc.) were in the form of 'Letters of Enthralling Interest received direct from Corporal Charles of His Majesty's Dragoons, who is an old reader of "The Gem Library"'. In order to simulate authenticity no author's name was given. Like the usual heroes of boys' books and papers Corporal Charles finds conditions at the front simply ripping. He is inclined to dance for joy on the occasions when he is able to volunteer for dangerous missions: a trip behind enemy lines to locate a hidden Krupps siege gun is a particular treat. For 1914, the British army seems surprisingly democratic: Corporal Charles is on matey terms with his jolly-faced old colonel who certainly never under-rates his rankers: '"Take four of our boys with you. That'll be enough for a score of Germans, I dare say."' Naturally it is—and to spare. On one occasion 40 British Dragoons successfully tackle 300 German Uhlans, capturing 42 food wagons as well as 170 German prisoners. There is a great deal of hearty handshaking and laughing congratulation from the genial colonel: '"Brave lad! I'm proud of you. I believe you'd have won through if I'd only given you 20 lads . . .".' Each episode ends on a reassuring note. 'What wouldn't a fellow do for a dear old chap like that? . . . I forget how many hands of famous officers we shook, and how many complimented us.'

'From the Firing Line'—with its sporty heroics and devotion between young boys and senior officers—is a pulp paper forerunner of *Tell England* (see Chapter V). Religious intensity and sex, however, are absent. These were barred from Northcliffe's juvenile publications. Just as well, perhaps, for at least in the *Gem* 'the hated Boches . . . mad, wine-soaked! Burning and robbing' aren't actually rapists too. The anonymous authors of Corporal Charles's adventures have to content themselves with opprobrious epithets like 'Prussian hogs!', 'the Kaiser's butchers' and 'Von Kluck's horde of barbarians'. It follows that Charles has 'a wholesome contempt for the German infantry, who fire from the hip and squeal at the sight of a British bayonet—though they're brave enough fighting defenceless old men and women . . .'. Real-life British soldiers on leave from the front often gave their children a different picture. Even the most patriotic and anti-German had a thoroughgoing respect for 'old Jerry' as a fighting man.

Though his style is less colourful than that of the *Gem* writers, Captain Brereton too succeeded in creating an attractive image of dugout life. For breakfast one ate, surprisingly, 'fizzling bacon, not to be beaten anywhere, bread that might have graced the table of a Ritz hotel, and jam that would have been the envy of any housewife'. In the vicinity were 'cinemas with the latest pictures from Lunnon, and concert parties made up of soldiers that goes about making the men laugh with their play-acting'. And—even more inviting—'. . . behind, don't you know, it's an eye-opener. Gals a-doin' this, gals a-doin' that!' These doings are more clearly and prosaically listed at another point in the narrative: 'driving pens or motor-cars, cooking, doing such work as loyal women may do in times of stress, freeing the men for the conflict'. Brereton was rather vague about the women's war effort, but evidently he was prepared to concede that the girls deserved commendation.

However loyal and attractive they might be, women and girls were usually considered boring in the context of boys' fiction. There was, however, an almost morbid interest in all kinds of masculinity. In the case of German soldiers, cruelty rather than strength was the keynote and they were supposed to be ugly not only in looks but in behaviour. One of Brereton's Tommies speaks of '. . . "this here greasy-lookin' German"', and Corporal Charles similarly describes a disguised enemy soldier: '. . . his round, greasy face and bullet head showed him at a glance to be a German'. John Buchan stresses the unappetizing qualities of the enemy even more heavily than the writers of the boys' papers. In *Greenmantle* Richard Hannay describes his first meeting in Berlin with Colonel von Stumm. He was '. . . a perfect mountain of a fellow . . . with shoulders on him like a shorthorn bull. . . . He was as hideous as a hippopotamus, but effective. Every bristle on his odd head was effective.' Of course encounters with Stumm *did* take place under circumstances which were unfavourable to Hannay:

> I was standing stark naked next morning in that icy bedroom, trying to bathe in about a quart of water [Buchan's heroes soon wilted if denied cold baths and vigorous exercise] when Stumm entered. I was half a head shorter than him to begin with, and a man does not feel his stoutest when he has no clothes, so he had the pull on me every way.

Naturally, however, excessive German brutishness has decadent undertones. Clean-living Hannay is affronted by the contemptible 'feminine' luxuriousness of Stumm's home. 'It was the room of a man who had a passion for frippery, who had a perverted taste for soft delicate things. It was the complement to his bluff brutality. I began to see the queer side to my host, that evil side which gossip had spoken of as not unknown in the German army'.

Buchan does try to be fair, however. Although in *Greenmantle* there are plenty of Germans clicking their heels like pairs of tongs and exclaiming 'God Strafe England!' occasionally one appears who is wholesome enough to merit a kind of narrative approval, even if this is expressed in dubious terms: '. . . clearly a good fellow, a white man and a gentleman. I could have worked with him, for he belonged to my totem.' There was mutual appreciation between Hannay and another German who 'liked the way I kept the men up to their work, for I hadn't been a nigger-driver [in South Africa] for nothing'. Of course, even without the provocation of being at war with them, Buchan tended to give foreigners short shrift. He frequently dismisses 'Dagoes, Jews and Teutons' for their insensitivity, but with unconscious irony says of the British: 'We call ourselves insular, but the truth is that we are the only race on earth that can produce men capable of getting inside the skin of remote peoples.'

Women usually upset Buchan's heroes just as much as those distasteful foreigners. In *Greenmantle* Hannay suffers the almost traumatic experience of having to share a car with a woman. 'I had never been in a motor car with a lady before, and I felt like a fish on a dry sandbank. The soft cushions and subtle scents filled me with acute uneasiness.' Hilda von Einem is not only a woman but a 'Teuton'; she disturbs Hannay so much that when he leaves her he doesn't feel clean until he has been soaked to the skin, enjoyed a good rub down and performed some dumb-bell exercises with two chairs. He even goes so far as to admit that '. . . every man has in his bones a consciousness of sex'. With Buchan's leading men, of course, it usually stays there; if they get married it is late in life, and to sporty, sexless women. There is one physical exercise that men of the totem do *not* indulge in to the point of exhaustion.

Richard Hannay in *Greenmantle* foils a German plot to lead 'the hordes of Islam' against the British, and in the weekly paper *Union Jack* Sexton Blake scotches the kaiser's schemes to bring other countries into the war against the allies. In 'The Refugee' (24 October 1914), Blake is working for the British Secret Service behind enemy lines in Belgium. Unlike Hannay he is master of the situation in encounters with a beautiful foreign adventuress, and remains indifferent to seductive enemy agents. Madame Renée Montera is the representative of an international gang prepared to sell to the highest bidder some papers of value to the British government. Blake gets hold of these, Madame Montera betrays him to the Germans and he sends the papers to safety by means of his wonderfully intelligent bloodhound, Pedro, who, limping and bleeding, breaks through the German line. By 1914 the Blake saga had been running for 21 years and some of its authors used to good effect the stimulus provided by the war. In 'The Refugee' Blake's inventiveness and Pedro's devotion make an appealing combination. Tinker, the boy helper with whom many readers must have identified, also plays a prominent part. He is given a temporary commission and leads an impressive cavalry charge against the German firing squad that is just about to execute Blake. In a 1915 *Union Jack* Sexton Blake intervenes to prevent the Germans from bringing China into the war on the side of the central powers. On this occasion the setting is Limehouse where the head of the Chinese Brotherhood of the Yellow Beetle agrees to meet the kaiser's spokesman in England. This is none other than His Imperial Highness, Prince Wilhelm (the German Crown Prince, and hopeful of becoming the future Emperor of

Europe). Blake of course has successfully skirmished with the
Hohenzollerns before; he deals with the crown prince just
as effectively as he has done with the kaiser in 1908 (see
Chapter I).

Sexton Blake is a patriot. When serving his country he
waives the large fees which the government is more than ready
to pay. Nelson Lee—another Amalgamated Press detective
who dismisses the enemy with panache—is similarly altruistic:
'"Not a penny, my dear fellow," said Nelson Lee, shaking
his head. "My services in that little adventure were only too
willingly given. . . ."' The little adventure is related in a story
entitled 'Twenty Fathoms Deep' (Edwy Searles Brooks;
Nelson Lee 25 September 1915). At this time the stories of
Nelson Lee and his young assistant 'Nipper' were the work of
several different authors. Brooks was the most successful. In
1917 he took over the series completely and continued writing
it for the *Nelson Lee* until the paper folded in 1933. E. S. Brooks
managed convincingly to transfer the free-lance detective and
his assistant to a school setting. (Lee became a teacher, and
Nipper a pupil, at St Frank's.) Brooks's forte, however, was
the adventure/suspense story, and the confines of school life
were not allowed to inhibit the exuberant nature of the
series.

The *Nelson Lee*'s special appeal for boy readers derives from
the fact that the action is seen largely from Nipper's viewpoint.
The 'young 'un' is not just the guv'nor's stooge, but a junior
partner in detection. In 'Twenty Fathoms Deep' Lee and
Nipper are anxious to retrieve from a sunken launch the secret
plans for a new British gun. But while they are waiting for
diving apparatus to arrive from London some enemy agents
try to forestall them. When the Germans discover that Nipper
is on their track they have no compunction about trying to
murder the boy. Nipper is drugged and put in the path of an
express train. Rescued in the nick of time by Nelson Lee,
Nipper is then naturally anxious to get even with 'these two
Germhuns'. (This term for the enemy is unusual in wartime
boys' papers, although it seems an extremely appropriate
expression of popular feeling.) Episodes in 'Twenty Fathoms
Deep' underline one of the many rules laid down by Northcliffe
for his writers of juvenile fiction: the prohibition on swearing or

doubtful language. When the officer in charge of diving operations finds that the Germans have tampered with his equipment he restrains his language for Nipper's sake: '"I had better not say what I think in front of you, my lad!" he said quickly. "You're a boy, and it is not good for boys to hear violent language.".' Only a thwarted enemy spy is allowed to swear 'under his breath, in pure, unadulterated German'.

British decency is contrasted with German ruthlessness on another occasion. Lee and Nipper have to prevent the Germans from reaching the launch. The enemy agents are preparing to dive and Nelson Lee would like to tackle them on a fist-to-fist basis; distance prevents this, and he confides to Nipper: '"Of course we could level our revolvers this very minute and drop both the scoundrels where they stand, but that isn't the British way. It's too cold-blooded...".' Nevertheless, it would have been efficient. The Germans apparently were unlikely to share these scruples. 'The slaughter of babies, the vile killing of hundreds of helpless people in the *Lusitania*, was not murder to the Germans.' Incidentally Nelson Lee's reluctance to shoot down enemies who are unprepared finds an echo in John Buchan's *Mr Standfast*. Hannay has the opportunity of killing Moxon Ivery, a German espionage agent who is planning to destroy the British army by the dissemination of anthrax germs. But Hannay doesn't shoot, although he has the spy in his revolver sights: it would be bad form, because Moxon is a sitting target at the time and unprepared for death.

A sense of fair play is prominent too in stories by Charles Hamilton, the Amalgamated Press's most popular boys' writer. In a climate of anti-German fanaticism that prompted people to go to ridiculous lengths, sometimes even having pet dachshunds destroyed, Hamilton makes the distinction between 'good' and 'bad' Germans. Harry Wharton, junior captain of Greyfriars School, points out in a 1916 *Magnet* that '"... there are some decent Germans—Handel and Beethoven were Germans, you know, and it would be idiotic to call them Huns"'. Wharton is disturbed by the persecution of Herr Gans, the hysterical but harmless Greyfriars German master. Some of the more odious members of the Remove are systematically planning to 'make him think that he's really off his dot'; and even the more reasonable boys jeer at him, put kippers in his Sunday hat and glue in his slippers. Things come to a head when 'the fat Herr' discovers a drawing of himself (in German army uniform) impaling a baby on a bayonet. According to Charles Hamilton such atrocities could be perpetrated only by the Prussians, and not by Saxons like Herr Gans: '"I veep mit shame tat men of Cherman blood shall do tose tings."'

Gans eventually proves his almost-British-decency by begging the Remove boys off a headmaster's flogging, and intervening to prevent the expulsion of Skinner, his most despicable tormentor. By his own admission—in answer to George Orwell's famous *Horizon* criticism of 'Boys' Weeklies'—Hamilton thought that most foreigners were 'funny'. The ineptitude of his French and German masters was a comic device to throw British spunk and tolerance into sharp relief at a level which might appeal to schoolboy readers. Bullying, however, was taboo.

Many of Charles Hamilton's *Magnet* and *Gem* stories were intensely patriotic: embezzlers, petty criminals and weedy, frowsting rotters were incredibly quick to answer their country's call. At the front they behaved with heroism and redeemed their past inadequacies. The Greyfriars and St Jim's juniors too managed to get behind the German lines with surprising frequency. ('"It would be a giddy adventure!" said Harry Wharton, his eyes glistening.') Although British schoolboys are always—eventually—more than a match for 'the horrid Huns', Harry Wharton, Tom Merry and their chums find themselves on more than one occasion facing an enemy firing squad. Their response is satisfyingly plucky: '"Keep a stiff upper lip," said the Bounder. "If we've got to face it, it's no good whining. Don't let the curs have the laugh of us."'

It is likely that Charles Hamilton, whose army service was curtailed on medical grounds, was sickened by the hypocrisy of politicians and the popular press. There is of course a particularly revolting smugness about stirring speeches and articles which exhort *other* people to go and fight. There are ironic reflections of this kind of humbug in Hamilton's wartime fiction: 'Some had come to the Anti-Conscription meeting to cheer, and some had come to "boo", and there was a party of determined-looking old gentlemen—over military age—who were there to heckle the speeches . . .' (*Gem*, 431, 1916).

One of Hamilton's masterly stories on the theme of vicarious recruitment is 'The St Jim's Recruit' (*Gem*, 364, 1915). This is by turns ironical and sincerely patriotic. Mr Railton, a young and popular St Jim's master, decides to deliver a recruiting speech to a crowd at a local football match. (This was a fairly common practice before conscription was introduced.) He appeals to the football enthusiasts as Britishers and sportsmen '. . . to back up our team—England's team in khaki . . . out there . . .'. Railton particularly addresses himself to Benny, a young carpenter in the forefront of the crowd, asking 'as a friend' why he doesn't volunteer. However, the young man's spirited reply—' "May I arsk *you* as a friend, Sir, why *you* don't go?" '—sets the St Jim's master thinking. The carpenter, with a family to keep, earns '2 quid a week', most of which he loses if he volunteers. Moreover '. . . the loss of a leg or an arm was terribly serious to a worker who depended on his limbs for his daily bread', whereas a wounded schoolmaster could probably take up teaching again. Mr Railton's half-hearted resistance—' "I have no training. If I should apply for a commission I should be refused" '—is succinctly dealt with by Benny. ' "Was you recommending me to apply for an officer's job Sir? . . . And can't you go as a private if I does?" ' Schoolmaster and carpenter leave the football pitch together for the recruiting office, followed by a score of other volunteers, to the satisfaction of the fictional schoolboys of St Jim's, and real-life readers of the paper.

There are touches of a more bitter humour in a St Jim's story of eighteen months later. In 'The Patriots of St Jim's' (*Gem*, 445, 1916) Arthur Augustus D'Arcy, an aristocratic junior, is lamenting that ' "the wah has been dwaggin' on long enough" ' because ' "our gweat statesmen are so busy lookin' aftah their jobs and their salawies that they haven't weally time for weflection" '. Tom Merry replies that '. . . "the war is a permanent institution. Under the new law, we're going to be conscripted when we grow up, and then we shall have to take our turn in the trenches. We've got to keep ourselves fit, or we shan't be allowed to go out and get killed." ' D'Arcy voices the hopeful view of the time that at least ' "This is a wah to end wah" '. But another junior prophetically suggests that ' "all countries will be governed by the same kind of silly idiots in the future as in the past. so there will always be a war, on and off...".'

Hamilton introduces farce as well as irony into his wartime stories with the exploits of Billy Bunter, the obtuse and greedy Greyfriars junior. Bunter's form-mates discover the fat Owl in a box room, surrounded by an enormous spread of preserves,

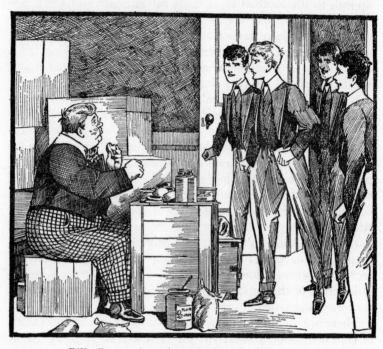

Billy Bunter ignoring wartime food shortages
From *The Magnet*, 1915

cakes, fruit, cold meat and chocolates. He is paraded round the quadrangle festooned with empty food jars, tins and bottles, and bearing a placard which says:

THE PRIZE HOG: This Animal Has Been Caught
Helping the Germans by Wasting the Food Supply.
PLEASE THROW SOMETHING.

In retaliation Bunter pretends to go on a fast to help the war effort, and patriotic members of the form feel obliged to join him. Of course, he has secret access to supplies of grub which the other juniors do not discover until they are feeble through lack of food. Incidentally a recurrent wartime advertisement in the *Magnet*—'EAT LESS BREAD'—adds point to this story: it appears among regular boys'-paper advertisements offering cures for red noses, blushing and stammering, and advice on growing taller and astounding one's friends by becoming an expert ventriloquist.

A great deal of the humour that occurs in boys' stories by Captain W. E. Johns is unintentional. Squadron Leader James Bigglesworth ('Biggles'), a first world war hero, was created retrospectively by Johns for the magazine *Popular Flying* which he edited for many years. The series is on a vast scale: there have been approximately 90 Biggles books, many of which are still in print. In 1975 a London Conference of Librarians decided to ban Biggles, a character now condemned as racist and chauvinistic, though in fact he is no more xenophobic or aggressive than the heroes of Buchan and other authors whose books still appear on the shelves of school libraries.

The early Biggles stories of the first world war are the most memorable, conveying something of the exhilarating, pioneer outlook of men of the Royal Flying Corps. Perhaps because these were originally written for an adult magazine their content is less facile than that of the subsequent stories aimed at increasingly lower age groups. There is no depth of characterization; attitudes are black and white, and the violence is that of the clenched fist and the quick, clean kill. Biggles is manly but not sexual. (He really has a great deal in common with Buchan's characters.) He experiences only one whimsical and frustrated romantic involvement. In a short story un-originally called 'Affaire de Cœur' Biggles meets Marie Janis (who turns out to be a German spy and almost causes his execution). She is described as 'a vision of blonde loveliness'. When she says, '"Please, Beegles!"' she unnerves him so much that he has to hurry back to his quarters on the pretext 'that his magneto is nearly shorting'. After the Marie Janis episode Biggles shows no further interest in women. (Years later he implies that his success as a deadly combat pilot and a reliable espionage agent is because he wastes no energy on sex.)

Biggles affects an attitude of contemptuous amusement

'The Germans broke ranks as the fighter strafed them'
From *Biggles—The Rescue Flight* by W. E. Johns

towards his enemies—'sausage-eating, square-headed sons of offal merchants'—but grim dog-fights between German and British air-aces are conducted with chivalry. In fact Biggles enjoys making all sorts of bizarrely chivalrous gestures to his enemies—and friends. 'A squadron of Uhlans watering their horses offered the next target, but for the sake of the horses he held his fire and satisfied himself by zooming low over them.' In another story he drops silk pyjamas behind the enemy lines for comrades who have baled out and been taken prisoner. And he nonchalantly lands on a German airfield to steal a live turkey for his men's Christmas dinner. Evading German fighters he flies home with the bird struggling and squawking in his cockpit until it is silenced by an enemy bullet. Of course the only thing that really matters in the Biggles saga is pace; as long as the skies are alive with German Fokkers and British Camels 'banking, wheeling, zooming, diving and turning to dive again' the stories will appeal to air-minded children.

Charles Hamilton, E. S. Brooks and other authors of fiction of the first world war wrote successfully for boys on very different themes in the following two decades. Several writers, including W. E. Johns and George Rochester—another creator of fictional flying aces—continued to exploit wartime situations. Their stories were read by a generation of boys who knew nothing of the actuality of the war, but who grew up romanticizing it. Many of them, of course, became the soldiers, sailors and airmen of the second world war.

V

PASSIONATE INTENSITY

Some Best-sellers of the War

The River of death has brimmed his banks,
And England's far, and Honour a name,
But the voice of a schoolboy rallies the ranks:
'Play up! Play up! and play the game!'
Sir Henry Newbolt, 'Vitai Lampada'

NATURALLY THE WAR produced a crop of best-sellers that
gave expression to all kinds of fashionable or retrogressive views
and provided a permanent shape for the basic myths whose
function was to transform and ennoble the raw essence of warfare in the popular imagination. For many people, these books
are still the standard works of fiction of the first world war.
In *Tell England*, probably the most representative novel in
terms of public-school honour and classic chauvinism, there
are no significant parts for the female characters who are
mentioned directly when they appear as tennis partners and
very obliquely when their rôle is to do with sexual initiation.
The book is relevant to our theme because its central characters
are schoolboys who never grow up.

The works discussed in detail below are all written by men,
and it is interesting to consider their treatment of women
characters where this is extensive: in no instance is it realistic.
The fundamental narrative attitude veers from adulation to
aversion. Richard Aldington's *Death of a Hero* is included here,
although it is much more complex and literary than the other
novels in this group, because of the author's extraordinary
contempt for the behaviour of women in wartime. In *Simon
Called Peter*, a very dull and unsavoury piece of romantic
writing, a particular group of women—prostitutes—is sentimentalized: to see this view in context, it is necessary to
an extent to consider the predicament and outlook of the
hero.

A. S. M. Hutchinson is another archetypal best-selling author of the period, and in at least two of his novels both the pattern of events and the narrative rhetoric are determined by the war. *If Winter Comes*, of course, has a male protagonist; but the theme directly relates to the experiences of three women. Hutchinson's standpoint is always traditional, to say the least. *If Winter Comes* has many failings of style and imagination; and *This Freedom* achieves what is possibly the most extreme expression of anti-feminism in a popular novel.

Tell England, published in 1922, became a best-seller because it pandered openly to certain romantic ideas of youth and its attitude to war. These are embodied in the persons of 'twin' heroes Ray and Doe, whose emotional closeness is symbolized by a common birthday and absurdly complementary surnames. The book was advertised as 'A Great Romance of Glorious Youth. In Two Episodes: School and the War'. The school is Kensingtowe, probably a fictionalized version of St Paul's, where the author, Ernest Raymond, was educated. The first section is entitled 'Five Gay Years at School' and the adjective has an aptness that was certainly not deliberate. In its debased or slang sense it is still relevant. Ernest Raymond himself was startled to recognize a homosexual element in the book when he re-read it in 1968: 'Another thing that is a wonder to me ... is the indubitable but wholly unconscious homosexuality in it.' (Quoted in Gillian Avery, *Childhood's Pattern*, Hodder & Stoughton 1975.)

In fact it is now impossible to remain unconscious of underlying homosexuality in the majority of highly-charged school friendships that were chronicled by various authors before the 1930s. No modern reader can fail to extend these authors' images to their most plausible conclusion, though it is obvious that the inference was not intended. It is a combination of narrative innocence and explicit description that makes this aspect of the stories so amusing. Our sense of wholesome behaviour has undergone a complete reversal, and we are amazed at the forms that friendship could take—or rather, at the terms in which it is presented: 'Perhaps Doe was a girl. After all, I had no certain knowledge that he wasn't a girl with his hair cut short. . . . As I produced this strange figure, I began to feel, somewhere in the region of my waist, motions of calf-love for the girl Doe that I had created.'

In cases like this it is simply the discrepancy between the author's implication and the actual implication that is startling. Evasiveness and dissembling give rise to a morbid, overwrought tone. At the present time, most readers prefer the subject to be treated sensibly: Kingsley Amis, in *The Riverside Villas Murder* (1973), gets the right note of forthright humour: 'Unconsummated meetings between the two were tacitly ruled out; Peter, at any rate, felt that their friendship as such missed being close enough by a small but decisive margin. Which was just as well; start getting fond of your sparring partner and you might end up a homo.'

In *Tell England* the build-up of incidents with a sexual undertone becomes almost farcical. One boy gets another into a corner and tells him, '"You're so pretty that I'd love to see you cry".' Doe remarks ingenuously to Ray, '"It was rather fun being whacked side by side, being twins".' Doe has a rather strange attitude to physical punishment in any case: '"Do you know, I really think I like Radley better than anyone else in the world. I simply loved being whacked by him."'

Radley is the athletic master whom the two boys admire. He has a habit of holding on to the hand that he has whacked, delivering at the same time a definition of honourable behaviour with many references to cricket. Radley is a 'lover of youth', no less than the jocular and effusive school doctor who concludes, '. . . "This is England's best generation. Dammit, there are three things old England *has* learnt to make: ships, poetry and boys."'

This pretty notion is elaborated in physical terms: '"I say, Radley, don't you think this generation of boys is the most shapely lot England has turned out?"' And, with an irony that was meant to have a deep effect on the sympathetic reader, Doctor Chapman adds, '"I wonder what use she'll make of them."' In 1922 the answer to that question was known: cannon-fodder. In a sense the book is a tribute to the dead schoolboys of the generation that was barely old enough to fight. The 'best' in this story are among the earliest to die, apart from Rupert Ray who had to survive until the last weeks of the war: the book is written in the first person.

The Kensingtowe boys aren't universally shapely, however. '"That's old Freedham's boy over there. . . . Shocking specimen."' At one point Edgar Doe is in danger of being led astray by the shocking Freedham: '". . . we—we tried everything together. We—we got drunk on a beastly occasion in his room."' Freedham is unattractive and subject to fits, but he succeeds in communicating to Doe his theory that 'Life is sensation': '"I still think . . . that Freedham's got hold of the Truth, only perverted; just as he himself is a perversion . . .".' In the brief interval between school and embarkation for the Dardanelles Doe and Ray experiment with kinds of 'sensation', mostly related to 'the things of the night' and 'the shameful doorway'. These emotive phrases are left to work their own effect. But it is on a motor-bike with 'the white dust of England' blowing into his face that Doe experiences bodily exhilaration most fully: ' "My godfathers, this is Life!" '

It is 'Life' by pointed contrast with imminent extermination. The first Kensingtowe boy to die is the dashing Pennybet, brave and outspoken to the end: '"By jove, I've had my good time— and am ready to pay for it—if I must. . . . If God puts me through it, *I* shan't whine."' This is the true public-school spirit in the imagination of Ernest Raymond. The unpleasantness of death is everywhere subsumed into the ennobling attitudes of the dying: the book purveys an adolescent idealism that owes much to Rupert Brooke's *1914* sonnets. The idea of death as regeneration, with the dead absorbed into some cosmic totality, was posited as an antidote to the realistic view that might have eroded the national morale.

Brooke was perhaps the most accomplished of the literary fantasists who relished the prospect of war, for whom mass slaughter could be regarded as an abstraction, a means of wiping out lackadaisical or degenerate elements in society. The purging was to take effect on two levels: apart from the actual deaths, the fact of fighting for a cause was expected to work the necessary transformation. Indeed, when war broke out, the British soldier appears to have derived remarkable encouragement from his sense of being morally in the right: in literature at any rate, mention of the word 'honour' could always be relied on to produce the correct response. Brooke's elevated sentimentality about war is expressed in a consciously pastoral,

poetic idiom; the same quality in Ernest Raymond takes on a
bluff fervour:

> 'Eighteen, by jove!' [remarked the colonel]. 'You've timed
> your lives wonderfully, my boys. To be eighteen in 1914 is
> the best thing in England. England's wealth used to consist
> in other things. Nowadays you boys are the richest thing
> she's got. She's solvent with you, and bankrupt without you.
> Eighteen, confound it! . . . Eighteen years ago you were born
> for this day. Through the last eighteen years you've been
> educated for it. Your birth and breeding were given you
> that you might officer England's youth in this hour. . . .'

This fatherly old poet, as Ernest Raymond calls him,
kindles a 'responsive excitement' in his impressionable recruit.
'"I think I half hoped it would be my high lot to die on the
battlefield."' (It is, of course.) The colonel's inspiriting
remarks are rephrased some time later by the boys' new
champion, Padre Monty. '"No army in the world is officered
by such a lot of fresh sportsmen as ours."' It is Padre Monty,
in his enthusiasm for the boys' spiritual welfare, who comes out
with the most memorable resolve in the book: '"I'm going to
send you down the gangway when you go ashore to this
crusade—properly absolved by your Church. I'm going to send
you into the fight—*white*."'

The high-church padre attains this objective by persuading
the two boys to 'confess' to him. The embarrassing business is
made worse for the reader by the padre's insistence on addressing Doe (Edgar Grey Doe) as Gazelle. ('"My dear Gazelle,
don't be absurd."') This section of the book is suffused with
banal sublimities—Goodness, Truth, Beauty and so on. These
are defined with a vagueness that was plainly meant to induce
a sense of infinity—necessary to accommodate the pseudo-
mystical aspects of the boys' deaths. When Doe is hit four times
in the waist, the dreadful cleric is ready with another piece of
high-flown sentimentality: '"Rupert, Edgar is dead. . . . And
there's only one unbeautiful thing about his death, and that is
the way his friend is taking it."'

The death-bed scenes in this type of war story appear as an
extension or refinement of the Victorian 'dying child' syndrome.

As a topical image the dying soldier boy could sustain with equal facility the notions of bravery and purity and incorruptible integrity that surrounded the stricken Evangelical waif. It proffered too the vapid consolations of a sense of heroic sacrifice: these could make sense only in a context that totally discounted reality, built on debased conventions of style and behaviour. *Tell England* re-creates the mood that may have

OFFICER (to boy of thirteen who, in his effort to get taken on as a bugler, has given his age as sixteen): "Do you know where boys go who tell lies?"
APPLICANT: "To the Front, sir."

From *Mr Punch's History of the Great War*, 1919

existed when war was declared; it takes no account of subsequent changes of feeling. The later war poets might as well not have written, as far as Ernest Raymond is concerned. His purpose was to give shape to the kind of idealistic chauvinism that Wilfred Owen had condemned:

> ... If you could hear, at every jolt, the blood
> Come gargling from the froth-corrupted lungs,
> Bitter as the cud
> Of vile, incurable sores on innocent tongues,——

> My friend, you would not tell with such high zest
> To children ardent for some desperate glory,
> The old lie: *Dulce et decorum est*
> *Pro patria mori.*

But these lines, of course, make nonsense of the view of death perpetuated in novels like *Tell England*.

Padre Monty is an apt successor to S. T. Radley in the boys' affections. Both men are decent, forthright, sincere, and given to the expression of uplifting sentiments. Each has his own clichéd metaphor to suggest the ineffable: with Radley it is cricket, with the padre the adjective 'white'. In fact the author relies heavily on these motifs to symbolize a noble and patriotic disposition. It is no accident that the famous epitaph from which the title is taken,

> Tell England, ye who pass this monument
> We died for her, and here we rest content

should appear over the grave of the boy 'Moles' White, sportsman and 'gentle giant' of Kensingtowe. (It is evidently derived from an equally famous Greek inscription to the Spartans who died at Thermopylae in 480 BC: 'Stranger, tell the Laccedaemonians that we lie here, obedient to their command.')

> The perfect words went straight to Doe's heart.
> 'Roop,' he said, 'if I'm killed you can put those lines over me.'
> I fear I could not think of anything very helpful to reply.
> 'They are rather swish,' I murmured.

In the work of writers less competent than Ernest Raymond the image of boys in the trenches can take on a startling incongruity. The Hon. Mrs Walter Forbes, for instance, envisages war in the terms of a fairy tale: '. . . Young Denham . . . looked like a baby whom a wicked fairy had snatched from his cot and dropped into some witches' seething cauldron.' *His Alien Enemy* (published in 1918), from which this quotation comes, is an interesting example of a war story in which none of the characters actually gets killed. Its dialogue is alternately jolly '. . . There was a moment's silence. Then Baby Charlton spoke. "By Jove! War!" he said' and sententious: '". . . a man's country is the country of his fathers; a woman's that of her heart".'

Young Denham looks like a baby, Baby Charlton behaves like one: war is plainly not a matter for grown-ups at all. It is rather closely allied to the concept of playing the game: 'playing for one's school is much the same thing as fighting for the empire'. The book is without a rational character to dispute this facile and inaccurate proposition.

Another public-school tradition, that of hero worship, provides a central theme for R. C. Sheriff's *Journey's End* (this play was first performed in 1928); but the author's objective is to indicate the bewilderment and misapprehension of many of the boys who went straight from the classroom to the fighting line. Propaganda and appeals to honour and manliness had made it fairly easy to conceive of the trenches as a kind of extension of the sixth form. Sheriff's hero, eighteen-year-old Raleigh, arrives at St Quentin expecting to renew his friendship with the senior Stanhope, whom he has admired at school. But Stanhope's nature has been changed radically: he is one of the young officers who can keep going only by being permanently drunk. On a simple level the play is about disillusion and horror—but Raleigh dies still behaving in accordance with the public-school code. '"It's awfully decent of you to bother, Dennis [he says to Stanhope]. I feel rotten lying here—everybody else—up there."'

There is an ambiguity of feeling here: we can either admire Raleigh for his team spirit or deplore his capacity for self-delusion. In romantic terms, Raleigh has to die before he has time to modify his false ideas. Innocence is slaughtered so that it may not turn to cynicism: this is the drift of the underlying concept, and it contains, again, a hint of the Victorian morbidity that killed off the 'angel-children' before they could be corrupted by worldly preoccupations. *Journey's End* has a sentimental basis, though it appears to take a realistic viewpoint.

More acceptable, perhaps, is the romantic view of death that sees it as the only possible end for those whose psychological capacities have been exhausted by the strains of battle. Like the hero of Erich Maria Remarque's *All Quiet on the Western Front* (published in England in 1929), experience of war has ruined them for civilian life. They have no means of resuming a 'normal' existence. The behaviour of soldiers on leave has been extensively documented: their sense of dissociation and futility was extreme. A mild form of shell-shock was nearly universal. The continual demands on soldiers to behave in a way contrary to their natural instincts could only have resulted in a deadening of individual purpose and sense of identity. In novels that make this point (like *Death of a Hero*; see below) death in battle is considered in an enlarged context that takes account of the mental state of the victims.

Simon Called Peter (Robert Keable, 1921) is the story of Peter Graham, a young army chaplain who loses his faith, goes through a great deal of soul-searching and finally becomes a mystical fanatic. The book is reminiscent of one of those girls' school stories with a faintly religious flavour and a title like *Cynthia Finds Herself*. Peter finds himself, but the process is tortuous, fervid and prolonged. To begin with, he is upset by displays of moral laxity in wartime France: ' "But how damnable, how beastly. ... It makes one sick!" ' However, this priggish view is modified rather quickly, and unthinking outrage gives way to a belated recognition of sexual necessity. ' "I am tired of play-acting. I've a body, like other men. Let me plunge down deep to-night, Louise. It will do me good, and it doesn't matter. ..." '

The biblical undertones become increasingly florid as Peter declares his intention to 'eat and drink with publicans and sinners'. The phrase occurs in a letter he sends to his well-bred fiancée Hilda. She is somewhat disturbed: ' "Peter is queer in some ways, you know" '. Her mother puts it more strongly: ' "My poor girl, he must be mad. Surely you see that, dear?" '

It is the end of the road for Peter and Hilda; but another girl—a high-spirited Red Cross nurse named Julie Gamelyn— is willing to take on the emotional burden of ministering to the confused padre. Julie is a madcap whose innocent naughtiness gives the sole touch of lightness to an overwrought narrative. The French prostitutes with their hard-luck stories provide the most marked instance of Robert Keable's tendency to idealize. He is out to preach the virtues of charity and compassion, and this can get dreadfully in the way of his sense of reality. '"You think me a bad girl?"' one *coquette* asks. '"No, I am not bad; I go to church. Le bon Dieu made us as we are; it is nécessaire."' 'Le bon Dieu' is invoked constantly by the holy street walkers. '"He is wise—ah, how wise!—it is not for me to say. And good—ah, Jesu! how good!"' another exclaims. These girls are meek and kind-hearted and emotional. They speak bathetically in a clichéd foreign manner: '"This love," she said, "it is one great thing. For us women it is perhaps the only great thing, though your Englishwomen are blind, are dead, they do not see. Julie, she is as us, I think. She is French inside. La pauvre petite, she is French in the heart."'

The plight of the French girls is attributed to the war: the deaths of their lovers or protectors or the destruction of their homes has driven them into the streets in droves. They have no other resources; they are objects for pity and understanding. They aren't commercially motivated, unlike the prostitutes described by Robert Graves (in *Goodbye To All That*, 1929); those could serve nearly a battalion of men a week for a short period and then retire on their earnings. In Robert Keable's novel they stand for vulnerability and incorruptible feeling, and provide a kind of Greek chorus to the more clearly defined characteristics of his heroine, Julie.

Charity for a fallen woman comes into A. S. M. Hutchinson's best-selling *If Winter Comes* (1921). The hero Mark Sabre ('old Puzzlehead') ruins himself socially and nearly lays himself open to a murder charge when he takes into his house a timid unmarried mother and her child. The girl, Effie, has been a servant employed by Sabre's wife and naturally people imagine that the child is his (he had been home on leave from the army at the time when it must have been conceived). His horrid wife chooses this moment to leave him, thereby strengthening the gossips' case. The innocent Sabre is flabbergasted when he realizes that Mabel too has read an obvious implication into his charitable act: 'His wife! Mabel! Was it possible? A vile, hideous, sordid intrigue with a girl employed in his own house? Effie! His wife to believe that! An unspeakable, beastly thing like that!'

D

Sabre has been rather short-sighted and stupid in this matter; now he sits down on a bed and repeats in a demented way, '"Seducer! Adulterer! I, seducer!"' Hutchinson's style has all the defects of subjective writing: there is no detachment, no irony, and little attempt to render a coherent or plausible emotional state. His hero's emotions are expressed in exclamatory outbursts: when Sabre is told of Effie's suicide (she has poisoned herself with oxalic acid and suffocated her baby) he repeats twelve times the phrase 'found dead'.

Sabre has an uplifting sense of nationality that is comparable to Peter Graham's obsession with God. He sees England simply as 'the most glorious and splendid country in the world'. Of course when war is declared his bursting heart takes up the chorus, 'England! England!' Disillusionment sets in, but the rhetoric continues. England is a

> ... huge and splendid animal something bewildered by the fury of the onset upon it. Shaking her head whereon had fallen stunning and unexpected blows... roaring her defiance; baring her fangs; tearing up the ground before her ... her dominion challenged; shaken, bleeding.
>
> England ...
>
> This frightful war....

One might add, this frightful prose: Hutchinson stirred by strong emotions is worse even than Hutchinson the social critic in the guise of the unassuming but facetious man-in-the-street. The latter pose was a common one in popular post-war writing: it was adopted also by the novelist A. J. Cronin, and in his case too it conveys an irritating narrative smugness and niggling sarcasm. Cronin's characterization of Jenny in *The Stars Look Down* (see Chapter VII) produces the same effect as Hutchinson's view of Mabel: the women are awful, of course, but we can't quite accept the evaluation of either novelist. In literary terms, the failing is one of wit. The facetiousness that passes for humour in fact has a deadening effect. The women's repugnant qualities are not presented sharply or stringently; they are merely reiterated in situations that illustrate but don't exploit them.

Mark Sabre's private fortunes are determined by his relations

with three women: Mabel, Nona and Effie. A section of the
book is devoted to each, and all three are invoked in the final
quarter. Mabel is the usual suburban housewife preoccupied
with gentility and totally unresponsive to her husband's rather
attractive whimsy. In the circumstances it isn't surprising that
Sabre should turn to a childhood sweetheart who has re-
appeared conveniently in the neighbourhood. Sabre is ambling
along on a bicycle, thinking 'puzzling thoughts' of his 'Penny
Green Garden Home, and of Mabel, and of Mabel and himself
in connection with the Penny Green Garden Home', when
his reverie is interrupted by Nona, now Lady Tybur, out
riding with her husband. Soon she comes to visit Sabre at his
office:

'. . . I like you best when you're thinking. You puzzle, don't
you, Marko? You've got a funny old head. I believe you
live in your old head, you know. Puzzling things. Clever
beast! I wish I could live in mine.' And she gave a note of
laughter.
'Where do you live, Nona?'
'I don't live, I just go on'—she paused—'flotsam.'
Strange word to use, strangely spoken!

Of course she is hinting broadly at the inadequacies in her
marriage; her husband is callously promiscuous, as it turns out,
and she and Sabre are rather tempted to commit adultery.
But Sabre's conscience restrains them: ' "Once we took a step
towards wrong, there it is for ever, and all its horrible things
with it—deceit, concealment, falsehood, subterfuge, pretence:
vile and beastly things like that." ' Curiously, it is the outbreak
of war that reconciles Nona to the platonic nature of their
friendship. Her husband has rejoined the Guards: ' "And you
see that whatever has been, and is, dear, he's my man to stand
by in this." '
This confusion of issues is a characteristic device of the
conventional best-selling novelist. Unlike the ephemeral
popular fiction of the periodicals, which panders unequivocally
to the more vapid type of fantasy, the best-seller has to evince a
quasi-intelligent approach. It has to appear to give reasoned
consideration to the serious questions it raises. Often in fact, it

shirks the logical development of the situations it posits. For an inner logic of its own it substitutes a facile endorsement of social conventions—and the reader is led to believe that the popular sentiment is really, ultimately, the most sensible (it pays off, after all, in the novelist's context). Best-selling authors have to manipulate their material to make it palatable to a large audience; each reader must be made to feel that the novel contains essential, simple 'truths' yet requires of its readership a degree of intellectual effort. The technical problems are enormous, but the author is helped by the public's willingness to come half way. And there are basic guidelines: the reader knows what to expect in the way of morals and social behaviour and sentiment, and must get it. It is only the presentation and the storyline that may be original or unexpected, though even this isn't necessary. Evidence of a flair, a 'way' with language that implies sensitivity, however, may help to put a novel in the best-seller lists—so long as it is blatant enough. The popular novel is consistent in presenting a clever, prettified but completely factitious substitute for the real thing. The reader is appealed to at the levels of intelligence, sensitivity, common decency and common sense—and all these concepts are subtly confounded. But the readers who make it a best-seller are not aware of this. (This applies only to 'general' popular fiction. Certain special categories, like the detective story, are not considered here.)

It can be done by taking two separate ideas and implying a connection between them—always with an emotional bias. There is no logical reason, for instance, why Nona Tybur's relations with Mark Sabre should be affected by the fact that her husband has become a soldier: her reaction is purely sentimental. The narrative defect is not that Nona's attitude is implausible—many women must have reacted like this—but simply that the novelist appears to condone it.

Hutchinson's prose style is effusive and repetitive. His novels are possibly among the most overwritten in the English language. *If Winter Comes* is heartfelt and showy—but the author's relish for emotional melodrama is really given full play in *This Freedom* (a falling bird stamped blind on the cover), published in 1922 and selling to the extent of 100,000 copies in the first year. The novel's heroine is Rosalie Aubyn, a 'new woman' whose experiences are followed from childhood to middle age. From the epigraph on ('With a great sum obtained I this freedom') the author's motive is plain: he is out to expose the weaknesses in certain feminist principles as he understands them.

It is possible that a reader might have a degree of empathy with Mark Sabre, whose troubles arise from a rather agreeable characteristic: a habit of giving serious consideration to the other chap's point of view. He is the traditional, middle-of-the-road Englishman, obstinate only in defence of the principle of tolerance. He is steadfast, self-effacing, and touchingly inarticulate in moments of stress: '"Look here——" Gulps. "Look here——" Gulps again.' In Rosalie's characterization, however, we are aware only of the novelist's bias: everything is geared to ratify the story's anti-feminist theme. (For an opposite viewpoint it is worth comparing this novel with May Sinclair's far more restrained and cogent stories, *The Life and Death of Harriet Frean* and *Mary Olivier: a Life*.) Hutchinson's thesis is simple to the point of absurdity: 'professional' women are flying in the face of biological necessity, and sooner or later a price will be exacted. They are violating the natural order, for reasons of envy or rashness or simple perversity. If they fail to marry, they will become odd old maids and take to drink; if they do marry, their husbands and children will be sorely neglected.

Ever since the beginnings of suffragette agitation in the 1860s, *This Freedom*'s theme has been familiar to readers of women's magazines; but even the most misguided or unfortunate of the magazine heroines were rarely subjected to the degree of narrative recrimination that is inflicted on Hutchinson's Rosalie. In sociological terms, of course, the book's appearance was opportune. It puts the case for sentimental conservatism. Women had just been enfranchised; *en masse* they had shown unexpected capacities in the course of the war; and many were reluctant to resume a passive and sheltered existence. The general post-war revolt against militancy, orthodoxy and authoritarianism had diffused a feeling of insecurity amongst the more reactionary sections of English society. Women's emancipation was just one of the issues that appeared to indicate a dangerous escalation in demands for social change.

Hutchinson's novel reassured its readers that traditional values were still worthwhile: Victorian ideas of chastity and motherhood and so on were re-examined and found comfortably relevant to life in the 1920s. The book's most pointed and lurid tragedy occurs during the short period of moral relaxation engendered by the war. Doda Occleve, a bored and wilful schoolgirl in 1917, persuades her parents to let her have a year's 'war-work'; inevitably (in terms of the plot) she becomes pregnant and dies from the after-effects of an abortion.

Doda's outlook and behaviour, as far as these are suggested by the author, seem typical of her generation; but Hutchinson chooses to attribute her death to the selfishness of her mother. She is Rosalie's daughter, and Rosalie has followed a career in banking, regardless of the welfare of her family. The origins of Rosalie's supposedly neurotic preferences are stated: as a child she has idealized the 'masculine' qualities of her aggressive and sentimental clergyman father. 'She did not love her father, for he was entirely too remote and awe-ful for love, but he entranced her with his marvellousness. This maintained also her perception of the altogether greater [sic] superiority of all males over all females.'

Rosalie is sent to boarding school; without tuition or encouragement she becomes interested in economics and applies her intelligence to the problems of starting on a career. Her early success is described in the following terms:

> She's left the school! She's living in the splendid house in Pilchester Square looking for a post!
> She's found a post! She's private secretary to Mr Simcox!
> She's left the splendid house in Pilchester Square! She's living an independent life! She's going to Mr Simcox's office, *her* office, every day, just like a man! She's living on her own salary in a boarding-house in Bayswater!

This much is plausible, if one ignores the patronizing tone and the cheap literary effects (Mr Hutchinson's purpose is to simulate the breathless quality of youth). But from now on Rosalie's character begins to deteriorate—she is less 'sweet', less charitable—and the author gets entangled in a string of

psychological inconsistencies. He is merely following a convention when he makes his heroine declare that she doesn't
intend to marry. But Rosalie's extraordinary hatred of men,
her sexual vituperativeness, are indicative of mental disturbance, nothing to do with feminism one way or the other. She
sees men horribly as various species of cat:

> Tabby cats—the soft fattish kind . . . sloppy, old-womanish
> creatures. Cheshire cats—the kind that grinned out of
> vacuous minds and that never could speak to a woman
> without grinning; the unattached men at the boarding-
> house invariably were of the Cheshire-cat cats. Tom-cats—
> the beastly ones with the lecherous eyes that looked at
> you. . . . elderly tom-cats . . . had small beady eyes, set in
> yellow. . . .

This Freedom is retrogressive in a literal sense. The war is too
close in time to suit the novelist's purpose: its use is merely to
give dramatic point to Rosalie's emotional neglect of Doda. Its
evocation is hardly precise ('This war!'). Her son, Huggo,
joins the army, but this episode is not given much emphasis.
The war helps to further Rosalie's personal ambitions, of course;
at the bank she takes on the work of six men, releasing them for
the front (and gets scant credit for it). In reality, the only
immediate improvement effected in the quality of English life
was the sudden, necessary relaxing of the standards that had
governed the behaviour of respectable young women. As
Vera Brittain wrote of a short journey undertaken in 1915: 'No
one, this time, suggested going with me to London; already the
free-and-easy movements of girl war-workers had begun to
modify convention'. 'Free-and-easy' for Hutchinson, however,
implied moral degeneration—an attitude that is conveyed in
his contempt for the shallow, smart young people whom Doda
admires.

There is one error that A. S. M. Hutchinson doesn't fall
into: Rosalie is not a feminist and takes no interest in the
suffragette cause. Her motives are at once, for the author, more
selfish and more excusable. She isn't deluded about women's
aptitudes in general, she has merely failed to recognize the
priorities in her own life. Like Robert Graves's sisters (*Goodbye*

To All That, 1929), she has been brought up to wish herself a boy, to be shocked at the idea of women's suffrage, and not to expect so expensive an education as her brothers. Certainly involvement in the agitation for political reform would have implied an outlook more perceptive and disciplined than the one Rosalie is lumbered with. But other popular writers created militant suffragettes—figures of fun—who came to the same conclusions as Rosalie in the end. This approach is more crude though hardly less distorting ultimately than Hutchinson's.

Vera Brittain, again (in *Lady into Woman*, 1953), has referred to the failure of reputable authors to give adequate acknowledgement to the extent of women's involvement in the war effort. Of course writers like Edmund Blunden, Siegfried Sassoon, Robert Graves and David Jones were recording their personal experiences of combat; apart from the ubiquitous prostitutes, women hardly come into the picture. Richard Aldington's novel *Death of a Hero* (1929), however, has several women characters who don't show up at all well. The first of these to appear is George Winterbourne's mother. Her son has been killed in action: 'In low moaning tones, founded on the best tradition of sensational fiction, Mrs Winterbourne feebly ejaculated: "Dead, dead, dead!"' Her next sentence is: '"They've killed him, those vile, *filthy* foreigners. My *baby* son."' It isn't necessary to quote any more of her remarks: her character is established. She is a vapid, gushing woman. Her behaviour is peculiar and not altogether convincing. Instead of taking the sentimental view the author has taken its obverse, and this produces a comparable weakening of realistic effect. This type of characterization is too extreme and unrefined to pass for satire: for that both incisiveness and detachment are needed.

Our distaste for Mrs Winterbourne's affectations, however, is intensified at once: her 'emotion at the death of George almost immediately took an erotic form'. This is plausible: it is neither admirable nor shocking, but a feeling of revulsion and contempt is conveyed by the author:

> ... the effect of George's death on her temperament was, strangely enough, almost wholly erotic. The war did that to

lots of women. All the dying and wounds and mud and bloodiness—at a safe distance—gave them a great kick, and excited them to an almost unbearable pitch of amorousness. Of course, in that eternity of 1914–18 they must have come to feel that men alone were mortal, and they immortals; wherefore they tried to behave like houris with all available sheiks—hence the lure of 'war work' with its unbounded opportunities.

The significant phrase is 'at a safe distance'; and the resentment and bitterness felt by soldiers against the non-combatants is understandable, though it is perhaps unfair to blame women in general for the social convention that kept them out of the trenches. (In some cases they got as close to trench warfare as possible. The phrase 'Killed in action' was inscribed on the graves of the nurses who died in the bombing of Etaples.) Many of the women war-workers were motivated, at least to begin with, by unambiguous patriotism: they were no more immune to propaganda than anyone else. Then, for the young women who had faced no prospect but enforced boredom in provincial towns and villages, the sudden encouragement to leave home and take up work must have had an exhilarating effect. In the circumstances this was inevitable. Sexual freedom, when it occurred, was merely an incidental benefit for both sexes—it wasn't used to gratify feminine delusions of immortality, but arose at least partly from a legitimate fatalism. With imminent death a probability for at least half of those concerned, there can have been no place for coyness or prudery. (The attitude is not peculiar to war, it is merely more widespread then. In another context the Irish poet James Simmons wrote: 'With death for sauce, what appetites / They bring to their spare hours.')

Unfortunately the sudden reckless repudiation of ideas of chastity led to a spate of unwanted war-babies. One popular French song puts it succinctly:

> Après la guerre finie
> Tous les anglais partis
> Les demoiselles seront occupées
> A soigner leurs bébés.

As Vera Brittain notes in *Testament of Youth*, the papers were
full of letters on this subject. Half of these came from

> people who are most unmorally moral, want to disgrace the
> poor girls as much as possible and enlarge the offence out of
> all proportion. . . . The other, the hysterical party, absolutely
> excuses the offence on the score of abnormal conditions . . .
> hold forth about the children of the heroes of Mons and the
> Marne (which they are not) and even makes suggestions of
> compensation so extremely favourable to the offenders as to
> encourage others to repeat the sin, and thus undermine our
> whole social and moral structure.

The mildly triumphant, wilfully unconcerned attitude to
pregnancy is typified by Ernest Hemingway's heroine in *A
Farewell to Arms* (1929); but Catherine Barkley isn't by any
means a fully realized character. She embodies a kind of
romantic phlegmatic quality; in the novel, she has no identity
that is separable from her affair with the laconic protagonist,
Henry. Her conversation is consistently personal to the point
of inanity—and her death seems not so much tragic as wasteful.
But Hemingway's idea of the complementary rôle of his women
characters is well known.

Richard Aldington's sympathy for the deluded and exploited
soldier has given him a rather jaundiced attitude to those who
escaped the horrors of battle. We can accept his forthright
condemnation of cant, but his own prose occasionally becomes
unrestrained, even rhetorical: 'Somehow we must atone to the
dead—the dead, murdered, violently-dead soldiers.' To talk
with vehemence of atonement and guilt and poison implies a
hysterical bias. His view of feminine wartime behaviour is
similar to that expressed with ferocity by Siegfried Sassoon. In
'Glory of Women' Sassoon wrote:

> You love us when we're heroes, home on leave,
> Or wounded in a mentionable place.
> You worship decorations; you believe
> That chivalry redeems the war's disgrace.
> You make us shells.

Aldington's other women characters aren't 'grotesques' as he puts it: they are merely products of the era, smart and frivolous and self-absorbed. Elizabeth and Fanny are George Winterbourne's wife and mistress: 'They both had that rather hard efficiency of the war and post-war female, veiling the ancient predatory and possessive instincts of the sex under a skilful smoke-barrage of Freudian and Havelock Ellis theories.' Actually, this comment is as conventional as the crass 'public school' view of women that the author repudiates: 'A rag, a bone, a hank of hair. Get rid of the sexual problem by teaching men to despise women, either by open scorn or by putting them on the pedestal of chastity.' This simplifies general derogatory attitudes to women; the view is accurately observed and Aldington is right to criticize it. However, his own 'predatory and possessive instincts' is one of those irritating, meaningless phrases that seem truistic only because they are too wide to be disputed.

Aldington goes on to expose the moral weaknesses of Fanny and Elizabeth, with emphasis on their irrationality and capacity for self-delusion. The airy sarcasm of the narrative at this point is reminiscent of the smug tone already noted in A. S. M. Hutchinson and A. J. Cronin: 'But in 1914 something went wrong with Elizabeth's period, and she thought she was going to have a baby. And then, my hat, what a pother! Elizabeth lost her head entirely. Freud and Ellis went to the devil in a twinkling. No more talk of "freedom" *then*!'

When Winterbourne is in the trenches he receives delicately bitchy letters about each girl from the other. 'I hear she is *much* attached to a brilliant young scientist . . .'; '. . . she was with such a charming young man . . .'. On leave, the shell-shocked 'hero' feels like a death's-head at a feast. Elizabeth reproves him: '"Remember, dear, you're not with a lot of rough soldiers now. And, please forgive me for mentioning it, but your hands and fingers are terribly dirty—did you forget to wash them? And you were rather rude to everybody."'

The women's extraordinary insensitivity and failure of imagination were surely not typical; but the author proceeds to indict the whole sex in the following terms:

And the women? Oh, don't let's talk about the women. They were splendid. Such devotion, such devotion! How they

comforted the troops! Oh, wonderful, beyond all praise!
They got the vote for it, you know. Oh, wonderful! Steel-true
and blade-straight. Whatever should we have done without
them? White feathers, and all that, you know. Oh, the
women were marvellous. . . . So splendid, such an example.

Parody is a legitimate device to elaborate or underline scorn, of
course; and the clichéd phrases of newspapers and popular
orators needed to be shown up. But in this case repetition
produces a laboured effect—and the target is so general that the
invective loses its point. The tone is merely warped. But
because *Death of a Hero* isn't an unintelligent novel, the narrator
frankly acknowledges his own prejudice. 'George Winterbourne' has pointed it out to him: 'He said the War had
induced in me a peculiar resentment against women—which
was probably true.' The attitude remains, however, and it
makes us uneasy because it isn't dissociated from the general
standpoint.

The structure of the novel is rather odd: the story is
summarized in the prologue and then developed in the rest of
the book. The style is deliberately eclectic: this was the most
obvious way to indicate various facets of the atmosphere in
England at this particular time. But it doesn't make for
integration. A colloquial tone ('George was pretty much
affected by this social-reform bunk') is followed by inflation and
sentimentality. When Aldington remarks, 'Dear lovers! If it
were not for you, how dreary the world would be!' the banality
is hardly mitigated by his consciousness of it. As parody, it is too
tentative to be convincing.

Parts of *Death of a Hero* are excellent: in particular the
sections that deal with Winterbourne's experiences in the
trenches. All the false romanticism that surrounded the war at
one time is unemphatically refuted. The author communicates
a sense of shock by a straight, impassive account of events.

On leave, Winterbourne rather aimlessly wanders into a
music hall:

All references to the superiority of the Allies and the inferior-
ity of the Germans were heartily applauded. A particularly
witty scene showed a Tommy capturing several Germans by

attracting them with a sausage tied to the end of his bayonet.
A chorus of girls in red pre-War military tunics sang a song
about how all the girls love Tommy, kicking up their
trousered legs in unison. . . .

Again, the comparison with Sassoon is inevitable: the outcry
against the trivialization of the soldier's experiences is implicit.
But in fact Aldington's straight description carries more
weight than the sudden, uncontrollable anger of the poet:

> The House is crammed: tier beyond tier they grin
> And cackle at the Show, while prancing ranks
> Of harlots shrill the chorus, drunk with din;
> 'We're sure the Kaiser loves our dear old Tanks!'

> I'd like to see a Tank come down the stalls,
> Lurching to rag-time tunes, or 'Home, sweet Home',
> And there'd be no more jokes in Music-halls
> To mock the riddled corpses round Bapaume.

In post-war fiction with a military theme, the movement
from elation to disenchantment is paralleled in the novels
that appeared between *Tell England* and *Death of a Hero*. The
mood of the former is that of straightforward romantic
chauvinism; in the latter a whole gamut of emotions has
complicated the narrative design. Guilt, anger and hysteria
('When I meet an unmaimed man of my generation, I want to
shout at him: "How did you escape? How did you dodge it?
What dirty trick did you play? Why are you not dead,
trickster?"') give way at last to a bitter outcry against the
duped soldiers: 'You, the war dead, I think you died in vain, I
think you died for nothing, a blast of wind, a blather, a humbug,
a newspaper stunt, a politician's ramp.' Looking back, the
author can find nothing admirable or heroic but the strange
intense platonic comradeship of the trenches, born of necessity.
When Winterbourne meets the troops for the first time he
feels instantly that 'these men were men . . . they had been
where no woman and no half-man had ever been, could endure
to be.' He goes on to declare, '". . . I swear you're better than
the women and the half-men, and by God! I swear I'll die

with you rather than live in a world without you"'. This
sudden idea of a bond of masculinity that transcends social
class and character distinctions is not in keeping with the rather
sensitive, low-key and unassuming personality that Aldington
has devised for his hero; but it does accord with a popular idea
of warrior companionship.

VI

AUGUST WAS A WICKED MONTH

Current Views of Women and Children in the First World War

. . .
> I thought that the war would last for ever and sugar
>   Be always rationed, and that never again
>
> Would the weekly papers not have photos of sandbags
>   And my governess not make bandages from moss
> And people not have maps above the fireplace
>   With flags on pins moving across and across—
>
> Across the hawthorn hedge the noise of bugles,
>   Flares across the night,
> Somewhere on the Lough was a prison ship for Germans,
>   A cage across their sight . . .
> Louis MacNeice, 'Carrickfergus'

As a subject for children's fiction, the first world war has not yet begun to exercise the fascination of the second. Its appeal is perhaps less nostalgic than historical; and its widespread nature makes it less appropriate as a focus of interest. Aspects of the war cannot easily be isolated to furnish the basis for a theme: in recent children's stories it functions as a general background or its course provides the whole movement of the plot. It cannot be split into sections whose names generate their own feeling, like Dunkirk or the Home Front. It is possible, too, that the children's war story has acquired fatal associations from the fervid patriotism of fiction produced at the time. Stories written in wartime dated quickly. Their sentiments had little meaning for post-war children, secure in a sense of nationality that did not have to be stressed. The antics of Brereton's or Strang's heroes became tasteless or embarrassing, and the absurd girl characters of Angela Brazil and Bessie Marchant imparted a laughable quality to the genre. Stories of 1914–1918 *were* written in the '20s and '30s (see Chapters

III and IV) but the theme petered out completely after 1939 and it was not revived until the late '60s. The obvious reason for this is the second world war which provided a topical background and later a retrospective setting which had not the old-fashioned connotations of the first.

For children at boarding school in 1914, life went on much as usual. Most schools were not evacuated (although one girl playing hockey was killed by a bomb dropped on Folkestone). Schoolchildren could help the war effort only by knitting socks or 'knocking off buns'; more dramatic involvement was confined to those excitable contemporary heroines who took spies in their stride and thought of the enemy as unspeakable huns. A temporary form of snobbery was instigated: children without male relatives at the front were at a disadvantage in social terms. When relatives were killed, however, the bereaved were approached by their friends with trepidation. In Penelope Farmer's *Charlotte Sometimes* (1969):

> . . . Charlotte almost bumped into Bunty coming out of Miss Bite's room near by. Her eyes were red all round and she was not looking at anyone, though she gave a sort of half-made smile at Charlotte. Charlotte half smiled back, as embarrassed as most people are at someone else's sorrow, not wanting by some mistake to make Bunty still more sorrowful.

This kind of low-key verisimilitude would not have been possible at the time, when children's writers were caught up in promulgation of heroic feeling.

In many real-life schools, the war was used to promote good behaviour. It became positively unBritish to step out of line. The moral pressure on schoolchildren must have been formidable, when the least transgression could be converted to a want of patriotism. Elizabeth Bowen, a schoolgirl in 1914, remembered: 'We grew up under the intolerable obligation of being fought for, and could not fall short in character without recollecting that men were dying for us.' ('The Mulberry Tree', *Collected Impressions* 1950.) At school, above all, it was necessary to conform, to fit in with the current mood, to uphold the qualities most valuable in wartime: courage, stamina, unquestioning conviction. Opportunities to display these came with air-raid practices and, as the food shortage set in, at mealtimes. And for sheer self-sacrificing drudgery there were the knitting parties: 'Celia and I have knitted countless pairs of socks for soldiers in horrid thick and scratchy wool which brings me out in a rash.'

Celia's friend Meg is the narrator of Penelope Farmer's other wartime story, *August the Fourth* (1975). This book is made up of Meg's recollections of the first day of the war—it is set retrospectively in 1916. Since it is part of a series (Heinemann's *Long Ago Children*) its length and style are largely predetermined but within these limitations its theme is effectively deployed. It makes the point that the state of being at war is not established suddenly or dramatically. It is a matter of minor disarrangements and undirected excitement. By the time one's priorities have been readjusted the experience is already being taken for granted.

Initially, the oddness is confirmed in small matters of behaviour. Four sensible children are allowed to go on a picnic on the understanding that they will be back by a certain time. They break the rules, they are naughtier than they've ever been, and return home expecting a storm to come down on their heads. Instead, their absence has hardly been noticed. Their mothers are preoccupied with older sons who have decided to enlist. A tennis party has had to be cancelled. A map of Europe appears on the wall so that the children can follow the progress of the war.

In the course of the afternoon they have come up against intimations of racial prejudice (three village boys and a girl abusing a shopkeeper with a German name), panic food buying, and death (a decomposing rabbit). They have noted the unusual closing of the level-crossing gates as a trainload of troops goes through. The instinctive patriotism of Cecil has been checked by his phlegmatic friend Hugh:

'It's bound to be over before you and he are old enough to fight.'
'Yes isn't it just our rotten luck.'
'Speak for yourself,' said Hugh. 'I'm not sure I want to fight in any war.'
'Coward,' said Cecil; about the worst thing you could have

called anyone, I would have thought. But Hugh remained quite cool about it.

'Not at all,' he said.

Of course it is impossible now to recreate the mood of the time without adding a present-day repudiation of its excesses. In this story, Hugh's is the rational voice: on two occasions Meg displays an attitude to death that borders on the platitudinous. 'Of course I'd rather he was still alive but the medal makes it easier somehow,' she says of her brother Robert. And on the last page: 'Cecil may be awful; I may be madly proud of Robert. But I'd still like to have one brother left, I think one medal's plenty for any family.' That remark hovers oddly between common sense and bathos, as though Robert were a commodity that had been handed over with a touch of exasperation and self-righteousness, 'Oh, very well . . .'. But the difficulty is to achieve an authentic yet acceptable tone. Many bereaved families *were* comforted by the award of medals for valour. On the whole, *August the Fourth* is unsensational and precise in its effects; everything is scaled down to fit the format, but the most common reactions and experiences are presented in outline. The book ends with a drawing of the two girls glumly knitting.

These are middle-class children, but the ubiquitous knitters came from all divisions of society. 'It was not always possible to read in the kitchen when she was able to have a few minutes to herself, because Mrs Harter expected Kate to take out her army knitting.' Kitchen-maid Kate, heroine of Gordon Cooper's *An Hour in the Morning* (1971) and *A Time in a City* (1972), experiences the war as a series of muted sentimental shocks, as other people's lovers or sons are reported killed or missing. The emotional tone of these books is consistently bland. They suffer, too, from a lack of sharpness in their social observation. Arriving in the city of Meldon to take up a new post, thirteen-year-old Kate Bassett sees a woman conductress: 'Before the war, no women had been employed by the tram company, but with so many men fighting in France, work which had previously been done only by men was now open to women of all ages.' No weight is given to this interesting development, Kate has nothing to say about it and neither has her creator.

Kate is an impeccably kind-hearted, boring young girl whose only ambition is to give satisfaction in her working capacity. She is one of the most insipid heroines in modern children's fiction. In her relations with others there is neither complexity nor tension. Her intelligence is superficial: she resents nothing and never presumes to be irritated. She is not socially mobile and in this sense her conception remains old-fashioned. As she waits on the guests of her rather aloof employer, she thinks that she 'would like to be able to wear a school uniform and to have the opportunity of learning Latin'—but this sudden feeling of deprivation is in no sense allowed to affect her outlook. Like the fictional lower-class batmen in the trenches, Kate Bassett knows her place: loyalty is the paramount virtue in this system, to family, employers, religion, class or country. Self-assertion is merely pretentious: there is no room for any kind of subversive feeling.

The people in these books aren't convincing because there is no allowance for ambiguity or self-interest in their behaviour. Anti-social traits are obliterated almost completely from the author's consciousness, and the result is a vagueness that is redeemed only partly by the authenticity of the background, below-stairs detail. The tone induces a proliferation of stereotypes: Miss Nell, bravely washing dishes in the kitchen after hearing the news that Sir Edward Carey had been killed in France; querulous Aunt Em whose abruptness hides a good nature. These culminate in a version of that image of wartime heroism that has become ludicrous through over-use: the well-bred lady who opens a concert or bazaar while holding in her hand the telegram that announces the death of her only son.

Kate's reactions are conventional to the point of complacency. On seeing two wounded soldiers 'she felt very sad when she realized that they had gone to the war as young, strong men and had come back to England so terribly changed. She wondered where they would go and what would happen to them when the time came for them to leave the hospital.' Of course she feels sad; of course it suits the author's purpose to say so; but the remark none the less produces an effect of vexation. It is all too smooth and easy; the fears and tensions and disturbances of wartime are not conveyed. Kate remains inadequate as a person and a symbol: her work-a-day nature is not neutralized or transmuted by covert acknowledgement.

Kate is a servant; in *The Children of the House* by Brian Fairfax-Lucy and Philippa Pearce (1968) we have an indication of the actual ways in which servants may be more fortunate than the children of their employers. The story opens with an escapade in the tradition of E. Nesbit and this has an irony that is soon apparent. Unlike the cheery siblings of Nesbit, these four have no cosy emotional relations with their parents. They have suffered an upbringing of particular rigidity and their scope for inventiveness or misbehaviour is pathetically curtailed. They have affection for one another and the servants do what they can: otherwise the life of Laura, Tom, Hugh and Margaret Hatton is appalling, a waste of cruelty and deprivation and worthless upper-class expectations.

Its limitations are sanctioned by Edwardian formality which also makes things easier, in a sense: when rules are defined so clearly there is less chance of spontaneous transgression. On a personal level the children's hardships come from a want of generosity in their father: proximity in this case has engendered nothing but mutual distaste. The book has an inner intensity that has nothing to do with its clear, dispassionate, often light-hearted style. There is no drama, only an understated triumph in the fact that Laura and the others are not warped or neurotic or even resentful. They survive the strictures of home life to grow into pleasant, well-mannered, spirited adolescents: and then the war kills three of them. Only Margaret is left, Margaret of the hazy understanding who clung to the others with unconditional loyalty.

The novel's implicit drifts and conclusions are managed remarkably. Time and theme are conjoined in the most economical way. The ethical point of the children's deaths could hardly have been realized if the setting had been different. As it is there is nothing morbid or gratuitous about this matter or the way in which it is related. On a practical level, death is the most common effect of war. Social disarrangement, the upsetting of destinies, is another effect. Margaret, who 'least wanted it' inherits Stanford Hall and it ends as an attraction for sightseers.

For girls like Laura Hatton, the war was truly an escape

route, irrespective of its possible culmination in a literal dead
end. Laura becomes a nurse and dies of hospital fever, and the
others too are given a wartime function except Margaret who
is intellectually unfit. Tom goes into the army and is awarded
a posthumous Victoria Cross. Sixteen-year-old Hugh is killed
in action at sea. All this is told briefly, in retrospect, and the
person to whom the information is given is Victor, the Hattons'
only childhood friend—an illicit one, because of his low social
origins (he was the son of a schoolmaster).

An upper-middle-class girl who has all the traditional
qualities of a heroine is Christina Parsons in K. M. Peyton's
Flambards trilogy: *Flambards* (1966); *The Edge of the Cloud* (1969);
Flambards in Summer (1969). Christina is endowed with courage,
determination, power, sexual attractiveness and ultimately
wealth—a combination that might easily have been disastrous
in terms of subtlety or realism. Two of the books, moreover,
have a lush setting: an ancestral mansion in the Essex countryside, overgrown with fungus, disintegrating, reeking of dogs
and horses and cluttered with the paraphernalia of hunting.
Add to this the facts that Christina is a female orphan of strong
character and that the era is late Edwardian and Georgian, and
we have all the ingredients for vapid romantic fiction. K. M.
Peyton, certainly, has a firm understanding of popular requirements, and in the novels' optimistic conclusions, the triumph
of feeling over convention, there is apparent a wish to accede
to the more facile expectations of the reader. But that is not the
whole picture. To the story-teller's competence is allied a
cautious good sense that checks the more obvious kinds of
inflation. It is only in outline that the plots seem unnecessarily
vivid or overblown. There is the girl's impression of the wild
old house and the impossible, crippled uncle; but the effect of
the images is qualified by narrative circumspection. There is an
elopement, but its fulfilment is deferred through the whole of
the second book: Will's attachment to Christina is of less
importance than his obsession with flying. The latter kills him,
of course: few fighter pilots survived the opening months of the
first world war. The widowed Christina returns to Flambards
to farm the land and restore to order the dilapidated buildings.
This homecoming provides a theme for the final part of the
series.

There is little sense of a country at war in *Flambards in Summer*. There are practical difficulties arising from the shortage of farm labourers, but this might have affected Christina at any time. Will might just as easily have died as a civilian in the

Drawing by Victor **G.** Ambrus for K. M. Peyton's *Flambards*

summer of 1914: at one point it was a toss-up whether it was he who had crashed, or his aviator friend. Christina is not in the least embittered or Teutophobic: she is helped on the land by a prisoner-of-war whom she regards in a way that is scrupulously sensible and humane. When an enemy plane comes down in a field she experiences a normal pity and revulsion. Only the child Tizzy can enthuse over killing: eight is about the upper age limit for jubilant, militaristic behaviour to remain agreeable.

Mrs Peyton's standpoint with regard to attitudes to war is entirely rational and fair to most varieties of contemporary opinion. It is true that she holds no brief for shirking or even conscientious objection; she is most in sympathy with those in whom enthusiasm exceeds a sense of self-preservation, but still a lack of common sense about fighting is considered almost as culpable as straight disinclination. Patriotism needs to be tempered with a realization of one's physical and emotional limitations.

A generous, unthinking wish to fight for king and country is what motivates the fifteen-year-old hero of *Thunder in the Sky* (1966)—and the author can only readjust Sam Goodchild's apprehension of the realities of the trenches, point out in a mild way the silly distortions of the popular press, give a balance to emotions that were threatening to get out of hand, but not alter her character's basic perceptions. Sam gets into the army in the end, using the calling-up papers of his brother Gil who has died heroically on a burning ship. In the course of the story Gil has exhibited foolishness and near-treachery. Again, we have a novelettish concept—this time, dramatic atonement: but in actuality it is underplayed and therefore effective.

Sam's patriotism is essentially childish to begin with ('He did not expect Manny to be killed, and when he thought of himself as a soldier, he did not think of dying as a soldier') and his transition to a clearer view is well contrived. The book has the same limitations as the *Flambards* trilogy: Mrs Peyton's concern with plot has made for a lack of suggestion, oblique connections and inner density. In each case there is a straightforward story to be told and this is managed without hesitancy or fuss. The reader's attention is engaged completely, but it is engaged on the topmost level only. The books aren't in the least evocative, and for this reason *Thunder in the Sky* reads more like an adventure than a wartime story.

To provide the action it has a network of spies, the carrying of messages across the English Channel, and this conventional element of the war story is neither sent up nor infused with melodrama. The treatment is unusual, in view of current scepticism about spies and their activities which has led to a kind of realism that has subtly farcical undertones. In adult fiction the successful spy story is either a high-powered romp along the lines of John Buchan or Ian Fleming, or a stylishly bleak piece of documentation in which a symbolism of office waste-paper baskets, rain-splashed window-panes and barbed wire is given full play. When it is written for children it has to take into account a long tradition of crime-prevention stories, with easy and improbable gratifications for character and reader alike on the final page. There are basic dangers that have to be circumvented, and this requires above all a large measure of narrative detachment. The young spy-catcher is merely a wartime refinement of the juvenile detective, with the objective raised from a local to a national level. The concept is naïve but potent in its effects, like the bases of all popular subjective fantasy. Certainly the children's spy story has flourished for more than 60 years, and it is only recently that it has moved towards conscious humour or even rationality.

In old-fashioned children's fiction the spies of the first world war were highly coloured and insidious. If male they were grumpy and not fond of animals, or given a veneer of suavity to hide that ruthless disposition. Women spies were vindictive, always liable to substitute a personal motive for a patriotic one, and inclined to glare and hiss when cornered. Sometimes the spies came in droves, insinuating their way into key positions in armaments factories, girls from the Black Forest speaking faultless cockney that took in even the hardened East-End workers. Only a sourness of expression or an inadequate handshake might alert the intuitive heroine to the falseness of her fellow machinist. There was always a thrilling dénouement, with the enemy aliens exposed but still behaving extravagantly, reverting in some cases to a conventional foreign idiom: ' "You flattered me when you suggested I was the leader. I am only the tool of another. Who it is that is at work against his country I leave you to guess. No?" ' (This example comes from a 1918 story, *Munition Mary* by Brenda Girvin.) Gradually the histrionic quality was toned down: the spies of the second world war had a saving moderation of speech and mannerism, though the circumstances of their subjugation were hardly less artificial. In the stories of Enid Blyton, Malcolm Saville and others we have the usual group of well-behaved children who run into difficulties but end by saving the lives of a crew of submariners or uncovering the plans for an outbreak of enemy activity.

In *Mademoiselle* (1973), Geraldine Symons has brought a new insouciance and buoyancy to the spy theme. There is respect here for no story-book convention, not even the one

Illustration by Alexy Pendle for Geraldine Symons's *Mademoiselle*

that the children must be shown to triumph in the penultimate scene. It is August 1914; war is about to be declared and Pansy and Atalanta are staying in Paris with a schoolfriend who is the daughter of a diplomat. Suddenly it becomes plain that the rather shoddy, emotional and unappealing French school-mistress (bogus, as it turns out) is spying for Germany. On her excursions from the house Mademoiselle is tracked with enthusiasm by Pansy, and methodically by Atalanta, in accordance with the natures of the two girls which have been established earlier (in *The Workhouse Child*, 1969, and *Miss Rivers and Miss Bridges*, 1971). Atalanta is formidable, pragmatic, interested in prison reform and committed to the cause of the militant suffragettes. Far too sensible to seem precocious, she has a way of speaking plainly and an inductive reasoning capacity that annoy and impress the more timid and frivolous Pansy. Atalanta has recognized her own limitations and discounted them. Of Louis XIV she remarks: ' "He wouldn't have wanted me for his mistress but I dare say he'd have been glad to make use of my brains." '

These unusual schoolgirls drink crème de menthe in a Paris café at night, they bump into the lower type of courtesan and Pansy imagines that she has inspired a reckless passion in a passer-by.

> 'Of course he's not following you. Why should he want to?' asked Atalanta bluntly. . . .
> 'He may be in love with me—love at first sight.'
> 'Talk sense, do. Is it likely that in Paris of all places, with the kind of choice there is, he'd pick on someone of fourteen who looks it?'

It isn't likely of course, and the man turns out to be a detective who is keeping Mademoiselle in sight. He is wearing a black beret, a purplish suit and yellow shoes with painted tops: ' "I suppose an Englishman might force himself to dress like that for King and Country in the call of duty," ' their friend's father remarks later. The adults in this story have everything under control: even Atalanta is momentarily discountenanced when the facts come out. ' "We were off our guard at a crucial point." For the first time she sounded sickened. Removing her spectacles, she glared blindly ahead of her.'
Geraldine Symons cannot resist the impulse to ridicule, in an exuberant way, the more exotic details of spying:

> '. . . it was written in invisible ink on the back of a snapshot of a small boy playing with a ball on a lawn.'
> Lydia gave a cry of mortification. 'One of those she showed us on the train! He had on blue rompers.'

There is a surprising inaccuracy in this observation but it does nothing to invalidate the humorous effect. It is fitting in present-day terms that snapshots of a friend's grandson should be in colour, but this would not have been the case in 1914. How did Lydia know that the rompers were blue? Would a small boy of that era have *worn* rompers? Even the word 'snapshots' seems wrong in the context. This is an interesting example of failure to distinguish between two opposing kinds of immediacy.

The tone of the exchange is right, however. Deliberate bathos can be just as amusing as the unwitting kind that occurs often in the work of unsophisticated authors. An example of this is to be found in 'Daddy's Gone to Fight!' (*Woman's World Library* No. 66) by H. G. Hill: 'And the soldier's wife knew then that all was over; that she was one of the lassies who must be left behind when the brave lads go forth to the war. And as she stood there . . . she did not know that her uncle Jim had promised to befriend her.' The effects are entirely different of course: in the first case the reader concurs in the author's repudiation of the cliché; in the second the repudiation is on one side and is expressed as mockery or stupefaction.

Mademoiselle certainly exploits the comic possibilities inherent in satrical exaggeration, but it is more loosely structured than the out-and-out parody of a discredited or over-used mode like the historical romance. Like the other stories featuring Pansy and Atalanta, its merits derive from a quirky realism and perverse but effective use of literary absurdities. When this spy is apprehended she behaves in accordance with the expectations of any reader of pulp fiction. She spits on the Bokhara rug— but the precision of this detail is enough to indicate the author's amusement and dissociation. Particularity does generate its own humour, provided its use is sparing.

Paris with its decorative iron-work and quay-side bookstalls is confidently evoked, but again there is little sense of impending war. When soldiers are mentioned it is difficult to envisage the old-fashioned peaked caps and the red-and-blue uniforms which they must have worn. This is a built-in problem of historical fiction of course: there is a fundamental conflict between authenticity and readability, and each book's success is related to the extent to which this has been resolved. The problem doesn't admit of any absolute solution. Few authors would choose to write in the style of another era, yet the modern matrix carries its own associations. The opprobrium that attaches to certain kinds of historical fiction can be traced to crude attempts to provide an instant time-solvent; the use of expressions like 'Gadzooks' and 'I prithee' was expected to transport the reader immediately to another century (in fact most readers are reduced to transports of merriment). The current sensible tendency is to treat the past as if it were the present, to play down its oddness and emphasize its quotidian nature. This is fine, but it does entail the sacrifice of a certain intangible quality of remoteness or preterition.

A straight view of soldiering is presented by Ronald Welch in *Tank Commander* (1972). In spite of the movement away from exclusiveness in children's fiction there are still books that will appeal to one sex only; and this is definitely a boy's story. The hero, John Carey, is the latest in a line of military figures drawn from one family and extending back to the time of the Crusaders (in ten books so far). The concept is orderly and logical and the practical, battlefield aspects of war are thoroughly examined. With history as recent as 1914, however, it is clear that military detail is not enough. The twentieth century demands analysis or development of character, however these may be modified to suit the requirements of the reader. In *Tank Commander* there is nothing but action and its repetitive effects: even death becomes boring when it recurs on every page. If a person is described in two or three sentences this is sure to be merely for purposes of identification: soon afterwards he will die in a grisly manner. Structurally, this is a weakness: characters are introduced and exterminated in succession. Finally the rather stolid hero is driven to remark that war is 'futile, wasteful and tragic'—not an unexpected conclusion, or one that is given much significance.

But John's function is not a critical one. Of his outlook we are told that he frequently thinks 'in Rugby football terms'— which implies only that he has attended a public school without dissenting from its ethics. He is entirely conventional: an officer trained to embody nonchalance and resolution in the face of enemy attack. The men may exhibit symptoms of cowardice or misunderstanding as the firing starts, but the officers are fixed for ever in an attitude of disdain, lighting cigarettes and chatting about the type of shell in use. Certainly the author has a good grasp of prototypical figures, but there is no development beyond these. The style of the book is sometimes peculiar: 'No waterproof sheets were carried by the men, only greatcoats, or by those who had not thrown them away and Jones cursed them furiously.' But at least it avoids the gruesome ambiguity of one children's pulp-writer: 'I suppose you heard what an awful cutting-up we got in the Arras shindy—five hundred of our chaps went west, and they've sent the remnants home as a nucleus for a new battalion.' ('Maisie's Battlefield Search', *Schoolgirls' Own Library* No. 262, Gladys Cotterill.) This sounds like one of those experiments using dead bodies strapped into cars to determine the efficacy of a type of seat-belt.

There is no place for women in *Tank Commander* and this is unusual in present-day terms: only in certain period stories for children was it felt that reference to an active female character might imperil the overall projection of toughness or manliness. (Toughness and manliness of course had their sentimental inverse, expressed in this case in a strange idealization of mothers and sisters.) Otherwise the novel reflects the current approval of realism and moderation: there is plenty of gore, and no hysterical chauvinism.

All these writers have been at pains to investigate the details of their subject. A thorough approach is taken for granted now; in earlier fiction it was often subordinate to the expression of patriotic feeling, usually amorphous, or the concoction of an 'adventure', usually improbable. In general the children's story has broken away from restrictions imposed by classification: an incident may take place at school, for example, but there are no more 'school' stories. On the part of authors there is a consciousness of pitfalls, clichés and stereotypes, that precludes amusement at their expense. Characters too are self-conscious in the positive sense of the expression. Often they are socially observant and aware of their own relation to society and this is valuable in a special way when the book is written with hindsight. It is easier to be objective about the past. The plight of an upper-class girl is perfectly expounded by Laura Hatton in *The Children of the House*:

'I'm a girl. I'm older than Tom, but it's Tom who will inherit Stanford. I'm cleverer than Hugh'—this had always

been agreed among them, without vanity on one side or
rancour on the other—'but he's the one who will be sent
away to school, to be educated properly, so that in the end he
can *do* something. I'm a girl; I stay at home; I wait to grow
up and be married off.'

No heroine of 1914 could have spoken with such bitterness and
finality—no children's author could have sanctioned what
amounted to an expression of radical dissatisfaction. The
attitude might have been recognized but it would have been
treated lightly to begin with, and modified painlessly in the
course of the story.

Of the four retrospective adult novels discussed below, two are
rooted in Ireland; two—like *Tell England* (see Chapter V)—
have no significant female characters but use the trench
locations to develop the theme of near-schoolboy friendship in a
community violently cut off from outside distractions; and
two have a slightly deceptive simplicity that almost puts them
in the category of children's fiction. It is interesting to compare
Susan Hill's *Strange Meeting* with *Tank Commander*, a book
written for children which we considered earlier in this chapter.
There is more crude soldiering in the latter, more gratuitous
slaughter and low-key heroism. The adult novel is distinguished
by remarkable subtleties of mood and characterization. The
restricted setting is used for a purpose; in the children's book
the structure is loose and the action always predictable. But in
neither story is there any place for civilian life or the wartime
experiences of women. This subject is left to a less accomplished
novelist than Susan Hill: Glen Petrie, whose *Coming-Out Party*
has a semi-documentary, sociological bias like many children's
books. In consequence the 'adult' episodes appear somewhat
dissociated from the main body of the text.

Ireland is the scene of action in Iris Murdoch's historical
novel *The Red and the Green* (1965), though events in Europe
and their reverberations are fundamental to the theme. Four
of the central characters die violently, three in Ireland and
one, Andrew Chase-White, at Passchendaele. Andrew is a
British officer on leave in Dublin at an unpropitious moment in
history, a week before Easter in 1916. He is there because he is

Anglo-Irish, a member of an interconnected family whose
political sympathies tend to fall sharply on one side or the
other, on the side of the British or that of the Irish rebels. Only
Frances Bellman, Andrew's fiancée, is at all confused in the
matter of allegiances. ' "I ought to be in uniform. But I don't
know which one to wear!" ' she declares, adding a layer of
ethical indecision to the already complicated issue of women's
rôle in war.

The central irony in the theme is the fact that Andrew's first
experience of action as a soldier should come at the moment
when he is forced into a confrontation with his cousin, Pat
Dumay. Pat is an Irish Volunteer, at present under the
leadership of Pearse and McDonagh, about to take up arms
against the British. In this novel, the personal relations of the
characters are extraordinarily outré and convoluted. The
revolutionary Pat Dumay, fanatical and intense and contemptuous of women in a way that borders on revulsion, is in fact
the object of the secret, deepest affections of several of his
associates, including his Aunt Millicent, a flamboyant lady
whom no one, not even the author, can take seriously. Millie's
sexual leanings incline towards incest—with her nephews in the
course of the novel, and with her half-brother, now dead, in
the past.

The author's usual tendency is to harry and push her characters into a situation superficially farcical or fantastic, but one
that none the less has implications of a deeply serious, complex
nature. In *The Red and the Green* the most heavily weighted
symbolic episode is the one that ends with Andrew, still in the
uniform of a British soldier, handcuffed to his fourteen-year-
old cousin Cathal Dumay, sitting lethargically on the floor of
the kitchen in the Dumay's Blessington Street house while an
Irish Republic is proclaimed by the rebels in the city centre.
'Frances stamped her foot. Her hands clawed at the muddied
skirts of her coat. She advanced on Andrew as if she would have
kicked him. "Your word of honour! Gave Pat your word of
honour! You ought to have shot him as a traitor! You've
betrayed your king and country. You've dishonoured your
uniform. How could you do it? I can't understand." '

In fact he has done it for personal reasons, miserably giving
in to Millie's blackmail; and Cathal has been put out of action

by a brother obsessively concerned for his safety. Millie, whose idea of emancipation 'is wearing trousers and firing a revolver in her own house', spends Easter week at Boland's Mill with the rebels, tying bandages on wounded men. Frances by this time has resolved her personal dilemma, deciding to leave for England in order to join a Voluntary Aid Detachment.

The moral structure of Jennifer Johnston's *How Many Miles to Babylon?* (1974) is simpler and rather less interesting. An Irish army officer is under sentence of death, and the substance of the novel is composed of the events preceding this personal disaster. The narrator, Alexander Moore, is an emotional casualty, only child of an Irish great house, living a particular kind of rarefied, limited existence until he becomes a soldier. His father is ineffectual and his mother is one of those cold, beautiful, autocratic women whose appearance in fiction somehow heralds a depressing note of unreality, a movement towards the shorthand of magazine fantasy. However, the inadequate parents are clearly responsible for the withdrawn nature of their son; the boy is driven to form an extreme attachment to a socially inferior, forbidden childhood companion, Jeremiah Crowe.

The story is one of friendship subjected to the ultimate irony: one friend is detailed to preside over the firing squad that is going to execute the other. Jerry Crowe is sentenced to be shot for desertion: the result of a muddle or misunderstanding combined with sheer incomprehensible carelessness on the part of the defendant. But Jerry's motives for enlisting have been devious in the first place: '"When I go back I'll be one of the fellas who really knows what the hell he's doing when it comes to fighting."' He is an Irish republican, out of place in the British army on every count, a boy whose experience of soldiering is confined to illicit manœuvres with a hurley stick on an Irish hillside.

There is no way that these boys can adjust to the conditions of trench warfare: and even for the sake of efficiency or minimal comfort they do not want to. 'I was afraid that one day I might wake up and find that I had come to accept the grotesque obscenity of the way we lived.' For the hero of Susan Hill's *Strange Meeting* (1971), on the other hand, the reality of the

trenches has obliterated all meaning and purpose in ordinary
life. John Hilliard is not indifferent or insensitive to the dangers
and discomforts of active service; but on leave, he is overwhelmed by the sudden realization that he wants 'to go back'.
This is no simple attitude derived from a wish for brute heroics
or the easy companionship of his 'men'; it contains an element
of resentment at the complacency and ignorance of civilians,
but this is not the whole picture either. It is more that experience of war has given shape and depth to a kind of alienation
that he has always felt. In the circumstances it is justifiable to
be affronted by futility or carelessness in the behaviour of his
home acquaintances.

Like Jennifer Johnston's novel, this is the story of an un-
usually felicitous relationship between two soldiers. It is far less
melodramatic, however; in every sense a more careful reconstruction of the brief violent life of the trenches. There is no
'class' issue to simplify the tensions in the central friendship.
These are most often productive, involving delicate responses
and increased self-awareness for both participants. The natural
charm and candour of David Barton are qualities especially
valuable to Hilliard, whose own nature is somewhat reticent
and austere. But Barton is more vulnerable to the corrosive
pressures of war. He cannot become acclimatized to the realities
of slaughter; his sensibilities are not deadened in the interest of
self-preservation—on the contrary, his resilience and sense of
judgement are subtly eroded, and in the context this is made
to have a more than personal significance. Some quality that
Barton represented is also being destroyed on a wider scale.
Hilliard is intensely apprehensive on his friend's behalf, and
with reason; the scheme of the novel makes it impossible that
Barton should survive.

For reasons of economy or emphasis, or simply because it has
no place in the pattern of events, both Jennifer Johnston and
Susan Hill have chosen to ignore the activity of women, even in
the areas where it would have been likely to impinge upon life
in the trenches. The narrator of *How Many Miles to Babylon?*
has lived for twenty-odd years without knowing any girls or
women but his appalling mother. John Hilliard has a mother
and sister but these do not play a large part in the narrative,
they have receded in significance along with the whole remote

E

incomprehensible civilian world. In *The Coming-Out Party*
(Glen Petrie, 1972), on the other hand, it is the life of civilians
that provides the essence of the theme: in particular the life of
Susan Middleton, an upper-class girl who voluntarily becomes
a worker in the engine maintenance sheds at Crewe railway
junction.

Susan is reminiscent of Vera Brittain's Ruth Alleyndene
(see Chapter II); she has a comparable intelligence, idealism,
lack of snobbishness and devotion to her brother, Toby, who is
destined to be killed in the trenches. In the matter of sex,
however, she is prepared to go further than Ruth Alleyndene
from entirely charitable motives, and this makes her a more
modern heroine but also raises questions of likelihood and
historical authenticity. Ruth's virginity was relinquished in a
mood of formidable integrity: she is a character devised to
illuminate the false priorities and hypocrisy of the time by
making a stand against them. Susan sleeps with young subal-
terns because it is the least she can do for them; her
own disinclination is irrelevant in view of the justifiable fear of
death that she is helping to alleviate. This is a creditable
attitude but it is not altogether plausible; no well-brought-up
girl could have been unaffected by society's view of her
behaviour; in some vital sense her personality would have been
complicated by feelings of guilt or by a defensive need for
self-justification. 'In the world where I was brought up,'
Charles Carrington noted, writing of this period, 'the female sex
was permanently divided into two classes: those who "did" and
those who "didn't".'

The weaknesses in Susan's characterization are noticeable
largely because neither the novel nor the heroine is exceptional.
Often in historical fiction the most memorable character is the
one whose views accord with modern ideas of rationality or
common sense, the person least conditioned by the untenable
pressures of a particular era. 'Ahead of his time' is always a
term of praise. But it is truly applicable only to the person
who is socially or psychologically conscious to an unusual
degree. In other cases it smacks of hindsight, an incomplete
assimilation, on the part of the author, of all the historical
facts.

Susan's determination to 'get her hands dirty' in her war

work is inspired by her brother Toby, an embittered young officer with an unreasonable contempt for the gentility of VAD workers. ' "They're tarts," Toby replied. "Upper-class tarts. They're as bloody ignorant about what it's like out there as everybody else in this bloody country. A clapped-out, illiterate French whore in an Amiens brothel knows more about what it's like than any bloody amateur lady VAD here at home." '

Upper-class girls 'cutting fast and loose' as soon as the eyes of their parents and friends are off them: this is the hostile view of women who rushed to join the Voluntary Aid Detachments. It isn't a complete fabrication, merely, as we have noted, an aggressive and unconsidered way of regarding a natural side-effect of the sudden freedom.

Class antagonism is a subsidiary theme of *The Coming-Out Party*, though it does not receive serious or extended treatment. The women workers at Crewe are ruthless and shockingly outspoken—'Had enough fuckin' passengers in this bloody shed'—but their resentment of Susan soon evaporates. Susan is 'a real lady'; the rough unpretentious girls are more to her taste than prissy Ruby, the ex-domestic servant with whom she lodges.

The incessant swearing and the total lack of patriotism in the girls' motives for volunteering to work in the sheds are slightly disconcerting to Susan; but soon she is saying 'bloody' with the rest of them and indulging in the delusion that she is 'meeting real people for the first time'. By and large the workers in the sheds are there for the money, and make no bones about it. Many women workers had been made redundant in the general disruption caused by the war, and it was not until 1915 that female unemployment levels began to fall, largely as a result of the take-over of occupations previously filled by men. ' "Reckon t'bloody war's made some changes for all on us. Nice to know what it's like to 'ave a bit o' money in t'pocket," ' one of Susan's thoughtless companions reflects.

When the war ends Susan's position is typical: she is one of the girls at a loose end, caught up in the spurious gaiety of the victory celebrations, disorientated and disenchanted. But it is hardly possible to take her predicament seriously since she is given such a bland and wooden character. Because it is *not* a children's book, *The Coming-Out Party* arouses expectations that are not realized.

In general, in both children's and adult fiction, the historical approach has meant that wartime behaviour can be viewed in perspective, with a finer perception of causes and effects. None of the above protagonists is carried away by untenable emotions. There is room in the books for muddle, complexity and inconclusiveness, so long as these are presented as aspects of reality and do not arise from narrative indiscipline. A sense of individuality is more carefully evoked, with oblique comment and suggestion that require a reciprocal effort from the reader. On the whole these authors have achieved an imaginative reconstruction of experiences that were commonplace but were not transcribed with sharp verisimilitude in the fiction of the time.

VII

BELOVED ENEMIES AND CUSSED FRIENDS

Some Romantic Fiction of the Interwar Years

You made me love you,
I didn't want to do it, I didn't want to do it . . .
Popular song

AT THE END of the first world war, there was little evidence
of the better and fairer world in anticipation of which many
men and women had sacrificed so much between 1914 and
1918. It was true that some women had achieved the vote and,
theoretically at least, greater career opportunities. However, in
a society beset by economic depression and unemployment
little progress was made towards improved living standards
and social security. The heightened consciousness and unifying
purpose of wartime quickly evaporated and divisions between
classes and the sexes were accentuated by a sense of lost
opportunities.

Many men and boys returning to civilian life from the forces
found it impossible to get work of any description, let alone the
jobs fit for heroes that they had been promised. Some of their
bitterness was directed against the independent wage-earning
women whose numbers had increased since pre-1914 days.
Whatever their inclinations might be, many of these women *had*
to earn their own livelihood, for they had few opportunities of
finding husbands who might support them. The 1921 census
showed a 1,700,000 surplus of women over men as a result of
the slaughter of the war years. As well as providing a focus for
the resentment of returning soldiers the so-called superfluous
woman was also the unfortunate subject of articles in the
popular press. Circumstances had denied her the traditional
rôle of wife and mother. She was also illogically expected to
forgo her right to work. Several newspapers went so far as to
exhort emigration. (Later on, Hitler's fascist state was similarly
dismissive of the interests of single women. One of the solutions

proffered for Germany's unemployment problem in the 1930s
was to force women out of industry so that their jobs could
become available for men.)

All this was reflected in fiction. In several books which
appeared in the 1920s and 1930s women characters were at
odds with the society in which they lived. They repudiated
long-established traditions, demanded interesting and well-paid
careers ('men's jobs'), and occasionally claimed the right to
become mothers even if they were not married. And, most
disconcerting of all, they decided to become the wives or
mistresses of men whose countries had recently fought against
England. In 1923 Hall Caine's *The Woman of Knockaloe*
expounded some of the problems encountered in love between
enemies—in this case a misunderstood Manx-woman and a
manic German prisoner. In spite of its farcical culmination in a
joint-suicidal death-leap (with Mona and Oskar 'eye to eye,
breast to breast, heart to heart' and singing 'Jesus Lover of my
Soul' together in both English and German) Hall Caine's
'parable' endeavours to present the subject seriously. The
author had been a pacifist but in 1914 he took up the allied
cause, convinced that 'liberty, civilization and religion were
threatened'. Honoured for his war service, knighted in 1918
and made Companion of Honour in 1922, Hall Caine was
dismayed by the harshness of the peace terms and the reparations which were imposed on Germany. He condemned these
measures for bringing about a situation that would lead to
future wars, and for showing a 'lack of feeling for the sanctity
of life'.

When *The Woman of Knockaloe* was published in 1923 rigid
1914–1918 attitudes to pacifism were already beginning to
soften. The war, of course, had been denounced, even while it
was in progress, by some writers of status including Bertrand
Russell and perhaps more surprisingly the soldier/poet Siegfried
Sassoon, who had been awarded the MC for gallantry in the
Somme Offensive. Disillusionment with post-war society
naturally led to deeper questioning of the ethics of nationalism;
but the preface to *The Woman of Knockaloe* suggests that Hall
Caine expected a hostile response to his 'plea for speedy and
universal disarmament'. Present-day readers are likely to be in
sympathy with the idea of the internationalism that Hall Caine

puts across, but his uneasy present-tense narrative produces a
sense of unreality, a disconnection between events. The author
seems unable to decide whether to write political propaganda
or a romantic novel. The language, as well as the story line,
is daunting; it is lurid and archaic in the manner of the
Victorian moral tale.

Initially Hall Caine makes Mona Craine the mouthpiece of
hysterical anti-German feeling; this is directed against the
German civilians, until recently resident in England, who are
interned in a camp built on part of her father's farmland on the
Isle of Man: 'She becomes conscious that behind the barbed
wire the men are looking at her with evil eyes and laughing
like monkeys. [This is not altogether unnatural: she *is* 'the
only woman among 27,000 men'!] Her flesh creeps—she feels
as if they were stripping her naked. The beasts! The monsters!'
They are also for good measure 'dirts', 'scoundrels' and 'scum'.
Mona relishes the prospect of 'the jolly good thrashing' which
the British will hand out to the German armies. Her antipathy
is sustained at such a high pitch throughout the first part of the
book that even her father—who is far from being pro-German
—feels compelled to reiterate, '"You're hard, woman, you're
hard"'. However, after Robbie (Mona's only brother) is killed
in action her father's repetitious refrain changes to '"What's
coming over thee, woman? What's coming over thee?"'
Mona is in fact beginning to succumb to the charms of Oskar
Heine, a German internee who comes each day to collect milk
for the men in his compound. In the context of romantic
fiction he is an untypical Teuton: '. . . tall, slim, erect, fair-
haired, with hazel eyes and a clear-cut face that has an open
expression. Can this be a German?' An added surprise is that
Oskar's voice 'is not harsh and guttural, like that of the other
prisoners but soft, deep and *human*'.

As Mona becomes more tolerant of the enemy, her father's
hatred assumes fanatical proportions. He advocates, for
instance, the destruction of 1,000 German children for every
British child killed in Zeppelin raids: '. . . let them be cast into
the fire and into the pit, that they may never rise again'. Mona
tries to reconcile the interests of both sides. She no longer condemns the Germans, and, with her brother's posthumous VC
pinned on her breast, she doggedly goes about the work of

running the farm. (Her father has been pretty useless since the news of his son's death brought on a stroke.) When Oskar hears that his ten-year-old sister in Germany has been killed in a British air-raid Mona comforts him in an extremely chaste embrace. It is of course witnessed by her semi-paralysed father, who works himself up into another seizure which proves fatal: not however until 'he falls on Mona with fearful cries— "Harlot! Strumpet! . . . Thy brother dead in France, and thou in the arms of this German! May God punish thee! . . . Curse thee! Curse thee!"'

Mona is harassed in various ways by the local community who turn against her after her father's denunciation. The lease of her farm and home is not renewed, and at the end of the war she is financially crippled by having to make good the dilapidations to the property caused by the presence of the internees. In a dream even her dead brother Robbie rejects her (piqued because the local dignatories have refused to include his name on a war memorial because of Mona's association with a German).

At first the lovers are not intimidated. They plan a new life together away from the parochial island—but their hopes are ground down in a series of anti-climactic events. When Oskar is refused the right to live and work again in England he is confident that the Germans will not be 'hard and unforgiving'. He sends his mother the happy news that he will be bringing a 'daughter home to love and comfort her . . .'. Her response is chilling, to say the least: 'Tell your Englishwoman from me that if she marries you and comes to this country she will be as a leper . . . rather than hear you had married an Englishwoman I would see you dead and buried.' It was not, of course, the best moment to expect the defeated Germans to overcome their bitter feelings about the British; even after the Armistice they were still being blockaded and many were half-starved. At length even America, 'the melting-pot of the nations', denies sanctuary to Mona and Oskar.

The author then embarks on prophecies about the future of Europe which have since proved dispiritingly accurate. He indicts the politicians for 'wrangling about their reparations', and goes on to predict that 'the little mother rocking her baby's cradle will have to pay the interest in blood and tears some day . . .' Blood and tears, in fact, engulf Mona almost immediately. She becomes temporarily unhinged by an Easter day sermon about Jesus dying 'of His own free will . . . for love' and, by dying, saving the world. She fires Oskar with enthusiasm for 'her great, divine, delirious project' and sealing their doom as well as their love with a first and last kiss they throw themselves off the most westerly headlands of Man. It may be helpful to readers to know that their deaths, if not actually instrumental in saving the world, at least 'touched the hearts' of the local mackerel fishermen who buried the lovers' bodies and built a lofty cairn memorial over them.

Pleas for greater understanding between nations were expressed more cogently by pacifist, feminist writers like Vera Brittain and Winifred Holtby—though their work occasionally reflected an unpalatable notion that was rife at the time. A few of the more intellectual 'superfluous' women took the compensatory view that the 'cream' of the nation's youth had been wiped out: the survivors, therefore, could only be second-rate.

The theme of love between enemies is tackled fairly realistically by Phillip Gibbs. Despite its underlying seriousness *Blood Relations* is written in a lively style which contrasts favourably with the rather dreary atmosphere of the author's later anti-communist stories. The hero is Count Paul von Arnsberg who matures convincingly in the course of the narrative. To begin with he is an uncomplicated militarist: ' "After all there is something heroic, don't you think, in a soldier's death for his Fatherland?" ' But by 1918 he has realized that few German or British soldiers have any idea of what they are fighting for. At the end of the war he has become that most contradictory of creatures, a soldier-pacifist, convinced that his generation has been duped by the politicians who promote untenable ideals.

Before the war, at Oxford, Paul has fallen in love with the sister of an undergraduate friend. Utterly English Audrey Middleton is a down-to-earth girl from Chiddingfold who at first is both amused and repelled by the formality of her Teutonic lover's wooing. But common sense is thrown off course by the extraordinary sentimentality which so many British people feel for anything remotely classifiable as 'Bavarian'.

(These Ruritanian associations still survive, despite Elinor M. Brent-Dyer's over-long series of Chalet School books, Ivor Novello's *The Dancing Years*—and Adolf Hitler's partiality for Berchtesgarden.) Audrey finds that her feelings for Paul cannot be disentangled from her romantic images of his country's 'marvellous mountains' and 'deep blue lakes', where 'the sun always shines and the fields were strewn with flowers'. She is enraptured by the prospect of visiting the von Arnsbergs' family schloss, envisaging Paul in his Bavarian costume—'a little blue jacket and embroidered shirt, and leather shorts above his knees, and white socks'. Guessing where this euphoria might lead, Audrey's conventional father tries to maintain the family pattern of holidays in England: '"Oh no, I don't think so, old girl!" said Colonel Middleton. "What about Bexhill as usual? Very enjoyable don't you think? Lots of golf. A nice band."' But Bavaria has the edge on Bexhill: Audrey and Paul are married in the early summer of 1914, a few weeks before the assassination of the Archduke Ferdinand. The von Arnsbergs talk incessantly of *kultur* and the German Soul—a kind of nationalism which Audrey at first finds 'mystical and mysterious'. (It not only conjures up shades of Siegfried, but cosy pictures of gnomes and wood-sprites.) But at the point when 'Our German Destiny' becomes synonymous with 'Our good German guns' and 'Our German God', Audrey has to point out, apprehensively, that the German God is also the one who won't let the English down in the event of armed conflict. Paul goes to the front: Audrey is left, bewildered and resentful, with her parents-in-law—and a new 'German' baby on the way. Her predicament, which has been shared by so many women, is clearly conveyed. Freshly married and hardly acclimatized to her new country, she is suddenly cut off from her English family and friends; no letters are allowed; she has no access to English newspapers. Audrey fears, correctly, that her brothers might be amongst Kitchener's first 100,000 volunteers. Eventually news filters through of her favourite brother's death in action: Paul's brother is killed by the English at Loos and Audrey is overwhelmed by the insanity of events. But 'all hatred left her . . . she had no ill will against German boys who were killing English boys. They were all victims of the same tragedy.'

Gibbs's descriptions of the breakdown of German society and social upheavals in England after the war are in their own way as lurid as his accounts of Paul's experiences as a soldier. (He sees mutilation all around him, is buried alive in the trenches and becomes a prisoner of war.) The humiliating peace terms and their crippling effects upon an economically dismembered Germany are spelled out. But with sudden illogicality —for it was, after all, male politicians who drafted the peace settlement—Philip Gibbs attributes the growth of materialism and the avoidance of social responsibilities to the *women* of Germany and England. A measure of the newfangled amorality is the number of 'painted women', who crop up frequently in the text, who have succumbed to 'the negro rhythms' of jazz, and its attendant 'dancing mania'. Actually men as well as women must have 'jogged to unceasing foxtrots which seemed to stupefy the senses'. However, according to Philip Gibbs, this pastime was particularly symbolic of the destructive aspects of femininity. The contrasting experiences of soldiers and women left at home had of course created barriers and resentments which have been mentioned earlier (see Chapter V). In *Blood Relations* one of Audrey's surviving brothers carries this bitterness to the point of self-pity and indulgence: '. . . these young women with frocks up to their knees have hearts like stone—cold and hard! Where is womanly tenderness? Where is the gentle creature who'll fondle me?' And another English ex-officer seems to feel that lower-class women are especially reprehensible:

> The working people had the time of their lives—lots of money, lots of emotion. They became quite used to the casualty lists. Little ladies married again before their boy husbands had been killed a month or two. Working women were quite glad when their husbands were reported dead or missing: the neighbours were so kind. It was a bit of drama for them in mean streets.

The same character also propounds—and amplifies—one distressing assumption that many children growing up in the 1920s and 1930s absorbed from their veteran soldier fathers: 'In England most of us believe that the only good Germans are dead Germans. After all their atrocities we regard them as Huns. Personally I think it's a pity we didn't kill all the German babies. They'll only grow up to make another war.'

The older generation of upper-class English survivors gloomily awaits the apportionment of their land by the estate-agents and the jerry-builders: they moan about income tax and the Labour Party that might 'come into power and wreck everything'. (Even as long ago as 1935 the party was threatening the same 'dreadful stuff about taking control of the banks and establishing a Socialist state' that it is still advocating in the 1970s.)

But Phillip Gibbs has more feeling for the *beau geste* than for basic political action. Like several other fictional soldier heroes, Paul von Arnsberg is deeply moved by a Christmas Day truce between British and German soldiers who have been hammering each other from opposite trenches. The image of 'Tommies' and 'Fritzies' shaking hands in No-Man's-Land, exchanging cigarettes and chocolates and singing each others' carols has also been a stimulus in fiction by Robert Graves, Henry Williamson, R. F. Delderfield and Hall Caine. In common with other disillusioned Germans Paul begins in the 1930s to gravitate towards Nazism, which seems to offer his country its only hope for economic survival and unification. But Audrey now wisely mistrusts 'all that nonsense about the Aryan race . . . all that mystical rubbish about the old German gods and the tribal instincts of the German folk'. The story ends when her son joins the Hitlerjugend ('I hate to think I have English blood in me') and Audrey, now more isolated even than in 1914, cries '"Paul! I want to die. . . . We're all marching towards another war. The world is going mad again."'

In spite of his tendency to overdraw characters and situations Phillip Gibbs was at least able in 1935 to write unequivocally about fascism, in contrast with many advocates of appeasement. Elizabeth O. Peter considers with hindsight the effects of Nazism on those who opposed it. *Compromise with Yesterday* is a romantic novel covering the period between 1911 and 1942. Its subject is an English family that has a remarkable aptitude for involvement with Austrians and Austro-Jews. Visiting 'the land of the Blue Danube and the Vienna Woods' shortly before the first world war Robert Deane, fresh from school, is deeply impressed by the hospitable, extroverted Austrians who spend their time dancing and playing their accordians 'with yodelling abandonment'. He is even more strongly influenced by Christl Somers, a dirndl-frocked, yellow-haired peasant girl whose innocent appearance is misleading. She knows just what she wants and gets it: Robert is seduced and, unknown to him, Christl bears his son Bertl who grows up to become a Nazi. (But—presumably because of his half-British background— Bertl has finer feelings and helps to save a Jewish youth from the Gestapo.) Robert's only other importance to the plot is that his 'quiet acceptance' of death 'in the loneliness . . . of an enemy's field hospital' at the Austro-Italian front creates a link between the Deanes and another Austrian family. Martin von Seefeld, a South Tyrolese officer who consoles the dying Robert, is an Anglophile. He has been educated at Rugby and is therefore able to strike the right note of understatement immediately: '"Hullo, old man! So sorry about this!"' Martin recounts the details of Robert's last moments to his sister Lorella, whom he visits in London—and predictably marries.

Though its starting point is just before the beginning of the first world war, *Compromise with Yesterday* was written during the 1940s; and in fact when the story gets to the second world war its atmosphere is more authentic (see Chapter VIII). Peter Löwe, the Jewish-Austrian boy whom Robert Deane's son Bertl eventually rescues from persecution, is an anti-fascist writer and the husband of Robert's niece Jill. Shortly after the Anschluss Jill is in hospital with a new baby when she learns of Peter's disappearance. The pernicious atmosphere of the police state is well drawn. Jill has to suffer the stone-walling and insults of officialdom. At last she begins to wish for news of Peter's death '. . . at any moment something must go crack inside me. It would be less terrible to know for certain that Peter was safely dead than to think that he may be alive and tortured . . .'. Martin von Seefeld, who is of course Jill's uncle by marriage, goes to Austria at Lorella's request to search for Peter. He achieves nothing—and is arrested by the Gestapo. 'A strange sequel to the long ago scene at Robert Deane's deathbed! Because of that meeting, he himself was now facing a firing squad of his own people. . . .'

Elizabeth O. Peter's marathon flirts on several occasions with the irony of nationalism that misfires. Robert Deane's only regret when he is dying in the first world war is that he had to fight 'as comrade-in-arms with the Italians, whom he didn't like, against the Austrians, whom he did'. When Peter Löwe is restored to his wife and child he and his family become victims of British bureaucracy. During the second world war they are resident in England. Technically they all are enemy aliens— even Jill, who like other British women had to forfeit her nationality upon marriage to a foreigner. They are subjected to curfew and allowed no radio. Peter is a well-known opponent of the Nazis but he only just manages to escape internment on the Isle of Man which was, of course, the fate of many naturalized German-British during both wars.

In the 1920s and 1930s problem-ridden fictional romances involving British women and German men were perhaps predictable expressions of disenchantment over the rebuilding of post-war society. Surprisingly the thorny subject of love between enemies was more compellingly conveyed in a 1942 wartime setting when the emotional climate militated against it. *Le Silence de la Mer* by 'Vercors' describes the reluctant beginnings of love between a German soldier and the French woman in whose home he is billeted. ('Vercors' was the pseudonym of Jean Bruller who played a leading part in the underground publishing organization *Les Editions de Minuit*.) The book was distributed in occupied France by members of the Resistance. Of course the idealistic young German, Werner von Ebrennac, becomes disillusioned: he realizes that the 'marriage of equals' which he envisages between Germany and France can never take place, and that the official policy of the Third Reich is to subjugate the French people. He is *désorienté*, and his only escape is to volunteer for active service at the front—in fact for death. A measure of the sensitivity of *Le Silence de la Mer* is that it could be read with appreciation by intelligent German, French and English people alike, at a time when racial animosities between enemies *and* allies were at their most acute. According to the preface 'Vercors' wrote this book 'as part of the effort to break the dreadful silence under which France had lain submerged ever since her occupation by the enemy'. A delicate mood is sustained throughout: every image, every conversation heightens the reader's awareness of the futility of aggressive nationalism and its ramifications. The heroine of the story is the niece of the narrator: but she is never named and is simply any woman in occupied France who has to keep the mundane business of life going despite tragedy and upheavals. Her passivity and resilience are symbolic qualities that relate to defeated France.

In the aftermath of the first world war several working women in romantic novels decided that their rôle was to change the fundamental structure of society. This of course demanded a great deal of self-conscious almost messianic renunciation of personal happiness. One of these dim but dedicated heroines is Mary Sarn in G. Cornwallis-West's *The Woman Who Stopped War*. Shocked by the deaths of her husband and brother, she proceeds to found a Women's Save the Race League, an infelicitously titled organization with the admirable object of preventing future wars. Mary points out to her supporters that '"at Geneva—where another League is labouring to achieve the same results as we ourselves—no nation is represented by a woman"'. However, the book does not put across a consistently feminist view. The leading women characters have little interest in careers, and indeed seem extraordinarily resentful that they have been 'driven in many cases to support themselves'. Mary starts her League in a modest way, whilst working as a mannequin. Eventually desperation to acquire the funds which are essential to put the League on an international footing leads her to become the mistress of an already married armaments king.

In novels of this type the voluntary relinquishing of sexual respectability is of course the greatest sacrifice that any woman can make; but it is stressed that the wife of Mary's lover has for some years been 'an inmate of a clinic in Amsterdam'—so Mary at least is not snatching Sir Edward Enthoven away from a conventionally happy marriage.

Edward lavishes money on his mistress, especially after she produces a son. He does not know that Mary is ploughing most of his millions into the Women's Save the Race League, though she makes no secret of her pacifist convictions. (Edward tolerates these as the harmless quirk of a beautiful woman who seems in every other respect endearingly deferential to male authority.) His tolerance breaks down when, out of curiosity, he wanders into a mass meeting of the League at Olympia, and discovers that Mary is its impassioned and eloquent leader. It is a bitter blow to Edward: he doesn't approve of women 'dabbling in politics' anyway, and has already sacked his kitchen-maid for attending a meeting of the League. He tries to smash the organization of these cussed women—but it is too late. War is about to be declared, and already groups of women all over the world are giving each other secret signals and knowing looks. As well as threatening their menfolk with the tactics of Lysistrata they are planning to go on strike in every other sphere of feminine activity. The prime minister of England, who had earlier confided to Edward that he didn't believe women could ever organize themselves, is appalled to find them walking out of their jobs and blocking the streets of London (and other capital cities). Edward has not been a munitions magnate for nothing; he urges the PM to use troops to clear the women from the streets—' "A lot of damned Bolshevists" '. However the prime minister has to admit that no modern war could be waged successfully without the supportive efforts of female 'clerks, shop-assistants, waitresses, teachers and factory-workers'. Mary's League has triumphed: international war has been prevented. Edward is a ruined man, as armaments have become a useless commodity. It only remains for Mary, complacent as ever, to persuade him that: ' ". . . you'll make other things just as well . . . There are heaps of things—harmless, useful things—that your works could turn out—railway wheels, golf clubs, motor cars and goodness knows what . . .".'

Netta Muskett's *The Painted Heaven* was published in 1934 and its leading character is also one of the 'surplus million' women. Like Mary Sarn, Anne Weston accepts a rôle that is daring and unusual in the context of romantic fiction: she becomes a successful business woman, and she has a child out of wedlock. In spite of the author's scorn for women who are 'always ready with transports of cheap emotion', this quality permeates the book. For instance, Anne is a snob: ' "I've had to work for Christine [her daughter] all her life, and sometimes I've felt I might as well have left her to get along as best she could at a council school and then as somebody's typist." '

Her attitude is unchallenged in the narrative view. This is reactionary to say the least; the goal of Netta Muskett's heroines is to be 'little, inconsequent, adored'. Men, on the other hand, are usually 'big' and 'reminiscent of the Greek God'. Women in *The Painted Heaven* are generally 'taken' by men after moments of passion in which lovers unconvincingly address each other as 'my dear'. The book opens with Anne characteristically making a prettified representation of the model at a life class: ' "Wouldn't you rather look at something beautiful than one of Nature's little mistakes?" ' There is a corresponding vagueness in Netta Muskett's prose: '. . . his eyes were grey . . . that grey which had only just missed being brown and which might equally have been blue or green. . . .' And Anne's laugh '. . . was neither a giggle nor a guffaw, but it had the femininity of the one and the heartiness of the other'.

With Anne it is not, as the blurb suggests, a conscious and courageous decision to go against the tide of public feeling by having an illegitimate child. She simply bungles her sexual relationships. Her fiancé John Denver is wounded in the first world war and spends over a year 'raving mad' in a German prisoners' hospital. Anne presumes that he is dead and tries to keep his memory sacred. But she is persuaded to have a short affair with a young Australian pilot who, it turns out, has 'a wife and kiddie . . . down under'. Though repelled by her own lack of faithfulness Anne next allows herself to be seduced by Captain the Honourable Hugh Galton RHA, who is engaged to Lady Letitia Fordyce, a client of Anne's. (She has by now built up a successful dressmaking and millinery business.) Hugh fathers Anne's child, but she would never dream of marrying him: '. . . we were not of the same social class for one thing'. Her relations with him spring from pity, for he has been slightly shell-shocked and of course his well-to-do fiancée doesn't understand him.

The resulting child, Christine, is a mixed blessing for Anne, and a major theme of the book is maternal sacrifice. In this area Anne's desire to prettify everything involves her in an extraordinarily complicated situation. Christine, as a young adult, falls in love with Nicky—John Denver's son. John eventually comes back into Anne's life: his wife is obligingly

dying of cancer, so Anne has a day or two of euphoria when she
agrees to marry John as soon as he is free. With amazing lack of
foresight she allows him to believe that he is Christine's father.
(In fact they never had sex together—or rather they never went
'on the strange journey together some day—some night'—but
John's period of amnesiac lunacy in Germany has left him
prepared to believe anything.) The drastic repercussions of
Anne's lie penetrate even to her slow-witted mind: she realizes
that she has make it impossible for Nicky and Christine to
marry, as they seem to be half-brother and sister. Obviously a
Stella-Dallas-like renunciation of her own happiness for the
sake of her daughter is called for, because Anne knows the
strait-laced John well enough to sense that he will reject her
once he learns that she has been 'despoiled' by another man.
Anne sees her crisis in terms of a Gethsemane: ' "Oh, God,
don't ask this of me! Not this! Ask me to give up anything
else, but not John, not my beloved come back to me after the
wasted lonely years!" And yet she knew, as a greater than she
had known, that she would in the end drink that cup.'

Although *The Painted Heaven* has irritating, pseudo-progressive
overtones Anne's unorthodox relationships certainly imply no
independence of thought on her part. When she reflects on
these it is in terms of 'the wages of sin'. A woman character in
Walter Greenwood's *Love on the Dole*, which was published
a year before Netta Muskett's book, is more convincingly
forced to repudiate convention. The story is set in industrial
Lancashire at the time of the post-war economic depression that
resulted in unemployment for three million people. Initially
Sally Hardcastle is a vivacious young girl who expects something more from life than her mother's 'everlasting battle with
the invincible forces of soot and grime'. Poverty is also expressed
through the dreariness of short-time working, the eventual dole
queue and the repeated pawning of already inadequate
wardrobes to buy food. Sally becomes restless for something
she has never known: a form of intelligent self-expression. This
restlessness is unassuaged by the vulgar attentions of blustering,
unimaginative young men like Ned Narkey who complain of
her discernment: 'Blimey, y'might be Queen of Sheba ... but
Ah've had enough o' your frisky ways.' There is a brief period
of fulfilment for Sally in her relationship with Larry Heath, a

socialist who loses his job because of his political activism and who dies of tuberculosis. The near starvation of members of Sally's unemployed family forces her to become the unwilling mistress of the local bookie and small-time entrepreneur. The author implies that this degrading solution of economic difficulties is at least preferable to matrimony in that particular social setting. For many working-class wives 'the vivacity of their virgin days' soon disappeared—as irrelevant as their 'afterwards utterly useless wedding finery'. The badge of marriage was perpetual shabbiness and a 'pre-occupied, faded lack-lustre air'.

The book also makes a cynical observation in connection with the success of women factory workers during the first world war. Larry Heath dismisses the so-called apprenticeship which many boy school-leavers are offered. He sees this as seven years of cheap labour for the factory owners: ' "Your apprenticeship's a swindle, Harry. The men they turn out think they're engineers . . . but they're only machine minders. Don't you remember the women during the war? . . . [they] picked up straight away what Marlowe's and the others say it takes seven years apprenticeship to learn." '

In D. H. Lawrence's *Lady Chatterley's Lover* (1928) the heroine's deflection from the traditional social pattern is, of course, well known. It is partly attributable to the effects of the first world war during which her husband has 'to be shipped over to England [from Flanders] more or less in bits', with resulting permanent paralysis of the lower half of his body. However, it is not only 'the cruelty of utter impotence' in Clifford that makes Connie Chatterley seek 'phallic tenderness' elsewhere. There is also disenchantment with his intellectual pretentiousness, and a repudiation of the anachronistic life she is expected to share with him in the isolation of his ugly ancestral home. To Sir Clifford Connie's infidelity with his game-keeper seems the ultimate in feminine perversity: ' "That scum! That bumptious lout! That miserable cad! And carrying on with him all the time, while you were here and he was one of my servants! My God, my God, is there any end to the beastly lowness of women. . . ." ' Clifford is represented as a 'perverted child-man' who is incapable of rational judgement of the usual responses between men and women.

Lawrence is effective in tackling explicitly but without crudeness the themes of sexual deprivation and fulfilment. Somerset Maugham's play *The Sacred Flame* is a challenging but less radical comment on the predicament of a woman whose husband has become paralysed. Maurice Tabret's spinal injury is the result of a post-war flying accident. He and his wife Stella are at least more affectionate towards each other than the Chatterleys and this warmth is expressed effusively. But it does not alter the fact that Maurice has become to Stella 'no more than a dear friend for whom I was desperately sorry'. He deplores the waste of 'all that beauty, all that superb and shining youth' of Stella's. '"Oh Stella, if we'd only had a little kid. After all, it's a woman's destiny to have children. You wouldn't have felt that you had entirely wasted your life."' There is a basic irony in this observation: Stella and his brother Colin are having an affair and she is actually pregnant.

Maurice's mother realizes what is happening and, rather than allow her disabled son's 'beautiful illusions' about Stella to be destroyed, she kills him by administering an overdose. Her action is in accordance with a pact between Maurice and herself that, 'if life became intolerable to him', she would help him to end it. The moral issues investigated in this play had a particular relevance to many families in the years following the first world war. There is of course the question of the right of voluntary euthanasia; and whether accepted standards of sexual morality within marriage could reasonably be applied when one partner had become impotent.

Mrs Tabret is supposed to have learned tolerance from her son's tragedy: '"I wonder why people don't see that morality isn't the same for everyone at the same time. . . ?"' But Stella, in spite of her own conflicting loyalties, thinks it 'horrible' and 'disgusting' when she finds out after Maurice's death that his nurse was in love with him. This—together with the fact that Nurse Wayland at first accuses Stella of murdering Maurice—produces some acerbic exchanges. Nurse Wayland rather petulantly exhibits the contempt that some working women feel for the privileged idle. Stella is similarly vindictive: '"I've often noticed that the average woman who works for a living looks upon it as a little miracle and can never believe that any other can be clever enough to do the same thing. I needn't have become a nurse, you know. I might have made hats or invented a face cream."' Stella's hypothetical choice of careers underlines her social milieu. Whatever difficulties the Tabrets and the Chatterleys had to contend with, these were not exacerbated by shortages of money or nursing and domestic help. For poorer families the problems of coping with paraplegic ex-soldier relatives, on minimal pensions, must have been appalling.

Officers coming home to change and challenge of a different nature are featured in books by popular writers including John Buchan and Dornford Yates. One which became a best-seller and remained in demand for decades was Warwick Deeping's *Sorrell and Son* (1925). Captain Stephen Sorrell MC meets every new challenge resolutely but head on with his rigid pre-war values. Sorrell is in fact portrayed as an enquiring individual who thinks everything out for himself. However, he inclines to a type of conservatism that seems hardly reasoned or reasonable. Like other heroes of between-the-wars best-sellers Sorrell believes that women are particularly responsible for many of the innovations that he finds most abhorrent. London, for instance, ceases to attract partly because Sorrell does not relish being at close quarters with 'that crowd of idle and superfluous women'. Mentally he also separates himself and his son from most 'ordinary' people—'the fool mob that might be asking for free wireless sets ten years hence'. It is implied always that Stephen Sorrell is 'a great man' who has suffered, and that he is unusual in having to make his own way in life without being in a position to benefit from nepotism or a private income. His progressiveness is largely a matter of being able to repudiate what he considers the hypocrisy of marriage. But Sorrell's unimaginative smugness must have made his own marriage a travesty. Certainly his wife had the sense to opt out whilst Sorrell was covering himself with glory on the western front. Of course she *is* superficial and ruthless. Warwick Deeping's fictional women have to be 'temptresses' and 'seducers' or— much more rarely—'sacrificial women who give to men more than men give to women'. They are certainly unlikely to be equal partners in any sexual relationships. One facet of Sorrell's individuality is his supposed, bland mysticism. This means that he occasionally meditates: '. . . a man's self sits and speaks with its very self'. When he is not reflecting on the (as he sees it) sleaziness of sex or the fecklessness of the lower orders—'the Labour dragon' and 'Socialist rot'—he is contemplating the flowers in his garden: 'You could take the little quaint face of a pansy between your two fingers and see the soul of it, the soul of all gentle, living things . . .'.

However, Sorrell's main preoccupation is the upbringing of his son Christopher (Kit). During the course of the story Kit matures from Open-faced Schoolboy to Brilliant Surgeon. It is true that he has difficulties on the way. The first of these arises when he is forced to attend classes with the 'common children' at a council school. To get him away from all this Sorrell takes the position of porter at a country hotel. (This is a fictional representation of the real-life plight of officers who returned to civilian life and were unable to find jobs in keeping with their educational background and social status. But Sorrell, of course, rises to the position of manager, and becomes the proprietor of a successful antique business.) Sorrell is soon able to send Kit to a good private school—where ironically he is again the odd boy out: his fellow pupils look down on him because of his father's menial job as hotel porter. So Kit has to be privately tutored. After university and medical school he is plunged into even more disturbing social challenges: he encounters women. First his mother tries without success to bring him into her fashionable world. However, Kit soon rejects her, along with '. . . all those beastly women' who have 'an unholy fascination' and 'a damnable beauty' . . . '"I can't help it, pater, but women are the very devil"'. Kit is prevented from becoming a misogynist by a brief relationship with a girl who sells programmes at a theatre. The author comments: 'There was a self-respect here, the self-respect of women who worked', but it is obvious that Mary's rôle is to be a sacrificial one. And when Kit, 'plucking the red fruit from time to time found the juice of it sadder and less sweet', Mary obligingly spares him the embarrassment of ending the affair by getting herself run over by a bus.

Naturally Stephen Sorrell has anxiously monitored his son's first sexual encounter. He is relieved to find that 'it has done him good'. It is a prelude for Kit's relationship with a different type of 'woman who worked'. Molly Pentreath has an upper-class background and she is also a successful novelist: 'Yes, she was brilliant and her brilliance troubled him. It hurt.' Predictably Molly and Kit fall in love—but she is opposed to the idea of marriage as she believes it will interfere with her writing career. They indulge in a series of futile clashes. Molly's views are presented in a somewhat overwrought manner: 'Pursued, she knew that complete capture cannot be tolerated by a woman who has her right to live. Even as the Amazons burned off their right breast in order to use bow and sword the better, so Mollie knew that a woman with a creative urge other than the urge towards motherhood may be happier with no breasts at all.' In spite of this extraordinary and extreme view, the lovers' incompatibility is soon resolved. Kit is in danger of dying, or of having an arm amputated, as the result of a virulent infection contracted whilst performing an operation. This naturally enables Mollie to get her priorities right. They marry. 'Half a house each . . . Your—atmosphere—as well as mine.' She continues to write novels (the couple are, after all, well enough off to afford help with the chores) and one wonders what all the fuss was about.

Warwick Deeping's assessments are trite and the style of *Sorrell and Son* is soggy and repetitious. But it encapsulates a whimsical mood to which readers responded between 1925 and 1953, when the book was last reprinted. It is difficult to understand the story's popularity with a generation for whom few of its issues could have been relevant. Perhaps its enduring appeal rests in the sentimental father-and-son relationship. However, in *Bestseller* (1972) Claud Cockburn suggests that its attraction did not derive wholly from its Sonny Boy overtones: '. . . the plight of Sorrell and his like was only a vivid dramatization of what the middle class felt about its general situation, and—this is the nub of it—has gone on feeling right up to our own day.' Whatever 'middle class' might, or might not, mean, this appraisal is surprising.

In popular fiction between the wars there were not only middle-class characters afraid of being submerged in the proletariat but plenty of men and women from the working class who were anxious to move up in a social sense. The behaviour of one of these characters is examined in *The Stars Look Down* by A. J. Cronin (see Chapter V). This was published in 1935 and the first part of the story goes back to 1909 when sixteen-year-old Joe Gowland declares, '"I'm sick of the whole bloddy pit anyhow. I'm going to slip my hook first chance I get . . . I want to get some brass and see a bit of life. . . ."' Joe's opportunism finds its fullest expression during the first world war when by blustering and conniving he becomes a munitions profiteer. Jenny Sunley is another youthful character in the book who dreams of escaping from her humble background: 'She was terribly genteel, crammed with etiquette culled from the columns of the women's penny journals.' Her efforts to achieve a more refined social status eventually bring about her death through venereal disease in a Lock hospital. This of course is a fate which in the book's context is predictable rather than ironic. There is, however, a baleful irony in the plight of Arthur Barras, who has repudiated the exploiting methods of his pit-owner father. During the war the sensitivity that makes Arthur want to improve working conditions for the miners also forces him to become a conscientious objector. He is subjected to the humiliation of a prejudiced local tribunal and subsequent imprisonment.

Go-getters of both sexes, and particularly those who did not make the required patriotic response during the wars, are portrayed with a degree of discernment by R. F. Delderfield in *The Dreaming Suburb* and its sequel *The Avenue Goes to War*. Though written in 1958 the action of these novels takes place between 1918 and 1945 and vividly reflects the social scene of the interwar years. In its preface *The Dreaming Suburb* makes the point that 'the story of the country-dweller, and the city sophisticates, has been told often enough; it is time somebody spoke of the suburbs'. Delderfield does so, with authenticity and humour, taking the outskirts of South London as his setting. Unlike most fictional teenage youths, Archie Carver, a 'glorified errand-boy' during the first world war, is frankly bored by the suffering of 'gallant little Belgium'. Unhampered by idealism he participates throughout the war in a mild form of grocery black marketeering. This brings him, as well as a great deal of extra money, a satisfactory sexual initiation with the attractive wife of a serving army officer. Archie eventually becomes the owner of a small chain of grocery stores—largely due to his marriage of convenience with the daughter of an

Italian sweet-shop proprietor. When the second world war begins he has planned ahead to exploit food shortages and restrictions. However Archie is not characterized simply as a stereotyped 'spiv': his unscrupulousness in certain directions is counterbalanced by his self-awareness, and by the affection that he feels for Anthony, the son of his unsatisfactory marriage. Anthony is a sixth former at a public school, a prefect and in the running for the captaincy. Archie's illusions about this aspect of his son's life are out of character: 'Hearthover, and everything Hearthover stood for, was . . . the chink in Archie's cash-box, and money could run through that chink as fast as it liked. . . . To Archie Hearthover was Harrow, the Glorious Fourth, Greyfriars and Billy Bunter.' But 'the old magic of Greyfriars and St Jim's' also overtakes Anthony. To his father's chagrin, his response to the war is in accordance with the best traditions of the *Magnet* and *Gem*. As his eighteenth birthday approaches he looks forward to joining up, despite the fact that Archie has cleverly worked out ways in which Anthony can avoid conscription. He enlists, gets the MC and is killed at Tobruk.

Just as Archie is a rounded-out and believable version of Joe Gowland, Elaine Frith is a humanized Jenny Sunley. She loathes the claustrophobic morality of her narrow-minded upbringing, and as a very young girl realizes her sexual potential over men. Purposefully she sets about harnessing this to further her well-defined material ambitions, and the war provides abundant opportunities in the shape of allied, rootless soldiers stationed near the Avenue. Delderfield skilfully pinpoints the curious separation of Elaine's life from that of most of her neighbours at a time when the prevailing mood is one of community solidarity. She is untroubled by public opinion of her proclivities: 'Marvellous what some women'll do nowadays for a pound of granulated and a tin of pineapple chunks, isn't it?' The provider of illicit groceries is of course Archie Carver. He and Elaine eventually settle down together, still opportunist and down-to-earth but in a curious manner true to themselves: and they are the most satisfying personalities in Delderfield's saga.

Actually it is Archie's father who is the leading character. Jim Carver is a tough but disillusioned first world war veteran.

'On the final day of the war he changed sides. From now on he was to fight his own people.' Jim witnesses a young boy's life pointlessly destroyed by 'a pot-bellied major, fresh from base, and thirsting for blood' who orders an attack on a German machine gun post just before the Armistice. For the next two decades Jim's private war continues although his allegiances shift; he moves from socialism towards communism; he becomes disillusioned successively by the white-collar strike-breakers in 1926, the trade union leaders, the League of Nations and eventually by the whole of the British organized Left, when they do little to arrest the advance of fascism in Europe. Ironically, after Dunkirk Jim finds himself lifted out of political despair by Winston Churchill, a man he had 'always disliked and mistrusted, the politician he had labelled as a typical autocrat of the ruling caste'.

Historical events are very differently evaluated by Henry Williamson in that part of his fifteen-volume *Chronicle of Ancient Sunlight* which is contained in *The Phoenix Generation* and *A Solitary War*. Like Delderfield's novels these were written after the second world war but they deal convincingly with the 1920s and 1930s. They encompass the disturbingly persuasive reflections of someone who is radically out of harmony with the economic and psychological structure of his own society. One of Williamson's books is dedicated 'to Oswald and Diana Mosley in friendship', and the author's account of a meeting of the British Union of Fascists organized by Hereward Birkin's (Mosley's?) supporters contrasts sharply with Delderfield's description of the same or a similar occasion. According to Williamson 3,000 communist 'roughs' intimidate Birkin's well-ordered supporters 'with missiles, including safety-razor blades pushed into potatoes', chair legs wrapped around with barbed wire and knuckle-dusters. Delderfield writes of cabbage-stalks and sodden balls of newspaper thrown by 'half-hearted hecklers' who are then set upon viciously by the officious Blackshirts.

But boyhood conditioning goes deep, and at least one part of the British cultural heritage about which these two writers *do* seem in accord is the work of Charles Hamilton. Phillip Maddison who in *A Solitary War* alternates between condemning the British establishment and vindicating Hitler's policies thinks with affection of an incident in an early *Gem* when schoolboy Tom Merry foils 'the machinations of the Germans' who plan to invade England in 1906.

The women in Delderfield's books have an independence which Williamson's heroines do not display. They are active and robust both in the services and at the home front. Characteristically Phillip Maddison considers the tendency of young women to worship male fantasy figures: 'illusions, which are the stronger because blood, or sperm, has not been tasted'. In Henry Williamson's books intelligent and experienced women too idealize the confused but coldly compelling Phillip. He and his associates are inclined even in wartime, and when they are supposed to be hard-up, to tuck into York ham and smoked pheasant from Fortnum and Mason; naturally they are rather contemptuous of the suburban life that Delderfield celebrates.

It is easy for an author to move from convincing portrayals of people in ordinary circumstances to the creation of patronizing cameos of 'the little man' or woman. Both Delderfield and Williamson avoid this more adroitly than Noel Coward in his 1932 play *Cavalcade* and his second world war film *This Happy Breed*. The impact of *Cavalcade* was tremendous: it is an above-and-below-stairs saga of England from 1899 to 1930, but events of significance from the relief of Mafeking to the slump of the 1920s are sometimes reduced to clichés. (There is even an 11am Armistice Day telegram announcing the death of a son in action.) From this distance in time it seems surprising that this rather stilted and selective view of the social effects of war could have been so well received. However, in the play every set-piece must have been transformed by the intensity of the audiences' response. *Cavalcade* also had a potent musical background. At the beginning of the 1930s a play that brought in 'Soldiers of the Queen', 'Land of Hope and Glory' and 'Nearer My God to Thee' was not likely to fail. Noel Coward *does* attempt to convey post-war disillusion as well as patriotic ideals; but in spite of the tableaux which *Cavalcade* provides of blind soldiers listlessly making baskets, or of jaded couples dancing together to monotonously insistent jazz numbers, the overall mood of the play seems ambivalent.

Other films and plays of the 1930s with war themes were even more bland. Their attitude was that the war had been

fought and won, and everything had been neatly parcelled up
and finished. Cinematically the first world war had become
simply a background for the adventure epic, or the sentimental
love affair. Even the songs of 1914–1918, which were extraordinarily poignant, produced a sense of security, of travelling
on well-trodden paths.

Europe's drift into the second world war is analysed per-
ceptively by writers like Delderfield and Williamson, but they
are of course able to assess it with hindsight. The Spanish Civil
War of 1936–1939 did inspire some contemporary fiction which
questioned complacency in relation to ideological conflicts. In
Ernest Hemingway's *For Whom The Bell Tolls* some of the events
that were so prophetic of the nature of future wars were
adumbrated: '. . . we have just seen the sky full of airplanes of
a quantity to kill us back to our grandfathers and forward to
all unborn grandsons including all cats, goats, and bedbugs. . . .'
For Whom The Bell Tolls did not appear until 1940 when the
second world war had already begun. Whatever their political
persuasions it was not difficult for people living in wartime
Britain to respond to the story of a conflict that so intensely
involved a civilian population. The impact of Hemingway's
book was consolidated by the distribution of the Hollywood
film in 1943. This had a special effect on women in Britain
and America. Thousands quickly adopted the short, bubble-cut
hairstyle which was so becoming to Ingrid Bergman who
played the part of Maria, the republican partisan. Short hair
was of course appropriate for women in the services and on the
assembly lines. Maria's hair had been shaved by the fascists
in degrading circumstances in the prison at Valladolid. Even
after her escape to join the partisans 'She would not speak and
she cried all the time and if anyone touched her she would
shiver like a wet dog'. The cropped appearance of her head was
to Maria a reminder of rape and humiliation. Shaving and
sexual degradation were again linked in 1945: after the liberation of France members of the Resistance made public rituals
of head-shaving, to brand women who had been intimate with
men of the occupying German army and administration.

Because of its concern with war of ideologies—which has
become the pattern of many recent conflicts—*For Whom The
Bell Tolls* has a topicality today, in spite of its 1930s setting.

There is a contemporary relevance too in Robert Jordan's strong sense of political alignment, which at the same time can accommodate doubt and unease. Robert, an American fighting with the partisans behind enemy lines, sees communism as

> . . . something that was like the feeling you expected to have and did not have when you made your first Communion. It was a feeling of consecration to a duty toward all of the oppressed of the world . . . as authentic as the feeling you had when you heard Bach, or stood in Chartres Cathedral. . . . It gave you a part in something that you could believe in wholly and completely—and also *do* something about. . . .

However, he questions his own intellectual idealism, and the rigidity of 'that so mutable substitute for the apostles' creed, the party line': 'sleeping with Maria' puts him once again in total relationship with another person and lifts him out of thinking in clichés 'both revolutionary and patriotic' like 'enemies of the people'. There are also convincing descriptions of reversion to prayer ('Hail Marys') by people under stress who have ostensibly repudiated religious belief in favour of Marxism. Hemingway brings across another situation common in every war—the vitality of romantic relationships that are likely soon to be curtailed by the death of one or both participants: 'There is only now, and if now is only two days, then two days is your life and everything in it will be in proportion.'

There is authenticity as well in the nature of the women's involvement in the war: Maria's is reluctant, passive rather than active; Pilar typifies the toughness of the stolid peasant inflamed with loyalty to a cause for which she will work or fight without reservation. This gives her the capacity to lead others—despite her husband's contemptuous remarks about partisans commanded 'by a woman with her brains between her thighs'. Both Maria and Pilar, however, find themselves playing the rôle of displaced survivors.

At the end of the first world war many women were in the same situation. Their response to the deaths of male relatives and lovers veered from despair to optimism: the hope of making a world that could justify the sacrifice of so many lives.

Katherine Mansfield in her *Journal* expresses this resolution in sombre terms:

> I think I have known for a long time that life was over for me, but I never realized it or acknowledged it till my brother died. Yes, though he is lying in the middle of a little wood in France and I am still walking upright and feeling the sun and the wind from the sea, I am just as much dead as he is. . . . Then why don't I commit suicide? Because I feel I have a duty to perform to the lovely time when we were both alive.

VIII

BACKS TO THE WALL,
HEADS IN THE CLOUDS

Working Women of the Second World War

> I'm only a wartime working girl
> The machine shop makes me deaf
> I have no prospects after the war
> And *my* young man is in the R.A.F.
> K for Kitty calling P for Prue
> Bomb Doors Open . . .
> Over to you.
>
> Louis MacNeice, 'Swing-Song'

ACCORDING TO WRITERS of popular song, nightingales as well as air-raid sirens were to be heard in Berkeley Square between 1939 and 1945. Curtailed love affairs and separation of families through service abroad, evacuation and air-raid fatalities led inevitably to a spate of sentimental fiction. However even in some of these excesses there were pockets of realism which conveyed the atmosphere of the period, an alternation between heightened intensity and slightly jaded doggedness. There was a great deal of authenticity in some of the novels which were written about women in the services or other forms of war work.

On the whole women's magazines welcomed the boost which wartime poignancy gave to their romantic fiction. Some journals, however, continued to play down the ramifications until after the end of 'the phoney war'. 'Whispers', the *Woman's Weekly* editorial page on 25 May 1940—just before Dunkirk—asks for readers' continued loyalty, although 'the price of our little book must go up to 3d next Tuesday: . . . because we have wanted to divert you and give you something different to talk about, we have not talked over much about this war. . . . It is not that we have a frivolous outlook. But we felt we were *helping* you more if we could beguile your minds into happier channels.'

Further cosy reassurance was given in Mrs Marryatt's advice columns and talks on 'Culture' and other topics by 'The Man Who Sees'. (These two contributors were still going strong in the 1978 *Woman's Weekly*: whiter-haired but sympathetic as ever, the problem-solving lady is more democratically known as *Mary* Marryatt, and 'The Man Who Sees' remains enticingly anonymous.)

In 1940 Newnes & Pearson's *Peg's Paper* also had an anonymous male morale-booster. 'Peg's Man Pal', however, struck a more matey note than the slightly remote visionary of *Woman's Weekly*, and practical matters rather than cultural chats were his forte. His columns had tempting headings like 'Keep Smiling' or 'A Bride's Problem': 'Peg's Man Pal gives some good advice to a girl newly married . . . but you will be interested whether you have a wedding ring or not.' Disappointingly this turns out to be nothing more exciting than a breezy injunction not to make new curtains in a hurry in case they should fit badly.

The other male characters of *Peg's Paper* however preferred action (usually unscrupulous) to words. For most of the magazine's run from 1919 to 1940 its conscientious but inept heroines were cast in the rôle of weak-kneed victims: 'She didn't see Danger—and when a rich man offered her a fortnight's holiday at a Riviera Hotel . . . she accepted'. Their dimness made them easy prey for schemers and seducers, as typical story titles suggest: 'Another Girl's Man', 'The Thirteenth Bride', 'Night of Shame', 'Too Young to Marry', 'Make Believe Fiancée', 'Forbidden Husband' and 'Twins in Sin'. Even when a blameless working girl managed to achieve marriage—her only goal—she was rarely home and dry. Her union was likely to prove bigamous ('Wife Without a Name', 'Her Baby Had No Name', etc.) or even more sinister. *Peg's Paper* specialized in the type of husband who has no scruples about selling his trusting wife to an Indian potentate or an Arab sheik: 'It was her wedding night . . . she had married the man of her dreams . . . too late, she found she was a BRIDE FOR SALE!' Even if she managed to contract a non-bigamous marriage and avoid becoming the unwilling odalisque of a desert rapist, the unfortunate heroine would almost certainly find her husband in a compromising situation on the day after the wedding: 'Shadowed Honeymoon; the man who had vowed to love her was holding another girl in his arms.'

Peg's Paper carried factual articles as well as 'great' and 'thrilling' fiction, but during the uneasy days of 1939 and 1940 it never lost sight of its declared aim of 'brightening the long blackout evenings'. In war as in peace it stressed that a girl's first duty was to make herself desirable in the hope that somewhere, sometime she would fall into the strong, protective arms of her non-bigamous Mr Right. Beauty features were always colourful, like the series of 'Desert Glamour Secrets' by Barbara Board. 'She will reveal how you can become as mysteriously lovely as the harem women of Arabia.' Little space was devoted to the old standbys of women's magazines: knitting patterns, advice on cookery and bringing up children. However, Nurse Janet, an ample, motherly-looking lady, gave her readers health hints and stressed the importance to beauty of 'evacuating waste', a theme echoed in the Bile Beans advertisements which promised not only to keep women regular in bowel movements but sylph-like in appearance. Whatever vicissitudes war might bring, Friday night remained 'Amami Night'—understandably, if this shampooing ritual really did produce the incredibly lustrous locks of the advertisement pictures. Publicity slogans for well-known cosmetics like Icilma, Snowfire and Outdoor Girl made attractive reading when no Trades Description Act existed to tone down copy-writers' flights of fancy.

Fashion advertisements often drew inspiration from the film industry: 'Dresses Modelled for you from Hollywood in rich velveteen at 17/9d [89½p] only; send 1/6d [7½p] deposit now.' Going to the pictures had acquired a new significance in wartime. Films provided momentary escape from boredom, austerity and the fear of bereavement. The readers of *Peg's Paper* must have enjoyed its long-running 'Gossip from Filmland'.

Naturally romantic difficulties received several pages of editorial attention. Madame Sunya, photographed in jewelled headband, heavy veil and flowing chiffon, gave astrologically slanted advice to the lovelorn. In spite of her star-spangled

F

appearance she was often surprisingly down to earth: 'The man
you are most likely to find happiness with is a fairly slight, dark
man . . . he will probably wear a uniform of some sort'. Not
exactly a rash prediction when uniforms were proliferating
daily.

Infidelity hotted up in wartime. *Peg's Paper* heroines were
flung into a maelstrom of seduction and bigamous marriage
as the boys in khaki, navy- and air-force blue marched in and
out of their turbulent lives. The curiously passive heroines
were set off by bitchy connivers whose glittering but hard-
skinned exteriors concealed no redeeming character features
whatsoever. They usually had exotic names like Fleur (if
foreign), or Gloria (if homegrown). On the whole the bitches
came off better than the good girls, at least until the last
episode, as Kitty Lorraine's 1939 serial 'War-Bride' illustrates.
Well-meaning Ann Fenner goes to France as a nurse and
marries Charles Miller, a handsome, wounded soldier. On
their wedding night he not only flirts with a French girl of
dubious reputation but is arrested as Carl Müller, a Nazi spy.
Soon afterwards, on the point of throwing herself into the
Seine, Ann is rescued by Brent Cadelle, an army officer whom
she promptly marries, believing that her first husband has been
shot. But—on the morning after her wedding night with
Brent—whom does Ann see beneath her hotel window? None
other than Carl of course—alive, and vigorously marching
away with a military police escort. And Ann's problems get
worse as the story continues.

Go-getting Gloria Vance, in contrast, thrives on romantic
complications. She has no qualms about involving blameless
Brent Cadelle in her divorce case and having him struck off the
medical register. Her object is simply to have a good time. 'To
red-headed, man-mad Gloria of the ice-blue eyes men alone
made life exciting. She decided at once that she must have a
uniform too' (on overhearing an RAF officer in a restaurant
complimenting the girl with him—' "Darling, you look an
angel in that VAD kit" '). In *Peg's Paper* the nursing image
seemed more popular than that of the women's services with
their undertones of masculinity. The magazine was not exactly
career-minded and slapping its fictional women into uniform
did not necessarily result in a positive contribution to the war

effort, as the behaviour of 'utterly superficial and deadly beautiful' Gloria Vance shows.

In Jessie Scott's 'Her Baby Had No Name' we find another victim of bigamy, Mollie Grant, '. . . just eighteen and facing the greatest disaster a girl can know'. The man Molly presumed to be her legal husband had 'swept her into a world of rapture' but then 'discarded her as casually as he might have done a pair of gloves'. And to add to the bleakness of Mollie's

From *Home Chat*, 1939

predicament, she is pregnant. Her difficulties are temporarily overcome when she meets Blake Dormer, a recently blinded RAF officer who mistakes Mollie for Dolores, his fiancée. (Living up to her foreign-sounding name, Dolores proves to be exotic but fickle. She has just gone off with 'a marvellous staff officer' who is giving her 'too wonderful a time to give up', but Blake does not know this.) Mollie accidentally bursts into his life just when he is expecting Dolores to arrive for their registry-office wedding. Mollie, who would 'give her very soul' for a name for her baby, takes advantage of Blake's blindness, pretends to be Dolores and marries him. (The heroines of *Peg's Paper* could make instant decisions where matrimony was concerned: and they never seemed to experience difficulties with trivial matters like conflicting names on birth and marriage certificates.) Mollie's new and fulfilling life of cherishing her blind hero-husband is abruptly shattered. When he regains his sight Blake is enraged at her deception and tears off to France where he is once more severely injured when his aeroplane is brought down. Not surprisingly he finds himself again being cared for by the devoted Mollie—a VAD now, nursing not only wounded service men but a broken heart, and guilt over her recent miscarriage.

As well as the *Peg's Paper* team, more competent writers have been strangely fascinated by the potent image of the strong but self-effacing heroine nobly standing by a blinded lover. In romantic fiction, her partner's loss of sight usually brings out a girl's best qualities, although paraplegia has the reverse effect, as illustrated by Constance Chatterley and Stella Tabret (see Chapter VII). Present-day readers might find it frustrating that Jane Eyre did not marry Mr Rochester until he was blind and mutilated; similarly Florence Barclay addicts might have regretted that the Hon. Jane Champion (hefty in body but all female fragility within) got together with artistic, beautiful Garth Dalmain only after he had been blinded in a shooting accident. The popularity of this theme suggests that some women, in fact as well as in fiction, were possibly motivated by power-lust rather than self-sacrifice in seeking maimed and dependent husbands.

Barbara Cartland would, one imagines, pour scorn on this chilling reflection: however her *Open Wings*, first published by Hutchinson in 1942, deals with this well-worn theme. At the beginning of the book Squadron-Leader Jameson (Jimmy) Braith is presented as the embodiment of almost everything a girl could want. As well as having 'a very slight look of Clark Gable' this dashing fighter pilot is the only son of 'one of the richest men in England—a millionaire even in these days'. Certainly these assets are slightly offset by the temporary limp and damaged arm resulting from his recent forced landing, but permanent disability does not affect him till later in the story when he is blinded after a ferocious air battle.

Lorna Overton, unassuming daughter of the vicar of Little Walton, is overwhelmed by Jimmy's confidence and masculine vigour. Lorna moves in a world of Women's Institute whist-drives, knitting parties, Sunday School, Girl Guides and Weldon's pattern books. Living in the country with no experience of air-raids she is at first largely insulated from the effects of war, though she does recognize that the influx of evacuees is adding to the work of their over-burdened local GP. Jimmy sweeps his 'Cherry Ripe' (the name springs from their first meeting when Lorna was picturesquely gathering fruit) into marriage, but this turns out to be far from ideal. Jimmy's self-indulgence is evident even when they are honeymooning in Cornwall at one of his family's large country houses. Out of harmony with the nation's prevailing mood of cheerful acceptance of austerity, Jimmy basely yearns for the Cap d'Antibes, for Biarritz and gambling. Lorna, who is used to the quietness of little Walton where '. . . the Overton family did not [even] possess a wireless', is naturally disturbed by this upper-class restlessness. It has further distasteful manifestations. Jimmy begins to flirt with Lorna's cousin Sally, fetching and feline in her ATS uniform. (Off duty her 'perfectly shaped legs' are 'encased in superfine silk stockings': it is of course too early for nylon.)

Despite the upheavals and challenges of war, which cut away a great deal of humbug in relationships between men and women, Lorna has difficulty in discussing anything important with her husband in a straightforward way: 'He had merely to touch her, to smile at her with that peculiarly charming, irresponsible smile, and she felt her heart turn over within her breast and knew that she could not withstand him, could only surrender herself without reservation into his arms. . . .'

This did, of course, make any kind of partnership or planning complicated. Lorna's status improves only when she is able to help the broken, savagely suicidal Jimmy to come to terms with his blindness. The solution is extremely simple: Jimmy's masculine strength and self-respect instantly reassert themselves when Lorna informs him in her genteel manner that '. . . so far as he [the gynaecologist] can ascertain, he thinks there is every reason to believe that I am going to have a . . . baby'. Hitherto

unbookish to the point of philistinism, Jimmy suddenly discovers dormant literary gifts. He becomes a playwright for the
BBC, a stable husband and father.

When *Open Wings* appeared in 1942 its exploitation of the
casually heroic, sexually exciting pilot fantasy figure must have
guaranteed its appeal to many women readers. Millionaire
Jimmy Braith was not of course 'just an *ordinary* fellow [who]
taught this heart of mine to fly', but with suitable verve he
conformed to the 'Silver Wings' image, endlessly sentimentalized in popular songs, plays and films to the irritation of many
real-life airmen. It is more difficult to understand the story's
present-day appeal but it was reissued by Arrow Books in 1971
and 1976. *Open Wings* lacks the colour and explicit sexuality of
more recent romantic novels and the dialogue is often naïve
or stilted. Perhaps its attraction rests in Barbara Cartland's
manipulation of the Cinderella motif. (There are, however, in
Open Wings some engagingly caustic moments which suggest
that the author is less sympathetic with Cinders than her
generally sugary narratives imply.)

The war demolished barriers between classes and the sexes
in an unprecedented manner, paving the way for the more
democratic society that began to emerge in the 1950s and 1960s.
After Dunkirk the image of British backs-to-the-wall solidarity
firmly seized the popular imagination and soon came to be
symbolized in the pugnacious leadership of Winston Churchill.
V-signing in unaesthetic siren-suit and growling out his
galvanizing speeches, 'Old Winnie' not only embodied patriotic
determination, but demonstrated political flexibility by obtain-
ing the support of many working-class people who had
previously regarded him as their traditional enemy. (Working-
class suspicions were revived in 1945, at the time of the 'Labour
Landslide' election victory, as Mary Rose Liverani remarks: 'I
knew who Mr Churchill was. He was the enemy of the workers
and in 1926 had shot all the miners dead when they wouldn't
work'—*The Winter Sparrows*, Michael Joseph, 1976.) She is of
course recalling a childhood impression.

The sometimes bizarre solidarity of 'the People's War' has
recently been conveyed by Spike Milligan in *Adolf Hitler—My
Part in His Downfall*, Michael Joseph, 1971, 'Now a Hitlarious
Film':

September 3rd, 1939. The last minutes of peace ticking away. Father and I were watching Mother digging our air-raid shelter. 'She's a great little woman,' said Father. 'And getting smaller all the time,' I added. Two minutes later, a man called Chamberlain who did the Prime Minister impressions spoke on the wireless; he said, 'As from eleven o'clock we are at war with Germany'. (I loved the WE.)

There are no *Tell England* overtones in Spike Milligan's snook-cocking record of his wartime experiences. Persuasive heroics were not—as in 1914 when enlistment was voluntary— necessary for recruitment. Conscription of young men was introduced at the beginning of the second world war. It did not apply to women until 1941, but on the whole they were quick to respond to government exhortations to 'Do Their Bit'.

To many women the idea of war service was exhilarating, with the possibilities it offered of escape from long-established or boring routines. In reality it often demanded mindless drudgery and hard physical work (the 1914 pattern was repeated in this respect: see Chapter II). In *One Pair of Feet* Monica Dickens describes the rueful but resolute spirit in which most women accepted these circumstances 'for the duration'. This entertaining autobiographical account of hospital training is far removed from the 'Carry On' farces of bedpan indignities or psychologically inflated ward sisters and matrons. At first the wide range of available war work made women's choice seem difficult and almost alarming. Monica Dickens records that every newspaper and hoarding beckoned and badgered healthy young British girls into the army, navy or air force; they were equally in demand by the ARP and AFS; also 'factory wheels would stop turning unless you rushed into overalls at once. . . . The Suffragettes could have saved themselves a lot of trouble if they had seen this coming. Men's jobs were open to women and trousers were selling like hot cakes in Kensington High Street.'

It was the war that established trousers as suitable all-purpose attire for women; not just a fashionable gimmick like the beach pyjamas, wide slacks or divided skirts of the 1930s. Wartime women's magazines illustrate many different types of these ubiquitous and highly functional garments, from dungarees and zip-up siren-suits to the durable but dispiriting ARP trousers in which some women seem to have lived ever since. As a concession to modesty most of these feminine pants were then fastened at the side: however the front opening now almost universally used in girls' jeans was foreshadowed in the early 1940s. It was not then considered attractive, as Monica Dickens notes in *The Fancy*, a book that deals with women employees in an aircraft factory. Freda, working on carburettors, emphasizes her tough, politically radical and 'mannish' personality by wearing pin-stripe trousers that did up in the front.

Monica Dickens decided to take up nursing only after careful consideration of the other wartime job possibilities. She dismissed the women's services because of the hip-spreading effect of their skirts and the unalluring prospect of black woollen stockings. Equally potent objections deterred her from offering herself to the AFS, becoming a 'clippie' or joining the Land army. 'One saw oneself picking apples in a shady hat, or silhouetted against the skyline with a couple of plough horses, but a second look showed one tugging mangel-wurzels out of the frozen ground at five o'clock on a bitter February morning.' And an experience of travelling to the west country with some demanding and disgruntled evacuees (one of whom had impetigo) had put her off the WVS. Although recognizing that attraction to nursing was often an adolescent phase like wanting to be a nun Monica Dickens reports dryly that she finally settled on this career after reading *A Farewell to Arms*. She had also been impressed by Madeleine Carroll's appearance in the film of *Vigil in the Night*. Her own hospital experiences were less romantic than Catherine Barkley's; and unlike Madeleine Carroll, she could not project serenity and glamour 'in a pure white halo cap, and glide swiftly about with oxygen cylinders'. But *One Pair of Feet* gives us an unpatronizing and accurate picture of 'ordinary' people under stress—their maddening lack of imagination, their bloody-mindedness, their frequent and surprising generosity. Monica Dickens shrewdly depicts the frustrations of an individualist caught in the rigid, hierarchical rituals of hospital life.

Despite the emergencies of war, some hospitals—except

perhaps when dealing with air-raid casualties—seemed almost hermetically sealed from its effects. Many nurses '. . . had no interest in anything that happened a yard outside the iron railings. They were only interested in the war as far as it affected them personally—shortage of Dettol and cotton-wool perhaps. . . .'

A fellow nurse expresses surprise at the interest shown by Monica Dickens in the war and in politics: 'I asked her what she would talk about [if] a German officer swaggered through the glass door to take over the ward. "I'd ask him if he'd had his bowels open," she said, and laughed coarsely.'

Immersion in their own work and disregard of the general progress of the war were typical of women engaged in other kinds of war work, too. This was partly due to gruelling hours of all-out effort: preoccupation with the job in hand might also have had an escapist function when the overall war news was— as so often—bad. Shirley Joseph's *If Their Mothers Only Knew* (her 1946 'Unofficial Account of Life in the Women's Land Army') reflects this compartmentalization: 'Apart from the fact that we were all doing a job which but for the war we should never have taken on, the war had very little effect on us. The majority of the girls took scarcely any interest in the progress of the fighting. . . .' And, according to Nancy Spain in *Thank You—Nelson*, this was true as well of the WRNS. 'One of the comforting or terrible things (according to which way you are looking at it) about being really desperately busy in the Service is the utter ignorance of other things taking place outside one's own little bit of war.'

Monica Dickens switched from nursing to aircraft production. In the autumn of 1940 'working on munitions' seemed the most vital contribution that women could make towards the war effort. The army still desperately needed re-equipping after Dunkirk, and in the Battle of Britain the RAF had lost planes at an alarming rate. Monica Dickens's factory experiences provide the background for *The Fancy*, in which different aspects of British wartime society are shown through the interwoven lives of ten women who work together on a factory bench, supervised by charge-hand Edward Ledward. At first Edward doubts his capacity to cope with his 'girls'. They range from a conscientious first-world-war munitions veteran to a flashy modern madam who radiates ripe sex. There is no inflation of the co-operative and sometimes incredible achievement of factory workers during this period. What *is* conveyed is the ghastliness of early rising, especially in the winter, to work yet another eleven-hour shift; the acrid smell of the draughty machine shop; the squabbles between women forced into uncongenial propinquity. There are also ironic references to the uninspired discussions of the Joint Production Committee, and the complaints of 'brother' and 'sister' workers at trade union meetings.

The book is full of images that reflect the wartime atmosphere as vividly as Hollywood's Veronica Lake tying her long blonde 'peek-a-boo-bang' tresses into a turban to take her place on the assembly line. In films it was easy for factory girls to look attractive in dungarees, but *The Fancy* indicates that in real life hygiene, let alone glamour, was difficult to attain:

> You were not supposed to go and wash your hands until five minutes before lunch-time. The 'toilet' ... contained six basins for about sixty girls. ... You could wipe your hands on a piece of rag and try to pretend that your lunch didn't taste of oil; you could run the three hundred yards among the sheds, fight your way in among the backs lined up at the basins like a litter of feeding pigs, and have a quick scrub with a hairless nailbrush and swill in someone else's dirty water ... or you could sneak out before the lawful time ...

(and incur the wrath of the foreman who occasionally posted himself outside the women's washroom). Monica Dickens's racy, down-to-earth narrative recreates other aspects of civilian involvement in the war—blackout rituals and compulsive listening to 'the wireless' news bulletins; the removal of iron railings for salvage, the use of 'envelope-savers', the carving up of football fields and dingy commons for allotments or barrage balloon sites. The 'fancy' of the book's title is rabbit-breeding—and it is a measure of the author's skill that she manages to make even this specialized activity intriguing to non-enthusiasts.

Similarly in *If Their Mothers Only Knew* Shirley Joseph writes about milking a cow, mucking out or harvesting with sufficient vitality to interest readers who have little appreciation of rural life. Her book is an interesting counterbalance to Vita Sackville-West's official account of the Women's Land Army. The 80,000 girls who went on the land were apparently the Cinderellas of wartime Britain: the song

> Ten bob a week
> Nothing much to eat
> Great big boots
> And blisters on her feet

summed up their situation. In addition to their basic 48-hour week they were required to work whatever 'compulsory overtime' their employers demanded, and some farmers expected a 70- or even an 80-hour week. They had no canteen facilities to eke out rations and accommodation was often primitive. According to Shirley Joseph a room with '. . . a chair, a bed, a wardrobe—and a lock' was often a luxury. Land girls received less money, shorter holidays and fewer chances of promotion than women in the 'armed' services.

Thank You—Nelson is Nancy Spain's lively record of her experiences as a WRNS driver at a base on the north-east coast. There is pride in her chosen service, and especially in her 'Lady Sailor' uniform, which she acquires only after several months of serving in unsuitable 'civvies'. (This pride is only slightly deflated when she is mistaken by several people for the district nurse.) In spite of romantic 'Jenny Wren' fantasies projected by the public and elaborated by romantic novelists, Wrens had often to be extremely tough. In her requisitioned civilian van ('FAMILY BAG WASH AND CARPETS BEATEN') Nancy Spain undertook a variety of unsavoury assignments. Her cargoes included smelly, gone-to-seed cabbages, unexploded mines and even, on one gruesome occasion, the unrecognizable remains of torpedoed trawler men *en route* for the mortuary. The tone of *Thank You—Nelson* is iconoclastic; but the patriotism which originally inspired Nancy Spain to join the WRNS is heightened, like that of so many of her compatriots, after Dunkirk. 'The hours I worked became impossible . . . I did not care. I should have screamed rather than admit it, but we were determined to blot Dunkirk and all that it stood for off the map.'

Nancy Spain persistently questions some of the men from the splintered, blood-spattered 'little ships' who helped to get the British Expeditionary Force home, although they are at first reluctant to discuss that 'hell let loose'. Their description of 'the fag end of the Brigade of Guards'—half starving, exhausted, under fire but still '... in line, heads up...' is moving in spite of its incongruity. A different but equally heartening picture emerges from another of their accounts. This suggests that the spirit of Angela Brazil, appropriately embodied in Arthur Marshall, was in operation at Dunkirk: '"Captain he was ... he's really a schoolmaster ... but he's made any money he has out of being a female impersonator."' His men 'weren't a bit keen' on crossing the beach, which was being machine-gunned continually by Messerschmitts but 'this schoolmaster fellow', though hit in the ankle by a bullet, staggers up to rally them: ' "Come on, girls," he calls. .... "Who's on for the Botany Walk?" .... Follow him? I'll say they followed him. When they came aboard they were laughing. So was I ...".' And apparently Arthur Marshall managed to keep them in good spirits all the way back to England. Later in the war his radio portrayal of 'Nurse Dugdale' provided amusement for a wider audience: a cross between hearty hockey mistress and pantomime dame, 'she' was the bracing antithesis of the *Peg's Paper* 'angels' in VAD uniform.

Norman Pett's Jane, from the *Daily Mirror*, 1940

Possibly the most celebrated member of the ATS was Norman Pett's Jane. The ATS was her first choice of service. As the *Daily Mirror* cartoon—and the war—progressed Jane temporarily joined several others with splendid impartiality. In September 1939 she is the khaki-clad chauffeur to a fatherly bemonocled colonel. Jane is soon transferred to MI5, and a little later seconded to naval intelligence. She spends a short time in the WAAF, but the air force is better represented in her saga by Freddie, an obliging spitfire pilot who drops out of the sky from time to time to extricate Jane from various predicaments. She helps with evacuees in the WVS and has a spell in the Women's Land Army. Jane also purposefully dons dungarees as a factory worker, carries off diplomatic missions abroad, routs black marketeers at home, joins the NAAFI and —finally—ENSA. No girl could have served her country more vigorously.

Jane raised the morale not only of British troops and civilians, but of their allies. The Americans dubbed her 'Britain's Secret Weapon of World War II'—but of course absolutely *nothing* about Jane was secret! She sheds her clothing with even greater frequency from 1939 to 1945 than during her seven pre-war years. However, Jane remains engagingly innocent, whether she is covered in nothing but seaweed, high-kicking in a front-line concert party, kissing a whole army battalion goodbye or simply hiding confidential documents in her cleavage.

Life in the ATS was presented with a degree of seriousness in Leslie Howard's 1943 film, *The Gentle Sex*; but although a popular song implied that people were 'whacky over khaki' (American pronunciation to make it rhyme!) the WRNS and the WAAF produced more attractive fictional characters. In 1944 Ursula Bloom's *Jenny W.R.E.N.* appealed to the average Englishman's and woman's fantasies of belonging to a race of sea dogs. (It is strange how deeply this feeling is embedded even in those of us who dislike cold water and are prone to sea-sickness.) *Jenny W.R.E.N.* (see Chapter III) was not an original title: it had been used for a novel about the first world war. In spite of its dashing, nautical background, Jenny's service life is not particularly adventurous: 'She had adored the life in the officers' mess, serving meals, pottering to and fro with this and that, handing potatoes, handing brussels sprouts, handing cheese.' (Quoted in *The Purple Heart Throbs*, Rachel Anderson, Hodder & Stoughton.) And unlike her first-world-war namesake, Jenny found that Cock Robin (fickle and fascinating Robin RN) was an unsatisfactory answer to a maiden's prayer. She settled instead for an unglamorous but reassuring naval doctor who '. . . wore his cap at the Beatty angle and . . . had freckles, surprising freckles on his cherubic face. The little Doc. came from the north, and when he got excited, he burst into Scotch.'

Sailors in romantic fiction have always projected nonchalant courage and compelling sex appeal. However, because of their daring and endurance in the Battle of Britain, RAF pilots took over these attributes from the navy in a great deal of contemporary fiction. The charisma of 'the Few' clung throughout the war to almost any personable young man who wore his air-force-blue uniform with sufficient panache to suggest *Per Ardua Ad Astra*. They had, after all, been likened by both the prime minister and the *Girl's Own Paper* to the Knights of the Round Table. The 'Silver Wings' remained untarnished even after the indiscriminate bombing of Dresden later on, when the allies were masters of the air and no longer played the rôle of David demolishing Goliath. Some of the lustre rubbed off on to the WAAFs—who also, in the public imagination, inherited the pluck and pioneering spirit of Amy Johnson. WAAFs carried out many important and highly responsible duties during the war and it is a pity these are not more adequately featured in the fiction of the time.

A recent story (1976) gives some colourful detail about the working background of these 250,000 'forgotten' women; but as *Sally, Diary of a WAAF* is written by a man (ex-pilot Paddy O'Neil-Dunne) inevitably the book's insights and technicalities are more relevant to life in the RAF. 'Ginger Roedale [Battle of Britain pilot, score so far eighteen German aeroplanes destroyed, six probables and three damaged] calls me his Toothsome Tootsie. He pesters and flirts with me to finish typing his dirty songs. Says they're more important to win the war than those binding Combat Reports.'

The hero of *Compromise with Yesterday* by Elizabeth O. Peter is handsome David Allen, a first-world-war fighter pilot who has become an air commodore in the RAF by 1939. For many women readers David must have typified the combatant but sensitive, Rupert Brooke-ish figure. (He never loses his 'sort of lost, searching look'.) He represents not only the vulnerability of youthful romance but the potency of remembered love affairs, sometimes 'more powerful, more relentless than the living presence, which might disappoint or cease to enchant'. Elizabeth O. Peter uses the clichés of wartime fiction; but skilfully enough to induce compulsive reading at a time when snatched meetings between lovers on leave and fear of sudden death formed the background to so many people's lives. David does not find happineess until the end of the book when lively WAAF sergeant Jacky Trevor wipes away the bitterness of his frustrated first-world-war relationship with her aunt, Lorella. ('Was he, like Faust, seeking a return of his youth?') *Compromise with Yesterday*, like Noel Coward's *Cavalcade*, is a family saga of two wars and the years between (see Chapter VII). It gets more deeply under the emotional skin than Coward, using similarly 'bitter-sweet' images. Scene after scene has a cinematic impact and intensity. It is surprising that Hollywood did not immediately translate it from story to celluloid.

WAAF Jacky is a practical young woman—typical of thousands who were getting on with the job of backing up the men of the fighting services. But Elizabeth O. Peter most genuinely recreates the atmosphere of the war when she concentrates on Jacky's and David's off duty moments: dinner at the Hungaria restaurant; Jacky's sensuousness in a black silk dress instead of her accustomed uniform, the sudden change from lighted café interiors to London's blacked-out shabbiness, and the surprising glamour of the scarred city, expressed through this and other contrasts. The sense of realism is intensified by the book's background use of popular music. David sings 'You Made Me Love You' to Lorella in 1914, and dances to 'the old Missouri Waltz' with Jacky in the 1940s. These songs and their settings convey the insecurity of people caught in an uncertain present—who have to look to the future for fulfilment, and to the past with longing.

Total involvement in the People's War was thrust not only on the women and children of Britain but, in different ways, on those living in many other countries. Although published as recently as 1964, Ursula Bloom's *The Ring Tree* discloses a greater awareness of the war's impact on the individual than her 1944 *Jenny W.R.E.N.* The atmosphere of the phoney war is accurately projected, and contrasted with the traumatic events that immediately followed it. The story begins in France during the summer of 1939: it is a young English girl's first visit to Paris and sixteen-year-old Fiona Betteridge savours the delights of evening apéritifs at the Café de la Paix and visits to the patisseries for rhumbabas and éclairs. She is staying with her middle-aged but volatile aunt, Camille—who has a 'high French bust and . . . ample hips welded by coutille stays'. When the war begins Camille's complacency is unruffled: 'War could not be so terrible . . . not for women, anyway. The Maginot Line would prevent war as it was once upon a time.' Similar faith in the Line and Britain's 'mighty fleet' exists in England, where Fiona's mother reflects on the declaration of war after returning home from church for sherry on the calm, lovely day of 3 September. Her sense of security is reinforced later by tea, sandwiches and a Fuller's walnut cake in the garden. 'She did not think that the war would change England so very much; it would still be England.' Even as late as early May when the Germans are overrunning the Low Countries, Camille is still saying, ' "We shall be all right" '. Thousands of people in France and Britain were of course clinging to that belief because the alternatives seemed too hideous to contemplate.

But Fiona and Camille suddenly find the atmosphere of Paris changing. Words like 'loot' and 'rape' are bandied about: the gradual exodus from the city gains momentum, as cars, lorries and handcarts loaded with families and their impedimenta begin to make for the coast. Ursula Bloom convincingly describes the nightmare journey to St Malo for Camille and Fiona, with Madame Julep and her little boy Etienne. (Only Fiona survives the journey.) German aeroplanes bomb and machine-gun the seemingly endless road: progress is further impeded by other refugees, wrecked vehicles, scattered belongings and the dead bodies of people and horses. The sense of unity which war often creates in a group or nation can equally be dispelled by its effects and by the instinct for self-survival. Fiona is appalled at having to ignore the injured and the dying in the desperate attempt to make progress; but—'This was the moment when they could help only themselves, and Camille knew it. The young girl did not.' Petrol runs out, they walk on mile after mile, almost at the end of their endurance. Just before Camille is killed in an air attack she has already reached the point where 'if death came it did not matter'.

Tragically many people in Hitler's occupied Europe were forced into situations where death became desirable as relief from suffering. Romantic fiction for women was disinclined to dwell on this aspect of the war, although plenty of films and adventure stories exploited its violence and degradation. The plights of the refugee and of the political prisoner are communicated without melodrama in Ann Bridge's *A Place to Stand*. The book was published by Chatto & Windus in 1951 but an author's note explains that it was planned about twelve years earlier: '. . . it treats, at first hand, of a brief period of recent history . . .'. Certainly her descriptions of the rootless life of a group of Polish refugees in Hungary just before the German take-over seem authentic. Her title is taken from one of Elizabeth Barrett Browning's *Sonnets from the Portuguese*:

> A place to stand and love in for a day,
> With darkness and the death-hour rounding it.

Stefan, from Poland, is about to go into his second exile, this time leaving Hungary to escape the Nazis. He and rich American Hope Kirkland are falling in love but he knows that he has no future to share with her. Theirs is an odd but of course typical wartime liaison. Hope has sufficient American practicality to accept the situation and let him go. But she suddenly finds herself at the centre of the escape plan for Stefan and his family: she gives her passport and identity documents to Stefan's sister Litka whom she slightly resembles. Consequently Hope is arrested by the 'Deuxième Bureau' (Hungary's replica Gestapo) in mistake for Litka. 'Hope Kirkland that night tasted a full dose of the bitterness of Hitler's Europe; she had taken on a European identity, and had a chance to learn something of what that meant.' Ann Bridge conveys the hopelessness of the secretly arrested political prisoner by low-toned descriptions of the ugliness of the environment. She doesn't dwell on the brutal questioning ordeals: 'Hope . . . stared about her for a moment in bewilderment—at the stained and dirty walls of the cell, scribbled over here and there with remarks in Hungarian, Polish, and Yiddish; at the high barred window, with a blank whitewashed brick wall close opposite; at the stinking urine-bucket in one corner. . . .' Hope's influential American background eventually impresses the Gestapo; and on her release she learns that Stefan and his family have got away successfully.

The early part of the book shows the growing influence of the Hungarian Nazis and how it insidiously begins to transform people's lives. Ruritanian overtones of gipsy music and flower markets take away some of the credibility, but there are gripping vignettes of the Gestapo searching for refugees on night trains to Istanbul. There is also a touch of authenticity in the way that Hope responds to the appearance of blond, confident soldiers of the German Panzer Divisions passing through Budapest on their way to subdue Jugoslavia: '. . . the girl found something horrifying about that display of power, of soulless mechanical precision, of anonymous inhuman efficiency. And yet there was a sort of magnificence about it too.' The author communicates the conflicting reactions of many women to displays of militarism: horror at its essence is sometimes coupled with reluctant exhilaration at its trappings and peripheral pageantry. It may be expressed simply in admiration of the RAF's stunting Red Arrows, the musical ride of the Royal Horse Artillery or 'the helmet and the plume' of the Life Guards at Whitehall. There is, after all, as Cicely Courtneidge has so often sung, 'Something about a Soldier . . .'.

Relations between women and fighting men is one of the themes of Vicki Baum's *Berlin Hotel*, published by Michael Joseph in 1944. In the wartime context this is unusual in its realistic treatment of German characters, who were not all mere cyphers strutting around in 'lion-tamer's boots'. The book has obvious similarities with the author's earlier best-selling *Grand Hotel* (filmed in 1933 with Lionel Barrymore and Greta Garbo). Again a variety of characters is brought into intense proximity in the lush but claustrophobic atmosphere of a large hotel—in this case 'an island' set apart for Hitler's élite. This is made up of German officials and notables working in Berlin and going to their country homes only occasionally, Quislings and collaborators and neutral industrialists. The hotel is under siege from air-raids—and the allied armies are already advancing into Germany on two fronts. The Third Reich's declining power is symbolized by the fading grandeur of the hotel's furnishings and the increased bickering of its ill-assorted guests. Ambitions for personal advancement are being replaced by furtive transfers of money to neutral countries and the finalization of escape plans.

The heroine is Lisa Dorn, a young, successful and suitably Nordic-looking actress. In spite of her naïve idealization of Hitler's person and policies, she is supposed to possess a shrewdness that contrasts with 'the sturdy, cowlike quality bred and trained into the average Nazi woman'. (During the war many English people came to believe that the whole German nation was made up of brutal soldiers and passive *hausfraus*.) Vicki Baum gives plenty of examples of Teutonic attitudes which seem to endorse this idea. Lisa's unimaginative lover is the shaven-haired Prussian General Arnim von Dahnwitz. He '. . . had never allowed his iron thigh muscles of an old cavalry officer to get flabby, and he was proud of them. Horses and woman like a firm knee grip, was one of his maxims.'

A further expression of Nazi 'Strength through Joy' was the fecundity that might result from the general's equestrian grip. In the words of flying ace Oberleutnant Otto Kaunders '. . . our major told us that every soldier who goes on leave and doesn't leave a pregnant woman behind has failed in his duty'. This is not so far-fetched as it may sound: Germany had made contraception illegal and in Hitler's anti-feminist philosophy the maternal rôle was glorified at the expense of career opportunities for women which had been drastically and deliberately reduced in the 1930s. Even when the war began to go against Germany, Hitler was initially reluctant to encourage women to take up industrial work, despite terrible shortages of manpower.

The other prominent female character in *Berlin Hotel* is Tilli, 'the bitchy little Gestapo informer'. Tilli is an ageing tartish hanger-on, suffering wartime shortages bitterly: she 'had to paste bad greasepaint over her grey, anaemic, vitamin-hungry skin, and to struggle with her bleached hair that screamed with brittleness for lack of nutrition'. She would, we gather, have sold her soul, her grandmother and of course her body several times over for some new shoes to replace her one disintegrating pair. At the beginning of the book the main characters are overdrawn but they are convincingly changed by events. Lisa finds herself protecting the hunted student resistance leader Martin Richter, and waking up to the real meaning of Nazism. Tilli is eventually sickened by her own opportunism, and at great personal risk she gets drugs for an old Jew who is dying painfully of cancer, and denied medical treatment. (It seems astounding that any known Jews were still alive in the Berlin of 1944.) Vicki Baum creates and sustains all the suspense elements of the chase and the struggle between 'goodies' and 'baddies' against the backcloth of a once invulnerable society on the edge of destruction. There is romance for good measure. Perhaps, after all this, it is churlish to complain that even the most patriotic British reader in 1944 might have queried one of Vicki Baum's assessments of the enemy: 'The German soul is . . . abstruse . . . full of darkness and with the face of a gargoyle. . . . Germans are forever yearning for the chain and the whip, because they are afraid of their own fathomless emotional furore and depth.'

In the early years of the war women's magazines were producing lively fictional variations on the theme of the enterprising girl in occupied Europe who outwits the Gauleiters or the Gestapo. These stories did not communicate the quality of the terrible ordeals endured by real-life women intelligence agents like 'Odette Churchill' who were arrested and tortured by the Gestapo. Odette survived fourteen interrogations and a period of imprisonment in Ravensbrück Concentration Camp. Subsequently she wrote: 'I am a very ordinary woman, to whom a chance was given to see human beings at their best and at their worst. I knew kindness as well as cruelty, understanding as well as bestiality. My comrades, who did far more than I, and suffered far more profoundly, are not here to speak.' (*Odette*, Chapman and Hall, 1950.)

After 1942 the bitterest invective of several women's magazines was directed against the Japanese—not surprisingly in view of their soldiers' record of atrocities. By 1943 *Britannia and Eve* and *Women's Pictorial* were reflecting the general listlessness brought about by several years of austerity, but even languor could not erode the will to win. (By then, of course, America and Russia had joined the allies and victory seemed assured.) Those were the days when a girl's best friend really was her sewing machine. 'With 36 coupons as our fashion ceiling we must be shabby, let's face it. But for goodness sake let us be shabby in a gay light-hearted fashion.' This is amplified in the following suggestions: the best parts of torn and split nighties should be quartered up and pieced together like a jockey's silks; readers should 'make the patches on panties and cami-knickers contrast gaily by using the flowered or patterned crepes of worn-out undies'; old jumpers could be renovated by stitching one's name on them in sequins, or adding heart-shaped tinselled pockets pierced by an embroidered arrow. With similar ingenuity cookery feature writers still managed to produce attractive recipes designed to eke out rations and provide variety. The advertisements in wartime women's magazines transport one back into the early 1940s as vividly as contemporary songs. It was a world of wedge-heeled shoes by Joyce, Herschelle square-shouldered coats and Goray pleated skirts. But for off-duty evenings there were still slinky 'little black dresses' with sweetheart necklines and a suggestion of swathing on the hips.

Male characters in the stories were naturally most often in uniform. RAF pilots were still presented heroically. In the domestic context of these magazines, however, after their intrepid raids over Heligoland they would return shot-up and exhausted—but in time for their children's birthday parties. American soldiers billeted in Britain were very much to the fore, exuding confidence: 'I want a place with a butler, and a ghost, and a moated whatsisname all round it. Armour in the hall and atmosphere. . . . Yes, sir, that's the sort of joint I want.' (He got it, too!) That lover of old England was GI Hank, 'long and lean' in the tradition of Gary Cooper. Although American soldiers were idealized in women's magazine il-lustrations most of those over here in fact bore little resem-blance to craggy Hollywood heroes. Their bland countenances prompted many East Enders to call them 'Baby faces'.

Before the war there was a great deal of mutual suspicion and misunderstanding between Britain and America. It was, apparently, 'an ordinary sort of woman'—Jan Struther's Mrs Miniver—who helped to break down American isolationism. According to President Roosevelt, she had 'considerably hastened America's entry into the war'. (Most people thought it was the Japanese attack on Pearl Harbor.) Before Mrs Miniver's advent, Hollywood's Englishwomen were either cheerful cockney charladies or daunting beauties who were all ice blue, rose pink and hydrogen peroxide. (English films hadn't done much better by them.) *Mrs Miniver* was published in 1939 and was in fact a reprint of a series of articles that had originally appeared in the Court Page of *The Times*. It shows the effect of the Munich crisis on a secure, middle-class family, and documents the worsening political situation that followed. The book ends in the early days of the war, but when it was filmed in Hollywood in 1942 it covered the period of the blitz. The air-raid sequences which must have done so much to impress the American public were unrealistic, less like bombing than firework displays which had got out of control. But in spite of the film's limitations Greer Garson managed to project a potent combination of intelligence and innocence in the character of Mrs Miniver. Jan Struther captures the mood of the time, though Mrs Miniver, with her cook, nannie, house parlour maid and charlady is hardly an average woman. She and architect husband Clem move gracefully in a world of shooting, sherry, dinner and week-end parties. But beneath the conventional veneer Caroline Miniver is given a slightly sceptical outlook. She takes an objective stand on important issues, unswayed by propaganda, retaining for instance her respect for certain German institutions and individuals. Her perceptiveness is expressed in a low-key way, in situations experienced by many people in England in 1939. She and her children attend a gas-mask fitting session when the approach of war seems inevitable: other families are there, and some of the younger children are terrified by the obliterating feel and ugly appearance of their masks. To their mothers, of course, this childish fear is a ghastly portent of worse horrors to follow: 'It was for this, thought Mrs Miniver . . . that one had boiled the milk for their bottles, and washed their hands before lunch, and not let them eat with a spoon which had been dropped on the floor.'

The war created uneasy alliances between people of many different shades of political opinion; for example communists who had initially regarded the war as a struggle between opposing oppressive elements began to support the allied war effort once Germany had invaded Russia in 1941. The problem for committed pacifists was less easily solved. After France's collapse in 1940, when Britain really faced the threat of defeat and destruction, many sincere pacifists found their position untenable. Also increasing evidence of Nazi policies of racial extermination converted some to belief in the necessity for armed resistance. Stephen Haggard (Rider Haggard's great-nephew) relinquished the pacifist view immediately after Dunkirk, as he explained in *I'll Go to Bed at Noon*, a published letter to his young sons whom he had sent for safety to the USA. It is interesting that this book, which strongly reflects Haggard's defeatist attitude, was allowed to be published during the war. Haggard felt that England and Europe really were about to go down into a dark age worse than any known to history. Read retrospectively the book is oddly moving. It is graphically written, but with a theatricality that occasionally touches the edge of hysteria. (Haggard was an actor, and his title is taken from one of the Fool's lines in *King Lear*.) The book conveys an impression that the author was rather more concerned with writing his own self-conscious epitaph than with the issues that were in question. (In fact he *did* die—fighting in the Middle East soon after he wrote *I'll Go to Bed at Noon*.) In spite of his nihilism, Haggard frequently displays the quintessential vigour of youth; and there are moments of insight which prompt this advice to his sons: 'Accept nothing, believe nothing, until a belief forces itself upon you, forces its roots into every cavity of your consciousness, and becomes an integral part of your way of thought.'

Stephen Haggard's apologia must have seemed irrelevant, if not devious, to many of the people who were putting so much effort into working for Britain's survival. However, doubts were expressed in other popular books. Eric Knight was a veteran of 1914–1918 and he served with the American army in the second world war. He too questions the validity of the military ethic. *This Above All* was published by Cassell in 1941 and filmed in 1942 with Tyrone Power and Joan Fontaine in the leading roles. Again Dunkirk seems to be the trigger point of deep, personal conflict. The book describes an improbable love affair between WAAF Prudence Cathaway and soldier Clive Briggs. (She is upper-class, constantly battling with the snobbishness that makes her think in terms of 'common private soldiers', 'workingmen's public houses', etc. He is aggressively from the people, and doesn't let her forget it.) After serving with the BEF in France Clive is totally disillusioned: he deserts and Prudence endeavours to persuade him to rejoin his unit. His final decision is never made as he is conveniently killed when rescuing a woman and child from a blitzed building. There is some challenging discussion of the comparative merits of British and German society: at one point Clive defends Hitler and attacks British decadence in a manner reminiscent of Henry Williamson. There is the conviction that—in both the wars—'someone had blundered': there is a sense of futility, and blistering condemnation of politicians, of the inhumanity that permits the sacrifice of soldiers' lives for a general's reputation. It is extremely strong stuff for 1941, but perhaps its emotive situations adequately counterbalanced the challenge. (*This Above All* certainly creates a different mood from *Lassie Come Home*, the book for which Eric Knight is best remembered.)

The poets of the second world war never caught the public imagination like those of the first, but American-born Alice Duer Miller's novel in verse *The White Cliffs* was widely read and quoted on both sides of the Atlantic. Critically, but with affection, she tries to convey to her compatriots the quality of life in Britain. Some of her lines crystallize the predicament of characters of the type created by Eric Knight and Henry Williamson who are

> Never more English than when they dared to be
> Rebels against her——

In this sense Williamson remains rebellious to the end. In his 1969 *Gale of the World* the *Chronicle of Ancient Sunlight* is at last completed. The text deplores the fact 'that they have hanged all those loyal generals and others at Nuremberg'. One of his female characters, Laura Wissilcraft, mentions 'a photograph of Hitler with the last of his faithful boys, outside the Bunker in Berlin. He looks worn-out, but he is so gentle and kind to those twelve- and thirteen-year-old boys'. If this is difficult to stomach, so is another of Laura's assessments:

A woman was a forked ex-quadruped, with breasts like bags slung from her collar-bones. By which the parasitism of human life was maintained. . . . Animals are shapely compared with women after twenty-five. Black brassières and French knickers—trap for John Thomas, Esquire—and finally cancer of the breast, from too much mauling. . . .

Henry Williamson cannot be classed with any other English writer about war, or women. He appears to see the two world wars of this century in terms of men's and women's evolution. Even when there is repudiation of his political and social interpretations one is impressed by his perceptiveness and enticed by his compelling images. Like Jefferies, whom he admires, Williamson has the capacity to look into 'the unseen world, which is the true world'. And there is his word magic, that inexorably links the reader's consciousness with the characters of his saga, the sexual complexities, the sacrifices of the Messines Ridge and the Somme, the animal symbolism, the interaction of past, present and future.

There is an apocalyptic ring of a different kind about the title of *The Last Enemy*. It is Richard Hillary's record of his part in the Battle of Britain as a fighter pilot; of being shot down, temporarily blinded and severely burned about the face and hands; of the long hospitalization that followed and the tedious but effective skin grafting by A. H. McIndoe. Hillary's purpose in writing *The Last Enemy* was to present an honest picture of the practical, unjingoistic attitudes which characterized most RAF personnel at that time. He hoped to dispel the 'Silver Wings' euphoria, the intense hero-worship of airmen in which many women and girls continued to indulge. For many readers, however, *The Last Enemy* had the reverse effect, and they made Hillary into a romantic, cult figure. There was a lack of literary heroes cast in the 1914–1918 mould. Richard

Hillary seemed to fit the bill, with his vigorous prose and his aeronautical achievements. The book expressed doubt about the justification of killing and the inequalities of our society, but it conveyed also a necessary exhilaration and confidence: 'I was released, filled with a feeling of power, of exaltation. To be up there, alone, confident that the machine would answer the least touch on the controls, to be isolated, entirely responsible for one's own return to earth—this was every man's ambition.'

Hillary's heroic image was enhanced when, soon after the medical patching-up so graphically described in his book, he returned to the RAF and was killed in a training flight. He was 23.

J. B. Priestley had reminded the aeronautical knight aces that they might have to come down to earth in more ways than one: they could well end up as door-to-door vacuum-cleaner salesmen unless a more egalitarian society was established after the war. This practical concern for the future was endorsed in 'For Johnny', the most popular poem of the war. At the time, however, public response to this poem was largely sentimental. Squadron Leader John Pudney wrote it on the back of an envelope in a London air-raid alert in 1941; Laurence Olivier broadcast it. In 1945, spoken by Michael Redgrave, it was the motif of the widely appealing Terence Rattigan film, *The Way to the Stars*:

> Do not despair
> For Johnny-head-in-air;
> He sleeps as sound
> As Johnny under ground.
>
> Fetch out no shroud
> For Johnny-in-the-cloud;
> And keep your tears
> For him in after years.
>
> Better by far
> For Johnny-the-bright-star,
> To keep your head,
> And see his children fed.

Johnny's children *would* be fed. The second world war ended in 1945 and the foundations of a new social structure were laid after the overwhelming Labour election win. The National Health Service, greater social security and more democratic attitudes towards education were established. Women played a more active part in reconstruction than after the first world war, and more vigorously than ever before they challenged the once accepted double standard of sexual morality. Improved techniques of birth control and increased career opportunities helped to bring about the beginnings of a freer, so-called permissive, society.

IX

DARK DEPARTURES

Serious Domestic Fiction of the War

Will it be so again—
The jungle code and the hypocrite gesture?
A poppy wreath for the slain
And a cut-throat world for the living? that stale imposture
Played on us once again?
                C. Day Lewis, 'Will it be So Again?'

INTIMATIONS OF WAR were sounded all through the '30s. 'The interval of time which divides us from the next war is almost certainly very short,' Stephen Spender declared in 1937 (*Forward From Liberalism*). At the beginning of the decade the progressive attitude was a kind of liberal pacifism; with the Italian invasion of Abyssinia and the Spanish Civil War there was a brief return to the heroic militarism of 1914, with impassioned outbursts about the defence of freedom. Political idealists went off to fight in Spain; but involvement was still voluntary. By the late '30s it had become clear that wholesale war was imminent and that no one in England could hope to escape its effects. Naturally attitudes to this were varied. England was still a place of radical social division and among the working classes there was a certain amount of pacifism based on simple disinclination to fight for the privileged minority that governed the country. The Labour party was divided on the issue since many of its leaders had renounced all ideas of pacifism at the advent of Hitler. Among the other classes, there were those who believed in appeasement at any price; those who were convinced that Nazism had to be resisted; and the small minority of fascists who found common ideological ground with Hitler.

Preparations for war were set in motion. The manufacture of gas masks was begun in 1937; a year later J. B. S. Haldane wrote a book on air-raid precautions, basing some of his conclusions on his experiences in Spain, and deploring the fact that the pets of rich people might be evacuated to safety while the children of the poor remained to be bombed.

For the lack of adequate protection for babies, Professor Haldane blamed 'the women voters of England', whose interest in public events like the coronation or the latest murder had prejudiced their children's chance of survival. This curious conclusion was a commonplace of the '30s: the women voters were held responsible for many social ills that they had failed to remedy. Dr C. E. M. Joad went even further than Professor Haldane: 'Before the war, money poured into the coffers of the WSPU [Women's Social and Political Union] in order that women might win the vote which, it was hoped, would enable them to make war a thing of the past. The vote is won, but war is very far from being a thing of the past.' (See *Three Guineas*, Virginia Woolf, 1938.)

War had not been done away with, in other words, because women, on the whole, continued to demand diversion in the form of scandal and fashion parades. They had failed in their task of reforming men's 'incurable . . . mischievousness'; and now they were too lethargic and stupid to badger their members of parliament into taking a serious attitude to the special problem of infants' welfare. However, after some encouragement, three women of slightly below-average intelligence were persuaded to lend their babies to Professor Haldane for the purpose of experiment with gas-proof boxes. One baby was snatched back almost immediately; one stuck it out for half-an-hour, and one for a little longer, with no ill effects. Professor Haldane offered to sell his box for £6 5s (£6.25p) to any mother who might want it. (In the event, of course, gas was not used against the civilian population; but the issue of gas masks and other forms of protection was no doubt of great psychological benefit.)

Professor Haldane's concern with air-raid precautions was the subject of one of 'Sagittarius's' parodies in the *New Statesman*:

What, teacher, can that object be inside a plate-glass drum?
It is Prof. Haldane whom you see, testing a vacuum.

Why are they hurling bombs so near that shelter made of tin?
It is a bombproof test, I hear, Prof. Haldane is within.

Oh, look! From yon balloon so high what dangles large and
    limp?
It is Prof. Haldane, we espy, air testing from a blimp.

Actually, Professor Haldane's book is full of sensible suggestions about the avoidance of panic and the basic precautions
needed to minimize risks. It is simply his assumptions about
women's lack of common sense that makes his tone occasionally
irritating. For the purposes of wartime activities, he divides
society into two categories: able-bodied men and everyone else.
'Where men must stay to do essential work in a dangerous area,
their wives and children would in some cases be urged to
evacuate, whilst arrangements were made locally for feeding
and otherwise caring for the men.' Some simplification is
necessary in the context, of course, but this is simplification
along the most predictable lines. Men useless in the kitchen,
women useless in any situation demanding resourcefulness
or courage . . . the image is retrogressive to the point of
falsification.

The issue of women's rôle in wartime was by no means
clear-cut. Conscription for women was introduced in December
1941, but it applied only to spinsters and widows between the
ages of 20 and 30; married women were exempted, even if they
had no children. In fact, the government made it easy for
mothers to work. The provision of day nurseries was carried
out with speed and efficiency, and remains as a startling
example of what can be done when certain pressures are
applied. By February 1943, 1,335 nurseries were operating in
Great Britain. Many working mothers, however, preferred to
leave their children with friends or neighbours. The facilities
existed, but propaganda had not been sufficiently intensive to
ensure that the nurseries would be filled.

In general, criticism of women's failure to change society was
muted during the war, when it must have seemed inappropriate
in view of their involvement in the national work drive. In
1914, Mr W. T. Massey was surprised by the women's response
to propagandist appeals (see Chapter II); to some extent the
pattern was repeated in 1939. The tetchy, anti-feminist tone
gave way gradually to a tone of adulation that is equally
unrealistic. In magazine articles and in semi-official accounts of

the women's services there is often an ecstatic, sentimental note that harks back to Thekla Bowser (see Chapter II) and the illusory idealism and cosy camaraderie of the Voluntary Aid Detachments of the first world war. The occasion called for rhetoric, and the rhetoric was trotted out. 'Mankind's darkest hour' was upon us, and it was up to the inhabitants of Britain to keep 'the flame of freedom burning'. Once again, the nation was surprised at the strength and determination displayed by its women: '. . . The so-called "weaker sex" tackled many exacting tasks hitherto reserved to men'. Once again, patriotism furthered emancipation—at least for the duration of the war.

In literature the aesthetic mood of the 'twenties was superseded in the next decade by a widespread political awareness and a social-realist approach to fiction, influenced by the techniques of Mass-Observation. (A movement started in 1937 to provide an unbiased record of every-day events.) It was an age of solemnity, when the novel was expected to provide sociological data or to make an appeal on behalf of some disadvantaged group. The functions of journalist and novelist began to overlap. There were some indications that the novel could even be replaced by autobiographical or documentary writing since these forms were more suited to the sober realism that contemporary taste demanded. The facts of day-to-day living, social behaviour, customs and expectations could be gathered and presented by anyone, as Mass-Observation was at pains to demonstrate. To qualify as literature, however, the fruits of reflection and observation had to be arranged in a way that would appeal to the imagination, express the true significance of the information conveyed, and form a complex narrative pattern. It wasn't the documentary writers who got most quickly to the root of contemporary matters.

> . . . there is always this something else in his mind that has perhaps always something to do with gun emplacements and this sort of thing that is rather Greek to me, and rather sad too in its unpleasant associations and the way it is so often driving a wedge between the sort of work that is men's work and the sort of work that is women's work, and all of that line of reasoning that is so much a part of unhappy

fighting times and of cheap newspaper correspondence columns. Phew, how I do detest this. Never again in England I think shall we breed exclusively masculine and exclusively feminine types at any high level of intelligence. . . .

Stevie Smith's *Over the Frontier* was published in 1938 and it sounds the note of foreboding that came to characterize late '30s writing. The 'nervous irritability that has in it the pulse of our time' is for Stevie Smith a general symptom of social and political malaise. Her three novels contain a great deal of social comment that is merely highlighted by the idiosyncratic, *faux-naïve* approach. In each the narrator struggles to come to terms with 'the hopelessness of the situation and the lack of what is sensible'. The expression is Celia's, in *The Holiday* (1949), and she is referring to the peculiar, ballad-like imagery of one of her poems; but the remark has a wider application.

Novel on Yellow Paper (1936) is simply a sustained monologue, in which the personality of the narrator (Pompey Casmilus) determines both style and content. The method is rambling, allusive ('the tyranny of the association of ideas, like I read in Max Nordau . . .'), fey and convoluted. To write from the inside like this, and still remain convincing and entertaining (as Stevie Smith does) requires a high degree of narrative control. The failings of obscurity and self-indulgence are skilfully avoided. The ingenuousness is deceptive; the humour occasionally has an *enfant terrible* quality but its effects are harnessed deliberately to heighten the shrewd and sensible observations of the central character. On a visit to Germany, Pompey reacts against the feeling of neurosis that is apparent to an outsider:

> Oh how I felt that feeling of cruelty in Germany, and the sort of vicious cruelty that isn't battle-cruelty, but doing people to death in lavatories.
>   . . .
>   Ugh that hateful feeling I had over there, and how it was a whole race was gone run mad. Oh heaven help Deutschland when it kicks out the Jews, with their practical intelligence that might keep Germany from all that dream darkness, like

the forests had got hold of them again, and the Romans calling their Legions back along the Via Aurelia.

Pompey's dislike of pomposity is the focus for her reflections on human foolishness and social usage. The tone is gay, exuberant and quirky, though in the second novel it is plain that dis-enchantment has set in. For an off-the-cuff record of the mood of the '30s, *Novel on Yellow Paper* is equalled only by Henry Green's *Party Going*, an extraordinary blend of humour and symbolism and precise documentation, that is completely authentic in feeling and also completely original.

The phoney war was the time when more casualties occurred as a result of the blackout than enemy action. War had been declared, but failed to get under way. It was also a time of grumbling, whining and resentment of authoritarian figures like air-raid wardens, who were held to blame for inconveni-ences that served no visible purpose. The foremost novel of this period is of course *Put Out More Flags* (1942). Waugh's satiric method is exactly appropriate to render the experience of anti-climax and frustrated patriotism. The opportunism of Basil Seal can be treated light-heartedly before his motivations take a more serious turn. He is one of those restless, disreput-able, upper-class young men who seem marked out to serve the country in an unofficial but high-powered capacity. The expectations of his mother and mistress are confounded, how-ever, when Basil moves to the country and takes on the job of billeting officer in lieu of Barbara Sothill, his sister.

He is fortunate enough to procure the services of the Connolly children, a dreadful trio who represent the full horrors of the evacuation scheme. Doris is lurid and oversexed, Mickey decapitates domestic animals and Marlene is continually sick. 'There the three stood, one leering, one lowering, and one drooling, as unprepossessing a family as could be found in the kingdom.' To Basil, however, they are a windfall. Various inhabitants of North Grappling and Grantley Green are pre-pared to pay moderate sums of money to be relieved of the presence of the Connollys. Basil's victims are elderly, refined and house-proud. The scheme works—until he trespasses on the territory of another billeting officer. He extricates himself, as usual, with aplomb. Waugh exploits the humour of fortuitous

G

conjunction to ensure the reader's sympathy for a hero who is on the make. Luck on such a scale not only generates enthusiasm on behalf of its recipient; its effects are extremely funny.

Put Out More Flags is a wartime, not a *war* novel. This important distinction was made by Elizabeth Bowen in the preface to the American edition of *The Demon Lover* (1945). The experience of combat was too close and too extreme to provide suitable material for fiction. ' . . . it is . . . likely that it [the war] has acted as a curb to the imagination, a check to the zest for living; . . .' P. H. Newby wrote in *The Novel 1945–50* (1951). His conclusion was that 'no good novel has appeared since 1945 to paint the horrors of war'. 'Horrors' is a strong word; in this context it suggests battle-field slaughter and mutilation and terror, and emotions that are inimical to dispassionate presentation. Nevertheless, the war produced good novels of the home front and the horrors of blitz and bereavement and evacuation. The most important writers of the 1940s—among others, Elizabeth Bowen, Evelyn Waugh and Henry Green—found their subject matter in the day-to-day experience of wartime behaviour. Unlike the situation of 1914–1918, the mood of the time was transcribed directly in imaginative, seriously intended fiction.

Contemporary fiction of the first world war was predominantly romantic or elevating in a way that appealed to popular taste (see Chapters II and V). Of course the later war had its share of myths and standard images: for example, the 'little' man or woman possessed of a steady, unostentatious courage and determination. But the declaration of war and its social effects were registered at once in intelligent fiction. To an extent, this happened because of the total involvement of civilians. War provided not merely the possibility of a romantic conclusion, an off-stage death for some young hero; it was responsible in all sorts of ways for changes and adjustments of the most prosaic kind. Families were split up in an unprecedented manner; children were taken from their parents and sent to live with strangers; men in reserved occupations went on working in danger zones while their wives and children were evacuated to safety. The women who chose to remain, and those who had no choice, were hurried into unusual occupations. Suddenly, the magazines were full of pictures of women in uniform: ambulance drivers, district wardens, smiling girls of the ATS, the WAAF, the WRNS. Ex-housemaids were photographed peering at their instruments in a way that suggested full understanding of the principles of anti-aircraft defence; ex-housewives and typists worked efficiently with gun equipment and barrage balloons. And readers of the *Daily Mail* listed 'women in uniform' as the most annoying aspect of wartime: they found this sight harder to bear than the blackout, the evacuation of businesses or the behaviour of the Ministry of Information.

The working lives of women did not become a major preoccupation of the serious novelists. Their business was to set the private imagination to work on the public events, to use the principle of selection to give meaning of a complex variety to each incident, to avoid the formulation of absolute moral decrees. Their women characters may work, but there is no objective description of this new circumstance. The quasi-documentary approach was confined, on the whole, to romantic or 'formula' writers whose heroines were persecuted by crusty spinsters in the women's services, who learnt to bandage wounded soldiers and drive ambulances bravely through the blitz. The authors of this type of novel or magazine story took the opportunity to assert, in one way or another, the view that 'British women are deeply feminine and will be glad when the war is over'. Their outlook is deliberately optimistic and generally banal (see Chapter VIII). Then, there was no didactic or industrious feminist author to assess the radical effects of widespread employment. In Elizabeth Bowen's wartime novel *The Heat of the Day* (1949) the women's work is related in a precise way to social position. Stella Rodney's is 'secret, exacting, not unimportant'—and it is left at that. Her occupation forms no part of the story; it places her merely, as a person of some ability. Louie and Connie, the lower-class girls, are drafted into factory and ARP positions.

The central character is Stella, middle-aged but still impressionable; well bred, well balanced but suddenly precipitated into a crisis for which she has no precedent, no formula to indicate the proper mode of response. She is told that her lover, Robert Kelway, is selling information to the enemy. This seems so preposterous that Stella is brought to a standstill; she takes no action for some time, and when she does act the movement towards disaster is begun, exactly as she has been warned. Faith in her lover will not permit her to take the accusation seriously; but the shift to belief is effected none the less. There is no dramatic moment of realization, merely a gradual acceptance of the fact. The lovers' last conversation is lucid and serious, and each finally shows tolerance and consideration for the other. The nature of Robert's treason is not spelt out, nor are his motivations made clear. This is in no sense a thriller, and the author is not concerned with the mechanics of spying. Treason is an effect of the time, an extension of the natural squalor and disruption of war. 'But they were not alone, nor had they been from the start, from the start of love. Their time sat in the third place at their table. They were the creatures of history, whose coming together was of a nature possible in no other day—the day was inherent in the nature.'

To represent a mood, to indicate the subtleties of a special response, conditioned by history—this is one of Elizabeth Bowen's objectives. Gradually the sense of London at war evolves, a 'particular psychic London'; the angle of perception is always oblique. Objects and scenes partake of the mental condition of the observer. A constant feeling of movement is achieved. Pure objective description has a static quality; in Elizabeth Bowen light of one kind or another is always at play.

The very soil of the city at this time seemed to generate more strength: in parks the outsize dahlias, velvet and wine, and the trees on which each vein in each yellow leaf stretched out perfect against the sun blazoned out the idea of the finest hour. Parks suddenly closed because of time-bombs—drifts of leaves in the empty deck chairs, birds afloat on the dazzlingly silent lakes—presented, between the railings which still girt them, mirages of repose. All this was beheld each morning more light-headedly: sleeplessness disembodied the lookers-on.

Stella's informant is Harrison, a man met at the funeral of a relative, a bleak, uncomfortable presence in the novel. Harrison with his slightly asymmetrical eyes, his charmlessness and

insensitivity, cherishes infelicitous ideas of an attachment to
Stella; and as a means of sexual persuasion he offers freedom for
Robert, for a short period at least. That he is in a position to do
so increases the distaste and exasperation that Stella feels. As a
secret service agent he is untrustworthy and indiscreet; but he
has not acted without calculation. Stella cannot betray him
without betraying Robert.

> 'Yes, I quite see.' [Stella says]
> He said with relief: 'You do?'
> 'Perfectly. I'm to form a disagreeable association in order
> that a man may be left free to go on selling his country.'
> 'That's putting it a bit crudely,' Harrison said, downcast.

This is social comedy at its most delicate and pointed, adjusted
finely to the pressures of the time. Of course it is Harrison's
behaviour that is crude, pushing and irresponsible; Stella is
merely stating the facts, with a degree of wit.

The irony is properly Stella's, not superimposed by the
author; another mode is necessary, however, when it comes to
the presentation of thick-witted Louie. Louie likes to be taken
care of; her parents have been wiped out by a bomb; her
husband Tom is in the army. She is vulnerable, or feels herself
to be, but lacks the physical qualities that attract protection.
'"It's not even as if [her friend Connie tells her, with contemptuous concern] you were a London girl." Louie nodded—
yes, there was that, again: she was a Kentish sea-coast orphan.'
For Louie, there is a comfortable pathos in the expression—the
irony is external, not Louie's or Connie's. The presence of the
author is felt: it is Elizabeth Bowen who gives an undertone to
the observation. It is significant that Louie 'has been' married
by Tom—even in this crucial relation she has made no move of
her own. She is deficient in knowledge, discrimination, *savoir
vivre*. Her innocence is not a positive quality because it derives
from dullness. She accepts her limitations only in the sense of
remaining unaware of them; becoming aware, she becomes
resentful and incoherent:

> '. . . often you say the advantage I should be at if I could
> speak grammar; but it's not only that. Look at the trouble

there is when I have to only say what I *can* say, and so
cannot ever say what it is really. Inside me it's like being
crowded to death—more and more of it all getting into me.
I could more bear it if I could only say . . .'.

Louie's abject naïvety can have only one result: pregnancy,
accidental and inopportune, an effect of a squalid liaison. But
Louie is treated satirically; she is in no sense a victim, merely a
muddler with a muddler's crude luck. Her soldier husband is
killed off-stage. In girls like Louie the capacity for survival is
related to a process of self-delusion. The baby, not Tom's,
begins to look like Tom.

Connie is altogether more shrewd and self-assertive. Initially,
in her dark blue ARP slacks, she seems to Louie to be 'one more
person empowered to tick one off'. But Louie soon becomes
acclimatized to the managing side of Connie's personality, the
latter girl a prey 'since childhood, to a repressed wish to issue
orders, blow whistles, direct traffic'. These women converse in a
curious stylized manner that represents perfectly the piecemeal,
makeshift quality of their existence:

'*Connie?*'
There came a hiss of breath. 'Well, what?' replied Connie
in a sharp sleepless voice.
'I couldn't hear you breathe.'
'Nor was I, till you go and make me.'
'What *were* you doing, then?'
'Trying what those Indians are said to do.'
'Which Indians?—You did give me a fright.'
'Fakers.'
'Whatever don't they do that for?'
'To attain themselves to the seventh degree of conscious-
ness.'
'. . . Anyway, what d'*you* want to be conscious like that
for?'
'I'm peculiar,' Connie said in a Delphic tone. 'If I'm not
to be one thing then I'd as soon be the other one hundred
per cent. I've never been so wakeful—must be something
I ate; nothing's pure these days. No, I'm not in pain, nor
is it fullness or wind, only the universe fevering round

inside my head.—Ever got a bicarbonate?—No, I suppose not.'

The author is being funny again at the girls' expense. But there is more than this to the contrived, elaborate, jumpy dialogue: it extends also to a constant documentation of the facts of bed-sitting-room, wartime life. The girls are ordinary; it is merely their presentation that is eccentric. With Stella there is less narrative dissociation; she is more on a level of sensibility with the author. This makes her less a subject for comic treatment, though it does not mean that her conception is chiefly subjective. Her character is defined exactly to the extent necessary to the plot. In the rendering of her feelings about the war, her repudiation of the ethics of treason, her revulsion at deceit, the voices of novelist and character are fused:

All that time, all the same, the current had been against his face. The war-warmed impulse of the people to be *a* people had been derisory; he had hated the bloodstream of the crowds, the curious animal psychic oneness, the human lava-flow. Even the leaden unenthusiasm, by its being so common, so deeply shared, had provoked him— and as for the impatiences, the hopes, the reiteration of unanswerable questions and the spurts of rumour, he must have been measuring them with a calculating eye. The half-sentence of the announcer's voice coming out of a window at News hour, the flopping rippling headlines of Late Night Final at the newsvendor's corner—what nerve, what nerve in reverse, had they struck in him? Knowing what he knew, doing what he did. . . . It seemed to her it was Robert who had been the Harrison.

In other words, his part had been dishonourable, disagreeable. Yet knowing what *she* knew, she had been prepared to buy freedom for Robert in the one way open to her—the traditional woman's way. It is not very important, merely a matter of subduing physical distaste. One wonders what Harrison would have got out of the experience—but Harrison's fantasies and expectations are not part of the theme. The question remains academic.

'If I had slept with him, [Stella asks] *could* he have kept you out of this?'

'What, did he say so? Naturally he would say so. You didn't try?'

'I thought I would, last night, but he sent me home.'

'You left it pretty late,' was his comment, abstractedly looking at her.

It is ingratiating Louie, blundering into the wrong night club in the dark, who saves Stella from the consequences of her last-stake decision. Harrison, irritated to a state of moroseness by Louie's patter, sends the two women off together, causing Stella an uncharacteristic moment of bewilderment. She is not in control; Harrison is not the fool she has taken him for; events will take their course without her intervention. All she can do for Robert is to hush up his treason. She is a woman of complex feelings, but at the back of it all there is support for the proprieties and conventions of her class, she is the sister and mother of soldiers for whom an aberrant view like Robert's is inadmissible. Ultimately, she represents a kind of civilized good behaviour that can allow for circumstances sufficiently to withhold condemnation.

In the stories that make up *The Demon Lover* (1945) a pattern emerges of curtailment, apathy or nervous dejection. Certainly Elizabeth Bowen's sense of an overcharging of a collective consciousness was acute: these stories examine the forms that its expression can take. Houses are closed, boarded up, bombed out of existence or opened to unaccustomed occupants; people are falsely cheerful, secretive, distraught, stoical or self-dramatic. With tenacity they pursue the past or take refuge in dreams or fantasies. 'Mysterious Kôr'—an imaginary city grows from a couple's lack of a place to sleep together; 'The Happy Autumn Fields'—a fragment of experience from the childhood of an unknown girl blots out for the bomb-shocked heroine the urgency of self-preservation. In the stories, everyone has taken up a new way of life:

'. . . But what would make it difficult for Joanna is having taken on all those hens. . . .'

'Yes, and I have evacuees——'

'But we won't talk about those, will we?' said Mary quickly. 'Any more than you would want to hear about bombs. I think one great rule is never to bore each other. . . .'

The conversation of the chatterers, the excitable or pretentious women, rambles on vaguely: 'One lives in a perfect whirl of ideas.' Foolishness in wartime takes on a new edge: it may actually constitute a danger, where there is access to information. But the silliest people are those who imagine special knowledge where none exists.

In all the stories there is a sense that tension, the immediate, dislocating tension of war, has been suppressed or interrupted by another, more personal, obsessional stress or access of feeling. This is matched in a curious way by the violent physical changes in the structure of the city, the day-by-day alteration of familiar scenes, the unnatural illumination of fires in the night. There is too much narrative control and discrimination for the stories to resemble a series of impressions; the writing is less subjective than this. The transmitted impressions—or rather, suggestions —arise as much as anything from the author's omissions: she knows where to stop. The emphasis is placed where the effect will be most telling. The stories have a 'double relevance' as Elizabeth Bowen herself wrote in a review of the poems in Cecil Day Lewis's *Overtures to Death*—'They have a poetic relevance to all time, and are at the same time relevant to our perplexing day'. (*Now and Then*, No. 61 [Winter 1938].)

There is little sense of the war in Joyce Cary's scrupulously objective and finely composed novel, *Charley is my Darling* (1940). In fact the actual effects of being at war are so muted that the country community treats the misdemeanours of its evacuees with conscious tolerance, even a kind of relief, believing that 'war, since it was a misfortune, ought to bring some hardships. . . . They complained of the vackies for leaving gates open, breaking the ripe corn, letting the pigs into the garden, but usually they added with various tones of resignation or bitterness: "But there, it's the war, iddn'it?" '

Fifteen-year-old Charley is one of a group of London slum evacuees, billeted on farms in a rural area and importing traditional street ideas of gang warfare, self-aggrandizement, ritual forms of bullying and delinquency. The children are not sentimentalized or, at the other extreme, treated censoriously: explanations are proffered without an underlying moral conclusion. The presence of the author is felt only to the extent that he is able to give shape to various emotions experienced by Charley: part of the boy's frustration is that he finds these incommunicable. His friendship with fourteen-year-old Lizzie, a half-deaf farm girl believed locally to be slightly retarded, results in pregnancy for the girl and further blame for Charley. He, however, resents with passion the official view that he has 'wronged' her—this seems totally to deprive Lizzie of individuality and worth. 'He is amazed by Lina's strange view of Lizzie. He has never thought of her as a poor country girl, unable to defend herself. To him she is Lizzie, a person full of odd and interesting characteristics.'

Charley is capable of complex perceptions but has no means to express them. Billeting officer, magistrate, teachers and police conspire to make him believe that his only hope lies in an exhibition of remorse. 'In two minutes Charley is once more in tears. He can't speak. But now, underneath this violent hysterical emotion, there is fury like steel, a deep, resolute anger. It is the protest of all his honesty against a lie, and a defilement.'

A quality the serious novelists have in common is an ability to affirm values without needing to instruct their readers. They are non-didactic, and in this respect, in the war years, they were slightly at odds with the mood of the time, when the whole nation was activated and sustained by a powerful sense of being in the right. In popular fiction the rights and wrongs of any issue were clear-cut, and a kind of moral shorthand existed to alert the reader to the proper judgement. In wartime, the easiest gratifications for the reader came from simple heroics, the instinctively noble or selfless or in some sense admirable behaviour of ordinary people. For many characters in fiction the primary objective was to attain a kind of physical courage, and the authors' aim to show how it could be done. At a slightly higher level of sophistication the emphasis was on moral heroism.

In Graham Greene's *The End of the Affair* (1951), the crucial event takes place in wartime, when the narrator's house is damaged in an air raid and he is trapped underneath the front door. The door is suspended above him, yet his body is bruised from the shoulders to the knees, 'as if by its shadow'. This is one of the unacceptable circumstances of the novel, the small impossible occurrences for which no explanation is suggested but the most fantastic one. To an extent the reader is left to make up his or her own mind; but the author's implication is clear and inevitably it has a deforming effect on the theme. The narrative purpose is to make an obvious moral statement: that genuine faith and its power to effect transformations can occur in unlikely places (this premise is of central importance in the work of Graham Greene); but in this case the ethical bias produces a sensation of uneasiness in the reader. As coincidences of a religious significance proliferate, the narrative moves on to a plane of abstraction that the novelist, for all his reticence and skill, cannot make convincing.

It is partly a matter of the reader's sympathy, or lack of it, for Sarah, the central character. Two views of Sarah are presented: that of Bendrix, the narrator, whose mistress she has been; and the image that emerges from her own diary which falls into Bendrix's hands and forms the third section of the novel. Sarah's behaviour is neurotic in a humourless, intense, exasperating way. She is a tiresome, unoccupied, high-principled woman, interesting only to the extent that her actions are radically misunderstood. She acts according to her own lights: in her the unappealing precepts of renunciation and wilful suffering are embodied. Instead of intelligence she has a kind of fortitude: in a moment of anguish she makes a bargain with 'God' and afterwards there is no way that she can deflect its consequences.

No way, that is, except the obvious, rational one: to accept that her impulse to pray has been hysterical. But this is totally at variance with the author's intent. The moment is one of intensity: the door of the house has blown in on top of Bendrix, and Sarah believes that he is dead. She offers to give him up if his life is spared: this is the starting point for the sequence of jealousy, incomprehension and misguided moral commitment that follows. In fact it is Sarah who has to die; and certain incidents that have a forced relation to her death, off-shoots of the miraculous, are given a wholly distasteful connotation.

The wartime background is not essential to the theme. It contributes nothing but a moment of danger (an accident would have done just as well), and an intensification of the usual murky, overcast, slightly dilapidated quality in Graham Greene's evocations of London. Sarah is married, and therefore not liable to conscription; besides, it suits the author's purpose to keep her as free as possible from extraneous interests or a means of self-expression. The details of environment or predilection are always relevant to the novel's basic idea.

In one at least of Henry Green's wartime novels—*Back* (1946)—the significant death has nothing to do with the war, it has taken place off-stage before the novel opens, though its reverberations are deep and extended. The death of Rose is magnified in the mind of Rose's lover, after his repatriation from a prisoner-of-war camp (with only one leg), until he cannot hear the word 'rose' uttered in any context without a shock of recognition that blots out sense. Charley Summers is a confused young man, war-shocked, inarticulate, falling rather grotesquely into modes of behaviour that don't accord in the least with his inner preoccupation. The novel is centred on one bizarre circumstance: dead Rose has a double, an illegitimate half-sister, Nance, and Charley at first cannot distinguish between the two girls though later his feeling for one is transferred to the other—or the process of fusion in his mind is completed. Rose is easy to betray, being dead; Charley's sense of disloyalty is obscure, however, merely a feeling of unease whenever he strikes a bluff attitude to pander to a coarse friend's expectations.

'I went down to the graveyard and, damn me, if I didn't run into her husband,' Charley told him.

'That must have been awkward,' Mr Middlewitch agreed. 'What happened then? Did you cry with your two heads together over the monument? You speak as if you knew the lad.'

'He's all right,' Charley said, seemingly a bit daunted. 'We had a bite to eat after.' Mr Middlewitch did not notice the reaction.

'And you had a bit of a chat? Compared notes, eh?'

'No,' Charley said. He frowned.

Charley imagines that Nance *is* Rose, that people are con-
spiring to keep the truth from him, that the girl has not died at
all but left her husband and son to become a bigamist and
prostitute. At the height of his delusion he attacks Rose's letters
with a pair of scissors, cutting out random phrases and sticking
them together to form a composite letter which he sends to a
hand-writing expert, together with a note from Nance. 'He felt
he had been extremely clever, till, all at once, he realized he had
destroyed, cut into ribbons, every letter he had ever had from
Rose. Then he despaired, blaming himself. But he could think
of no other way to get an expert opinion. And he knew Nance
was really Rose. And, after all, that had killed her letters.'

A comic pattern is constructed from Charley's bewildered
desperation. Part of Henry Green's method is to cause his
characters to act in accordance with a predetermined image of
themselves: they are fixed in postures of gentility, jocularity,
winning unscrupulousness and so on, and one result of this is
that they are always slightly at cross purposes with one another.
Since they speak primarily to assert the particular quality that
each values, their reactions sometimes have no more than an
oblique connection with the statement uttered, and the effect
of fragmentation thus caused can be extremely effective.

'How you people manage to dress as you do,' [Nance said],
in a hard voice, at his city suit. He thought, 'Oh what have I
done? She's out of her mind.' His mouth went dry as he
realized, next, that she was completely self-possessed. He
reached for his cup. He did not know how he would be able
to lift this. He tried to take heart because she had given him a
saucer with it.

'That's right. Drink that, then go,' she said.

'My God,' he said, as he dropped it. He had been afraid
he would.

'Now look what you've done,' she said, and rushed out into
the kitchen for a dish-cloth. 'Here,' she said, throwing this.
He mopped at his trousers. 'And what about my covers?'
she asked. He stumbled to his feet, began dabbing at the
chair.

'Rose,' he said low, his back still turned to her.

'What's rose?' she asked frantic.

No other novelist has made such original use of the clichés that simple-minded people rely on, the irrational assumptions they parade with so much conviction. Henry Green harps on the common phrases until their fundamental oddness is exposed. This technique is paralleled in the structure of the novels, when a seemingly commonplace but somewhat curious incident or idea is pursued until it takes on the symbolical weight of the whole theme (the aunt with the dead pigeon in *Party Going* is a good example). The movement of the action is unified by the queer thread that runs through it. In *Caught* (1943) it is the obsession of a subsidiary character with the fact that he may, inadvertently, have committed incest with his sister.

The sister of Fireman Pye has become unbalanced, she abducts a small boy from a toyshop and has to be put away. The boy is the son of Richard Roe, the central character, and Roe is drafted to Pye's station in the wartime AFS. From nervous embarrassment, Pye cannot speak to Richard without making some 'dark reference to his sister's little trouble'. ' "A woman I was born and bred up with wronged your wife," ' he says, not knowing that Richard's wife is dead. The guilt that he feels in Richard's presence leads on to the other, primary guilt: as a village boy, before the first world war, Pye has made love in a dark lane with a girl whom he now believes to have been his sister. The idea becomes more and more persistent:

> 'What d'you make of this moonlight, I mean in the black-out?' Pye began again. . . . 'D'you mistake objects in it, 'ave you taken one person for another?'
>
> . . . Richard thought he could risk a joke.
>
> 'What have you been up to, then?' he asked. 'Going up to the wrong girl?'
>
> 'You mightn't be so far out at that,' Pye said. . . .

The squalid, disorganized or horrifying lives of the characters are juxtaposed with unexpectedly lyrical evocations of the wartime spirit. Couples 'gorged with love' emerge from the double bedrooms of plush hotels; the wives of soldiers travelling to Portsmouth are 'dragged along the platform hanging limp to door handles and snatched off by porters in the way a man, standing aside, will pick bulrushes out of a harvest waggon load of oats'. At this time, the fire service was second only to the air force in the public regard: 'Auxiliaries were often given money by old ladies, they were stood drinks by aged gentlemen. . . . Street cleaners called Richard "mate". Girls looked him straight, long in the eye as never before, complicity in theirs, blue, and blue, and blue. They seemed to him to drag as they passed.'

The women AFS workers in the novel are tense, outspoken, and generally incompetent: Mary Howells the inefficient cook, for example, whose daughter is in a state of post-natal derangement. The prolonged period of inaction, before the bombing starts, affects the spirits of everyone: gossip, speculation, squabbling and dissension erupt in small outbursts. (A similar state of frustration is experienced by characters in Brian Moore's novel *The Emperor of Ice-Cream*: see Chapter XII). None of Henry Green's characters is especially admirable or reprehensible; in this respect his novels are completely free of a moral bias. To an extent the central figures share a lack of intelligence, an inability to function outside the limits of a particular convention (only the elderly hero of *Concluding* has a complex sensibility): instead they may have a certain sharpness, a knowing or forthright disposition.

Loving (1945), the most highly wrought and decorative of Henry Green's novels, is set in Ireland 'where there is no blackout'. The characters as usual suffer from fixed ideas: Miss Burch the housekeeper tells her girls that they are lucky to be here at the castle 'particularly when over at home they were all being sent into the army to be leapt on so she honestly believed by drunken soldiers in the darkness'. The servants are all English and the war affects them in various ways:

'Whatever's the matter with you these days?' he asked.

'I'm fed up I shouldn't wonder. . . . It's the war most likely,' she said pouting. 'I shall have to get me out of this old place.'

'You don't want to talk like that my girl. Why we're on a good thing here all of us. Trust Uncle Charley, he's seen some. There's a war on, the other side. You don't want none of it do you? And there's the grub question. . . .'

The servants do not take a wide view. War causes nothing but inconvenience, worries about IRA opportunism and the arrival of troublesome relatives. The cook's nephew Albert is tolerated because of his special status as a refugee 'like the Belgians we had in the last war'. When he strangles a peacock his aunt explains, '"Children is all little 'Itlers these days"'. Only the owner's wife finds cause for happiness in the war: with her husband in the army she can sleep with Captain Davenport, which she does incautiously so that Edith the housemaid surprises them in bed. This episode is at the centre of the theme, in devious ways it has a significance for the entire household, and various connections are implied by means of symbolic objects, a ring that appears and disappears, a dead peacock and the live doves and peacocks that surround the castle.

The little community is isolated in a way that forces its members to have strong reactions to one another. Edith and Raunce, the butler, become engaged; randy Kate has to make do with a defective Irishman for her lover. There is an erotic quality in the friendship of Kate and Edith: 'Kate began to stroke up and down the inside of Edith's arm from the hollow of her elbow to her wrist. Edith lay still with closed eyes. The room was dark as a long weed in the lake.' In fact, an erotic undertone is inherent in the whole drift of the novel; like the comparable poetic feeling it doesn't become explicit at any point, largely because no character is capable of giving it expression. Characters and symbols are equally part of the narrative arrangements; the author keeps his distance.

Satire is not altogether comfortable when it works on a complete inversion of usual ideas and outrageously upsets the expectations of the reader; it is too easy to achieve effects in this way, at least to begin with. *Love on the Supertax* (Marghanita Laski, 1944) is based on this principle: it is a story of 'the needy and the dispirited . . . the fallen and the dispossessed': in other words, the suffering dukes and duchesses of Mayfair. Poor aristocratic Clarissa, the underprivileged and underdressed heroine, is captivated by the thought of meeting 'a real worker'. Sid Barker in his blue serge suit, with his air of confidence and his habit of addressing everyone as 'comrade', seems to fit the bill. But social differences create a problem from the beginning.

'In the classless society,' Sid said sternly, 'the capitalist children will be as good as ours are.'

'But until then,' insisted the young man, 'would you yourself be quite happy to see your children playing with scrubbed little brats from Park Lane?'

Marghanita Laski is poking fun at the idiom of romantic fiction when she says of Clarissa 'never before had she been kissed by a worker, and now it seemed to her that her wildest dream was coming true'. And in effect the whole vapid course of the magazine story is parodied. The pseudo-moral is that the silly girl has failed to realize that class barriers cannot be transcended. Vulgar clothes, a humble attitude, familiarity with the catch-phrases of communism are not sufficient to get Clarissa a desirable job as a factory worker. ' "We regard it as a privilege to work here, and we have to be very careful to see that this privilege only goes to the right sort of person and isn't abused," ' she is told with firmness. Sid leaves her for sound-principled, working-class Lou; her brother Eustace is arrested in connection with black market offences, and the family mansion in Curzon Street continues to decay. But Sir Hubert Porkington, a persistent baronet, is waiting in the background with his legitimate grievances to arouse Clarissa's enthusiasm on behalf of her own class.

'. . . I should very much have liked to have shown you my country house.'

'Tell me about it,' said Clarissa politely.

'The government have commandeered it,' said Sir Hubert savagely, 'as a rehabilitation centre for incontinent evacuees. I should not care to tell you about it now.'

Handsome Sir Hubert finally reveals himself as leader of an organization that is working clandestinely to establish a Second Capitalist International after the war; and weak-willed Clarissa proceeds with enthusiasm to transfer her allegiance to this body, abandoning without a qualm her ineffective adulation of the rising workers. 'And so we may leave [her], clinging confidently to the arm of her betrothed, looking backwards, fearless and unafraid, into the Past.'

The trouble with this amusing novel is that its satire is indiscriminate, the objects marked out for attack are so varied that the effect of the author's social criticism is disseminated, and in a sense weakened. The narrative object is to push all dangerous or dead-end views to such an extreme that their absurdity will be apparent to everyone. For quite long stretches, however, the story reads like the type of fiction it is meant *not* to be; the reader is pulled up only by a sudden startling observation that is often rather fey: 'Travel by omnibus was one of the exotic pleasures to which Sid had accustomed her.' In fact it is the unobtrusive details underlying the satiric conception that enliven the narrative: the hardship caused by wartime shortages of food and other commodities; the books of French verse, in a left-wing flat, lying negligently 'on a low birch table'; the 'massive breasts' of a working-class mother. On the whole the method of comic inversion and ridicule is simply not adequate to express the political pressures of the era. In its last pages, however, the novel does provide a remarkably accurate enumeration of the groups most likely to benefit from social evolution:

> . . . the vast majority of young people whose opinions always tend to react against the established order . . . the mass of older citizens who, in the ranks of the various Defence Forces and more particularly under aerial bombardment have discovered a sense of equal comradeship that seems to them better than the pre-war social inequalities. Then there are the workers, before this war indigent and unemployed, who are now earning munificent wages and fear that peace may thrust them into poverty again. There are the married women who have been released from the drudgery of house-keeping into profitable jobs, girls who have been freed from parental restrictions by the demands of the Services. And lastly, there are the fighting men themselves, who always believe that they are fighting to come back to a brave new world. . . .

The irony is that the speaker is Sir Hubert Porkington; he is listing the types of people whom he hopes to reach through the columns of their own newspapers in order to nullify their potential for disruptive action before it can be formulated. This pinpoints the facts that it is easy to influence public opinion and that trickery on a gigantic scale sometimes *is* perpetrated. But the narrative tone is not incisive or restrained enough to provide a useful social guideline.

In terms of reality, it was true that many Labour party supporters were sustained by idyllic visions of a Red utopia, while conservatives struggled to re-establish the kind of environment that had existed before the war (in some cases, before the earlier war). No policy based on such premises could be realistic. 'It [the war] had eroded practically every traditional social barrier in Britain' (Anthony Howard, 'We Are the Masters Now', in *Age of Austerity, 1945–51*, 1963). The emphasis was on movement forward, rebuilding and clearing up of wartime débris. The key novels of the post-war era were those of the new town, the new university, new social arrangements and opportunities for advancement—novels like *Scenes From Provincial Life* (in spite of its 1939 setting), *Lucky Jim, Room at the Top*.

New kinds of realism meant that the women in these novels on the whole lacked style: this quality was confined to the narrators and often was degraded into brashness, an ability to take risks or an abundance of self-confidence. Contempt for women was a prominent feature of 1950s fiction though it came in various guises: recognition of one's girlfriend primarily as a social asset, irritation with her silly foibles and pretences, blame for her failure to be tolerant and free-thinking. Certainly the problems of women who had been made redundant after the war did not get much of a showing at this time. The whole range of women's social difficulties, from lack of encouragement to train for a career to the sense of panic of the house-bound mother, were not even recognized until Betty Friedan in the USA had investigated the causes of female malaise and published her findings in a study that was to have many offshoots, *The Feminine Mystique* (1963). 'There was a strange discrepancy between the reality of our lives as women and the image to which we were trying to conform,' Betty Friedan wrote. This basic observation had a radical effect on literature in the '6os and '7os: the psychological difficulties of women became an accepted theme for treatment in fiction in a way that had no connection with traditional 'women's' reading. In some cases there was a backward look to the conditions that had existed in the war and early post-war years.

X

THE CHILDREN'S WAR

Juvenile Fiction of the 'Forties

'Well, I don' see why we shun't have one, too', said William
morosely. 'Grown-ups get all the fun.'

Richmal Crompton

THE WAR OF 1939–1945 was aptly dubbed 'The People's
War' because of the strong sense of community involvement.
In children, especially, patriotism was intense and uncomplicated, and from the beginning girls as well as boys were
enthusiastic in their efforts to participate. Contemporary
stories provide a lively reflection of this identity of purpose in
boys and girls; there is a coming together of the sexes in work
and play which is far more evident than in fiction produced
between 1914 and 1918. Children of course were generally less
disturbed by the reversals of war than their parents. Conditioned by history lessons and stirred by official propaganda
they felt certain that whatever happened Britain would win the
last battle. All over the country pubescent boys and girls
cherished fantasies of marching shoulder to shoulder with
Winston Churchill and the Home Guard, to resist the Nazi
paratroopers on the beaches and in the cities until victory was
achieved. (Some mothers, however, were silently resolving that
at the first sign of invasion they would burn their sons' army
cadet uniforms and keep their would-be heroic offspring safely
at home under lock and key.)

There were plenty of realistic ways in which older children
could help the war effort; they acted as messengers to the Home
Guard and ARP, collected salvage, joined fire-watching rotas
and gave voluntary help to the Red Cross. All these activities
have been featured in fiction of the period. But it was the
evacuation scheme that had the most profound effect on many
children's lives, and the subject has been treated extensively in
literature, both at the time and retrospectively.

The Evacuees (edited by B. S. Johnson, 1968) brings together a selection of wartime reminiscences. From the diverse accounts of the contributors to this volume some common factors emerge. The authors are all aware of the particular vulnerability and resilience of childhood. They note, too, the strange cattle-market process of selection by hosts when the children had arrived exhausted and bewildered at reception centres. Many evacuees were billeted on families whose standards of behaviour or morality they found incomprehensible. This was due to distinctions of class as much as environment. Details—like the proper mode of serving jam—could cause confusion. Gloria Cigman writes: '. . . I remember one day visiting the largest house in the village where two children from the slums of Soho had been billeted. I watched the younger child, aged about ten, taking jam from a silver dish, with a silver spoon, and putting it on to the edge of his plate before spreading it on his bread and butter with his knife. . . .' Michael Aspel found his new life in Chard 'Narf smashin' after sooty Wandsworth. The local juvenile population, however, often resented the invasion of their territory and sometimes failed to behave with tolerance: '. . . for us "vaccies" there was no cordial welcome from the local kids. All they extended to us was a fast-moving fist between the eyes.' But Londoners could give as good as they got. Even the most rarefied minority groups were not easily intimidated. Michael Aspel records that some Chinese evacuees from Lime-house '. . . were given the title of "Dirty yellow Japs", and came in for merciless hammering from our hosts, which they didn't take with any oriental calm. . . . They yelled "git orf" and hit back.'

As well as increasing the self-reliance of many children, evacuation brought a variety of initiations. Young boys bragged of real or imagined sexual attentions from foster-mothers. The defencelessness of children in remote reception areas was central to the theme of Joan Temple's play *No Room at the Inn*. Freda Jackson's portrayal of the brutish landlady may have had an effect on parents in danger zones: many children were brought home to face the known horrors of air raids rather than the unimaginable hazards of evacuation.

The image of the evacuees was subjected to a whole range of treatment in the popular culture of the war. Sentimental at one extreme—'Goodnight children everywhere, your mummy thinks of you tonight'—it was rough-and-ready at the other: in the comic-paper *Knockout*'s 'Our Happy Vaccies', for example. Kitty Barne strikes a moderate note in *Visitors from London* (1940). The title is significant: in spite of its authentic touches this story projects a country holiday rather than a wartime atmosphere. Taking in evacuees seems rather a lark to Gerda, David, Jimmy and Sally Farrer, who stay in Sussex with their aunt during boarding-school holidays because 'Daddy and Mummy' are 'in India'.

There are lively descriptions of rushed preparations. Cups, cutlery and domestic equipment are borrowed wholesale, and straw-stuffed mattresses are made pending the delivery of government-issue beds. After several false alarms the evacuees arrive by bus complete with babes in arms, gas masks in card-board cases and their statutory iron rations—bully beef, condensed milk, chocolate and biscuits. Altogether the Farrers accommodate four families of mothers and children. These are of course Londoners—either of the cheery cockney variety or those who moan about missing their trips 'up west' to the 'pictures' and 'restrongs'.

The Farrers at first find their noisy, untidy visitors over-whelming. Tensions arise between guests and hosts, and the author's acceptance of middle-class standards of behaviour is clear from the text. The Farrer children use the boarding-school jargon of the period, and there are narrative references to *boys'* 'knickers' and 'stockings': of course the visiting children would have called these garments trousers and socks. Some-times the author goes too far in her efforts to express the evacuees' excitement; the clichés of town/country distinctions are used without discrimination: 'I ain't never seen sheep before, not without they're dead at the butcher's'. . . . 'Can we go outside them gates? Is it free? . . . It's a bit of all right, the country is. I never bin before. . . .' (Richmal Crompton deals better with this convention: in one episode, William, apeing a town child, asks moronically '"What's grass?"') The tone of the book is low-key and reasonable, to the point of dullness. The characters never indulge in humorous heroics like those so pre-valent in children's fiction of the first world war. Expressions of patriotism are restrained, as when Lily Tipping adopts a piglet:

'What shall you call him?' asked Sally.

'George. After the King,' said Lily, with only a moment's hesitation. 'We got to be loyal now there's a war on.'

Most of these evacuees return to their homes after two or three weeks. The families did not like being split up, and husbands who had remained in London soon tired of looking after themselves. (In real life evacuees did of course drift back to the cities. Many children had the experience of being evacuated several times—and yet finding themselves in London again for the Battle of Britain, the blitz and the flying bombs.) The few who stay disperse to private billets and one boy goes to work with the local shepherd. The Farrer children prepare to return to boarding school, and the book ends on a note of anti-climax.

Towards the end of the war the subject is examined more thoroughly by Kitty Barne's sister-in-law, Noel Streatfeild, already well known for her unsentimental children's stories. *Saplings* (1945) is a book for adults, and it contains no trite conclusions and no evasions. For its central characters, the children of a secure, middle-class family background, psychological disturbance occurs as a result of the combined stresses of bombing and evacuation.

Another notable children's author—the ageing Angela Brazil—took up the theme of evacuation in 1941 with *Five Jolly Schoolgirls*. The title has an anachronistic ring, and in fact it is slightly misleading. The narrative tone throughout is heavily admonitory, and the usual gymslip high jinks associated with Angela Brazil are subdued in this story. The girls of Dunfield High are sent away to a safe zone, where five are billeted on Mrs Norton, 'an anxious mother and housekeeper'. This lady accepts the extra work with some misgivings. However as 'All her friends in Greenford were having similar experiences, and, as many of them were obliged to receive children from slum areas, she counted herself comparatively lucky in having members of Dunfield High School quartered upon her'.

Occasionally the style harks back to 1914–1918. Soldiers are called Tommies, there are 'nigger minstrel' songs and earnest discussions of Cornish piskies and astral beings. The girls still worship brothers and friends in khaki whose tales of life in the army inspire them 'to knit garments for the troops, a form of war work they had been inclined to neglect'. Two of the five schoolgirls eventually go further afield—to South Africa and the USA. '"But I shan't learn to talk through my nose, as you seem to imagine. I've told you I'm going to cultured people."' Angela Brazil writes proudly that 'The British are born emigrants and ready to colonize anywhere overseas where the Union Jack flies'—but the book implies that it is more patriotic to stay in England:

'I'm going to be a land-girl and "Dig for Victory",' explained Margery.
'And I wouldn't desert the old country for any safe billets,' approved Doreen. 'I'll stay put here, and help all I can, and proud to do it, and wave a Union Jack with my last breath.'

P. L. Travers (author of *Mary Poppins*) turned from fantasy to realism in 1941. *I Go by Sea, I Go by Land* is an account of the evacuation overseas of two English children. James and Sabrina Lind are shipped off to America soon after the air raids begin, when an early invasion of England was expected. (An official scheme to send British children to the Dominions and the USA was started at this time. By July 1940 CORB—Children's Overseas Reception Board—had received 211,000 applications, but only 2,664 children emigrated before the *City of Benares* was sunk in the Atlantic on 7 September 1940. Seventy-three of its child-evacuee passengers died. With the dangers of long sea journeys so tragically underlined, the scheme was wound up. However, it is estimated that at least 14,000 British children were privately sent overseas. Many never returned to their original homes, and the profound effects of this type of evacuation can hardly be estimated.)

In P. L. Travers's story, the excitement of the Atlantic crossing in convoy is clouded by apprehension. U-Boats are spotted in the area and the radio brings news of heavy air raids on England. The sense of fear is conveyed with restraint and authenticity. Sabrina overhears snatches of adults' conversation about the worsening war situation, and because these are only half understood their menacing quality is intensified.

When they reach America, the details of James's and Sabrina's new environment are convincingly described. They are impressed by the faster tempo of life and the constant availability of out-of-season foods: '. . . you can get strawberries and cream in America all the year round instead of only in June—think of that! You can't wonder the Americans are proud of their country.' Although they are comfortable and safe in the USA the children still have to come to terms with wartime insecurity; for instance, not knowing what might be happening to their parents in England during air raids.

The realities of war, of course, were brought home to numberless children all over Europe and Asia; but initially at least the prospect of air raids simply added to the exhilaration of life. Gas masks, fire-fighting equipment and so on merely afforded opportunities for horse-play, in the non-serious context of children's fiction:

> AIR RADE PRECORSHUN
> JUNIER BRANCH
> ENTRUNCE FRE.

'They'll come if it's free,' said Douglas, with a tinge of bitterness in his voice. 'They always come to free things.'

Cock-eyed patriotism is a suitable quality for Richmal Crompton's William, a boy who is extravagantly determined to have a say in the affairs of his elders. The wartime William books (beginning in 1939 with *William and A.R.P.*) were nothing if not topical. The hero and his outlaws get involved with poison gases, bandaging and decontamination: 'Ginger's mother . . . came upon the disgraceful scene—a wild medley of naked boys on the lawn, wrestling and leaping about in the full play of the garden hose, manipulated by Ginger. Their clothes, which they had flung carelessly on the grass beside them, were soaked through. . . .' At this point the parents intervene to close down the junior branch of the ARP and William's enthusiasm has to find another outlet. Forbidden to play with his gas mask, he muses bitterly on the 'jolly good times' that should result

"GET OUT OF THIS AT ONCE!" THUNDERED THE SECTION
OFFICER. "HOW DARE YOU COME IN HERE! DON'T YOU
KNOW THAT YOU'RE TRESPASSING?"

Illustration by Thomas Henry for *William Does His Bit* by
Richmal Crompton, 1941

from unrestricted access to respirators: 'I bet they [the adult
ARP workers] bounce out at each other in their gas masks,
givin' each other frights. I've thought of lots of games you could
play with gas masks but no one'll let me try.'

The gas mask is actually rather sinister in appearance, and
many younger children found it frightening. William's attitude
is healthier, if equally unrealistic. In the course of the war,
however, the respirator became so familiar that it ceased to
affect children one way or the other. Before this happened it was

seen as a comic object by another popular children's author, Charles Hamilton, who as Frank Richards was still writing the *Magnet* Greyfriars stories (see Chapter IV). In a May 1940 issue, just before the paper shortages caused the *Magnet* to fold, Hamilton is cheerfully envisaging an improbable air raid on south-eastern England. Harry Wharton & Co. are staying at Eastcliff Lodge, home of a British intelligence agent, at present operating in 'Hunland'. On the roof of the lodge a 'spy of the Gestapo' is signalling to enemy planes. When the bombing starts the juniors make tracks for the cellar, but Billy Bunter remains in bed, snoring off his latest gargantuan meal. Harry Wharton has to awaken the irascible and inept Fat Owl, and help him to find his respirator:

'Lend me a hand!' howled Bunter.... 'I ain't going to be gassed and slaughtered and murdered just to please you!'

'Here it is!' exclaimed Harry, grabbing up the gas mask container from a table.

'T'ain't in that!' gasped Bunter. 'I keep toffee in that!'

Another rumbustious young patriot is Jane Turpin, the heroine of a series of books by Evadne Price, who tends to follow in the wake of William. For Jane and her boy chums Pug and Chaw, respirators become the helmets of the improvised uniforms in which they do battle with imaginary spies. The trio's own exercise in decontamination requires a victim, and the series has already provided one: Amelia Tweedale, the horrible and sanctimonious daughter of the vicar of Little Duppery. This unfortunate child is soaked with mustard and onion juice (representing gas); her clothes are removed forcibly and she is clapped into a gas mask which effectively mutes her protests. Next she is handled roughly and her body is smeared with thick motor grease and cement powder.

In effect William's behaviour is rather less vicious, and the muddles that result from his misapplied enthusiasm are always funny. He unofficially evacuates a couple of children from a safe rural area. Wearing a saucepan for a steel helmet and using a tin tray as a shield he tries to remove a suspected unexploded bomb from outside the home of a friend. He fights fires and collects scrap iron for salvage, despite lack of co-operation from

Drawing by Frank R. Grey for
Evadne Price's *Jane at War*, 1947

the local adults. Like Jane Turpin he is instrumental in having
fifth columnists arrested.

At a more realistic level the stories of William and Jane may
indicate how the war affected the lives of middle-class families
in suburban England. Supercilious Marjorie Turpin, Jane's
sister, learns to drive an ambulance and frivolous Ethel Brown
takes up ARP work and later becomes a VAD. By 1941
(*William Does His Bit*) the Brown family have lost their cook
to the ATS though they still cling to Emma, their housemaid.

Robert, William's elder brother, 'is on night duty at the warden's post': shortly afterwards, however, he appears as a second lieutenant in the army. As a soldier he is diffident rather than heroic—but William blithely ignores this fact. He boasts of Robert's imaginary capture of Hess and his plans for the downfall of Hitler.

Gang warfare between evacuees and host communities is a proper subject for farcical treatment. In one episode precocious Violet Elizabeth, the terrible child of the William books, has a birthday party tea of pre-war proportions. A visiting self-styled expert on child psychology encourages the guests to eat frugally in order to save some of the food for the deprived evacuee children. Her homily has the reverse effect: 'As one man the little guests fell upon the feast. . . . [They] had suffered at the hands of the . . . tough young guys from the East End of London whose methods of warfare were novel and unpleasant . . . and the thought that their tormentors might profit from their abstinence urged them on to yet greater feasts of gastronomy.'

Jane Turpin's family is forced to take in a horrible evacuee called Horace ('Orris) Shutter, a boy who swears, hides the baby, puts field mice in the cooking and displays Nana's knickers all over the village. He also hangs his foster-mother's top denture outside the front door and telephones her from a call box to say that her husband is dying after a car accident.

Generally the humour of these stories was whole-hearted and invigorating. Ridicule of certain situations, and of course of the Germans, helped to alleviate children's fears of invasion; and in the comic papers the process of outrageous caricature and slapstick farce was quickly adapted to the needs of the time. Hitler's Chaplin-esque appearance and *Sieg-heil*ing, goose-stepping followers were a gift to the children's cartoonists. The *Dandy* featured a long-running strip about Hitler and Goering, 'Adolf and Hermie, The Nasty Nazis,' obsessed with the search for food: 'I have der pain in der breadbasket'. After Italy had declared war on Britain Mussolini was similarly debunked in the *Beano*: 'Musso the Wop, He's a Big-a-da Flop!'

Songs which echoed the style of the comic papers found

favour with many children who delighted in the unpretentious and the vulgar. Slogans and catch-phrases proliferated, each good to raise a laugh: recognition and response was a simple way of enforcing community solidarity. Generally children preferred the down-to-earth phrase—'You've Had It!'—to the high-flown: 'Freedom is in Peril, Defend It with All your Might!' A wry, humorous spirit was in evidence everywhere, a kind of knowing cleverness that was sometimes expressed in topical graffiti. Government propaganda notices were particularly liable to receive rude, handwritten addenda: when request bus stops were introduced, for instance, a notice appeared to instruct the public:

> Face the driver, raise your hand
> You'll find that he will understand.

And someone quickly added

> He'll *understand* all right, the cuss
> But will he stop the bloomin' bus?

But certain aspects of war were intrinsically shocking, not at all suited to brisk or humorous treatment. In air raids, for instance, people died or were mutilated; contemporary children's fiction frequently ignored this circumstance, although it has been emphasized, sometimes needlessly, in some of the stories written retrospectively. When death did occur (usually off-stage) the narrative tone became mawkish or reverential. It was a dangerous area for children's writers at the time, and usually they left it alone. On the whole the most irresistible wartime subjects were evacuation and spy-catching. As a theme, the latter was improbable but appropriate: it could be made to represent the extra dimension of excitement that the war engendered in young people.

It appealed even at the nursery level. Mary Plain, the anthropomorphized little bear created by Gwynedd Rae in 1930, 'lends a paw' during Britain's time of need. Like other lively story-book heroines, Mary finds that an excess of zeal can lead to disaster. 'Help' for a workman results in the misuse of a tin of paint; and really it does no good to anyone when the little bear constructs a 'seaside' from ARP equipment (sand and water). But when it comes to fundamentals like catching spies Mary *does* succeed. She helps the Home Guard to catch a fleeing enemy agent whom she knocks over by throwing herself out of a tree.

With equal presence of mind two small girls capture another spy by rolling him in a rug and sitting firmly on his stomach (in Noel Streatfeild's *The Children of Primrose Lane*, 1941). As

Title page by Irene Williamson
from *Mary Plain Lends a Paw*, 1949

the author points out in her preface to a later edition, during the early '40s every child in the country knew what was the proper action to take if a suspected German parachutist appeared. In the story, the children's suspicions are aroused by the curious English of a supposed deserter. According to widely shown propaganda films, the most adept German spy was bound to give himself away eventually through mispronunciation or failure to understand colloquialisms. Percy Westerman, in *By Luck and Pluck*, suggests that spies and fifth columnists behind the allied lines after the D-Day landings were caught out in the same way. A young English subaltern interrogates two young boys found in surprising circumstances in Normandy:

'Hang it all! I can't say the beastly thing myself! I'll have another cut at it. "The Leith Police dish—dish . . .".'

'You mean, "The Leith Police dismisseth us," sir!' announced Toby. . . .

'It used to be a catch phrase used by the police when they suspected a man of being drunk. . .'.

'Good enough!' exclaimed the subaltern. 'It's one of the phrases we try on Hun spies. It's claimed that no German could speak it without giving himself away.'

For Dorita Fairlie Bruce the issue was even more simple. In *Toby of Tibbs Cross* (1943) the teenage heroine is convinced that '. . . however much he may try, it is difficult for a German to look like anything else'. A disadvantage—to say the least—for those engaged in espionage for the Fatherland. In real life, of course, the problem was not so clear-cut. It might seem an easy matter to unmask German agents who said 'zh' instead of 'th'—but enthusiastic young patriots soon realized that many of the refugees and soldiers who had come to Britain from the occupied countries were similarly handicapped. This kind of complication never arises in the spy-catching tales of Dorita Fairlie Bruce. Once they are recognized, the enemy agents are quickly put out of action: 'There's a German spy lying doped in the drawing room, and I'm almost afraid he may be dying! And—and if he is, it will be I who have killed him, and I—I don't quite like the idea somehow.' Anne Willoughby, in *Dimsie Carries On*, has in fact used her herbalist training to good effect and administered a massive dose of sedative. There are, by the way, indications that Dorita Fairlie Bruce did not really approve of women in uniform. One character in this story *is* in the WRNS, but the author's sympathies lie with Anne Willoughby, who is doing her bit as a civilian. Dimsie Gilmour points the moral in conversation with her doctor husband: 'Apparently my war-work is to consist of carrying on with my daily life, only more so.' She has heavy domestic commitments, of course, but this is not true of Tabitha ('Toby') Barrett.

Toby is diverted from joining the Women's Land army by Charity Sheringham, a young farm-owner who doesn't employ labour through government organizations but 'prefers to go about it in a more personal way'. The interview between

H

prospective employer and employee therefore appropriately
takes place at Fuller's restaurant in London's Victoria Street.
Toby notices amongst the passers-by '. . . . quick-stepping
Wrens, efficient damsels in khaki with smart peaked caps
crushing down their curls; a bunch of WAAFs.' These whimsi-
cally described service women prompt Toby to exclaim: 'It
takes all sorts to win a war . . . and I am not that sort.' She
does, however, concede that 'they are splendid'.

Toby of Tibbs Cross is a story of determination and ingenuity:
two inexperienced young girls run a farm successfully in spite
of labour shortages and damage by air raids. Toby for instance
promptly converts a bomb-crater into a silage pit. The Dunkirk
evacuation is integral to the plot—but the country's half-
stunned, half-proud reaction is unconvincingly expressed. No
straightforward teenager, however moved by the event, would
describe it in these grandiose terms: '. . . That's where the
small boats have gone to, Charity! They are plying between the
beaches at Dunkirk and the big ships lying off, snatching our
men out of Hell, with enemy planes machine-gunning them the
while! The thing's magnificent beyond words. . . .'

The Nazi agent in *Toby of Tibbs Cross* is well cast in relation to
the book's agricultural background. He is the local 'lumbering,
red-faced vet' whose caddish method of destroying British
morale and food supplies is to inject a mysteriously effective
'cow plague' into every animal that comes within range of his
syringe.

There are no spies in Dorita Bruce's *Nancy Calls the Tune*
(1944) but it includes another stereotype—the conscientious
objector—who invokes an equal amount of narrative recrimination. The story is set in Scotland; deserter Gordon Macrae
hides in the organ loft of his minister brother's kirk. He is
discovered by Nancy Caird, another of Dorita Bruce's freshly
grown-up, healthy-minded girls. When the man claims pacifist
views, Nancy's reply is a contemptuous 'Tuts!' To suit the
story's positive patriotism the conscientious objector has to be
portrayed as parasitic and generally lacking in sensitivity. He is
'one of those modern products whose gender is hard to discover
in a passing glance'. The affected youth appears in a long
negligé tie of an unusual peacock shade, and his black hair is
'long enough to wave untidily over a broad, white brow'.

Naturally the implication is that no 'real' man could accept the pacifist view. Nancy's robust rallying fails to achieve the desired character transformation. This is left to the Luftwaffe: Gordon's pacifism goes 'up in the smoke' of the first air raid that he experiences. Soon he is bursting to get back into the British army 'with a good tommy gun in my grip'.

Children's fiction was not the place to examine irresolution and ideological doubt, especially at a time when the country's mood was one of gamely 'getting on with the job'. But the more enquiring reader might have been irritated by over-simplified characterizations and their propagandist effects. Antonia Forest is one of the few children's authors who has managed to indicate without banality the character complexities of someone who betrays his country. However the action of *The Marlows and the Traitor* (1948) does not take place until just after the war; and Lt Lewis Foley—an instructor at Dartmouth Naval College—is not pro-Nazi: he is working for the communists. Foley is described by an acquaintance as having 'no loyalties, only enmities. I don't think for a moment he's an ardent communist. I think he's only in it, because he gets a peculiar kick out of being on his own against the rest of us. He always did.' The combination of ruthlessness and decency that motivates Foley is highlighted by its effects on Peter—a Dartmouth cadet—who realizes that Foley is involved in espionage. Antonia Forest goes against the mainstream of juvenile war stories too by expressing the ghastly impotence that many children feel in critical confrontations with adults:

> Peter clenched his hands under the table and tried to think of something—*anything*, from stabbing Foley to the heart, to driving holes in the bottom of the *Talisman*. But he knew he couldn't hope to match Foley if it came to physical violence; he still felt hot and ashamed when he remembered that moment when Foley had flung him aside as if he had been matchwood.

Peter's frustration is a quality that many readers will recognize, although of course there is a satisfaction of a more obvious kind to be found in stories of child spy-catchers of the traditionally dogged-and-undaunted type.

Malcolm Saville's *Mystery at Witchend* (1942) offers several examples of the latter. Some London children are evacuated to Shropshire where they found a society known as the Lone Pine Club. In search of adventure, they are fortunate enough to meet up with a plethora of German spies. Intrigue and excitement are helped along by convenient fogs, and the air resounds with the peewit calls of the Lone Pine Club and the owl hoots of the enemy agents. There are authentic evocations of the period— hints of wartime food shortages, 'Daddy' in the RAF, and Home Guards with bicycles doing manœuvres. Basically, however, the central emotion is simply the children's pleasure in camping and woodcraft. This has a more light-hearted touch than the Baden-Powell variety, which of course was still inspiring Guiding and Scouting stories in the 1940s.

Catherine Christian, who from 1939 to 1944 edited the Girl Guides' Association's official journal, produced two attractive wartime stories with a Guiding background: *The Kingfishers See It Through* and *The Seventh Magpie*. Of course tracking, signalling and Girl-Guide grit assume a special significance in the spy-catching context: 'You kids have got to stop playing at Guiding, and *be* Guides, not because you want to, or I want to, but because England is going to need you. . . .'

At the beginning of *The Kingfishers See It Through* the Guide company is broken up because its captain goes off to do war-work. The Kingfisher Patrol continues on its own, like the London Prides, a patrol of cockney evacuees. The Londoners resent the 'stuck-up' behaviour of the Kingfishers—but the trailing of a spy-ring of carrier-pigeon operators brings both patrols together. These Guides take their responsibilities seriously, but they come up against a problem that has bothered many fictional children who uncover espionage: no adults will listen to them. '. . . if we report it the Police here'll just say it's Girl Guides playing games or something . . .'.

The Seventh Magpie is a story of the Guide International Service, an organization that arranged for Guides to do rehabilitation work in the occupied countries towards the end of the war. This book in fact recreates the expansive feeling of late 1944 and 1945: ' "It's going to be a lovely summer and the war's going to end, and everything is going to be marvellous . . ." chanted Paddy, dancing up and down with her bulging haversack bumping against her, to the extreme peril of the patrol milk supply she was carrying . . .'. The leading characters learn how the Girl Guide movement has survived under fascism by going 'underground'. (In *The Big Test* [1947] Catherine Christian records that even in Auschwitz a Belgian ranger symbolically clung to only one personal possession, her Guide badge, by hiding it in her mouth whenever she was searched; and Guiding managed somehow to continue in Weihsien, a concentration camp run by the Japanese in the Far East.)

In England too the Guides coped with problems arising from wartime conditions: for example travel restrictions meant that sometimes the annual camp had to be held on the local vicarage lawn instead of in the country. Their capacity to improvise had even more positive effects in the creation of Guide mobile canteens. These grew from 'blitz cooking' in ovens which had been put together from bricks and iron door-scrapers.

The *Girl's Own Paper* and the *Boy's Own Paper* were still carrying on. By 1940, however, both magazines had acquired a new liveliness, a patriotic tone unlike the oppressive fervour they had projected during the first world war. But echoes from 1914 persisted. In Gunby Hadath's serial 'Grim and Gay', the central character Cranmer is searching his public-school buildings for a younger boy who is missing during an air raid. The raid is so violent that Cranmer longs to take shelter and give up the search but '. . . like some shining Excalibur withdrawn from its sheath . . . in that moment . . . it rushed upon Cranmer for certitude that against the battle raging over his head he was fighting the last, fierce battle for his own manhood'. He wins it, of course, and in the process saves the Speech Room ('all that old timber, and the wonderful panels with the old Boys' names carved on them') from burning. With appropriate pluck and presence of mind he hammers out a message for help 'on the big drum of the OTC' which is conveniently at hand.

The *BOP* celebrated the activities of the various junior cadet corps, along with their parent bodies. Its favourite armed service, however, was the Royal Air Force. Generally its fictional heroes were too concerned with practical matters to indulge for long in Cranmer's type of introspection. Still going strong and now a squadron leader in the RAF, Biggles tersely conveys the mood: 'Frankly, Scrimshaw, we haven't much confidence in fellows who grab a bottle when things get sticky.... Make up a party with my fellows.... They'll do anything you want to do, but they don't brood and they don't booze—those are the only two things we bar.' And, of course, sex! As far as possible the magazine continued to keep female characters out of its stories; but, perhaps for reasons of wartime economy, the *GOP* and *BOP* began to use the same blocks for features urging readers to save paper, collect salvage, etc. So girls and boys were shown together in at least one kind of useful, wholesome activity. At this time several Biggles adventures were serialized in the *BOP* before appearing in hardback. Captain W. E. Johns was then a recruiting officer for the RAF. Through the *BOP* and *GOP* he presented an extremely colourful picture of service life that must have seemed attractive to many readers. Apart from fiction he wrote regular articles on many aspects of aviation for both papers: 'Jottings from my Logbook' in *BOP* and 'Between You and Me and the Joystick' in *GOP*. In March 1942 he wrote an obituary for Ernst Udet (published simultaneously in the boys' and girls' paper). This German air ace had shot down Johns's plane in Germany during the first world war. When Udet committed suicide he was one of the heads of the Luftwaffe. Johns had sufficient restraint to refrain from making political capital out of the event.

The remarkable popularity of Biggles prompted the Air Ministry to suggest that Johns should create a fictional girl aviator as part of the WAAF recruiting drive. Flight Officer Joan Worralson duly appeared in the *Girl's Own Paper* of October 1940. No other young woman could have expressed the post-Dunkirk and Battle of Britain spirit more suitably for this attractive but conservative periodical. 'Worrals' was extremely responsible (during her schooldays she had been head-girl and was 'inclined to be studious when not on the playing fields'); but she can be imperturbable, quick-witted and intrepid when the need arises. 'Excitement is like a drug. The more you have the more you want, and when you can't get it the old nerves begin to twitch.' Like the Biggles saga, the tales of Worrals move quickly: searchlights 'beam questingly', flak 'sparkles menacingly'; a dull or serious note is rarely struck.

Perhaps because he was writing for a new, female readership Johns took more trouble with the Worrals stories. (By the 1940s his Biggles adventures must have become a sinecure.) His heroine's exploits had the added spice of Johns's rather facile brand of feminism: '"Men! They can take care of themselves, but we're poor little waifs who can't be trusted to find a way home unless the sun is strong!"'—snorts Worrals, in response to the CO's doubts about her ability to handle an aeroplane in snowy conditions. However, in the first book of the series after a successful crash landing Worrals is overcome to the extent of fainting. Biggles, of course, would never have behaved like this.

The stories had a special appeal for girls who idolized RAF pilots for their Battle of Britain triumphs. The peculiar exhilaration of flying is conveyed even when Worrals is simply returning an old Reliant aircraft for servicing: '. . . for the sheer joy of it Worrals roared through the solitude, the aircraft skimming the cloud tops like a dolphin in a silver sea. . . . Then she drew the control column back and climbed steeply towards the sun . . .' (Worrals incidentally was only seventeen and a half at the time.) A different and less palatable kind of wartime excitement is also expressed. The *Girl's Own Paper*, in spite of its enthusiastic patriotism, normally left killing to the boys. However, as the war progresses Worrals becomes increasingly callous about having to shoot down the enemy: 'A sort of frenzy surged through her. . . . Exultation seized her as she saw her shells going home.'

On the whole, however, the *GOP* is at pains to point out the differences between girls' ambitions and those of boys. Referring to a psychologists' report in 1941 the paper informs readers that boys dreamed of getting VCs and flying over Germany, 'but little girls dreamed of fairies and strange countries, and older ones of being evacuated to wonderful romantic places . . .'. Nevertheless the *GOP* contained articles on the exploits of 'women with a will' like Amy Johnson (who had recently died while ferrying planes for the Air Transport Auxiliary) and Sabiha Goeksten, the Turkish aviatrix. The domestic tone of an article about doggie gas masks and the problems of pets in air raids is quickly counterbalanced in the next issue by 'Dogs of War'. This rather daunting story about a Nazi attempt to fly

rabid dogs into England to destroy morale was written by
Pauline Gower who was at the time head of the All-Woman
Squadron of the Air Transport Auxiliary. She wrote several
flying stories for the *GOP* but her main contribution to aviation
literature is *Women With Wings* (1938). This is an account of how
she and her friend Dorothy Spicer trained to become pilots, and
later ran their own air-taxi service. The book brings across the
exuberant, pioneer feeling which is often associated with flying
in the 1930s. The introduction is written by Amy Johnson, and
on one occasion Pauline Gower and Dorothy Spicer borrowed
one of her Gipsy Moths. However, in spite of relating several
joy-riding anecdotes *Women With Wings* stresses that 'A good
pilot takes no risks'. The women who graduated from giving
the public 'five-bob flights' to becoming air-ambulance and
ferry pilots during the war were not dare-devils. Pauline
Gower's book includes a chapter of advice for the 'would-be
aviatrix' about training facilities and job possibilities: 'Most
young women of today have exchanged the word "hobby" for
"career".'

In the *GOP* saboteurs are at it again in *The Mystery of H.Q.*
(by Elizabeth Tugwell). A serious leakage of information to the
enemy from an army signals HQ 'somewhere in England' is
traced to an ATS major. The spy network is tracked down and
broken but the traitorous woman escapes. This story ends with
the reflections of a male lieutenant of signals: '. . . it would
have been rotten to arrest a girl . . . the penalty for that sort
of thing is death, you know . . .'. In the first world war—in
spite of public outrage at the German execution of Nurse
Cavell—girls' fiction had displayed less tolerance of female
secret service agents. In 1918 the heroine of Angela Brazil's *A
Patriotic Schoolgirl* asks the headmistress if it is 'right to forgive
the enemies of our country'. Mrs Morrison's reply—'When
they are dead'—is typical of the kind of uncompromising
patriotism that was then recommended to adolescents.

As well as his aviators Johns produced another war hero in
Gimlet, the commando; but he never achieved a fraction of the
success of Worrals and Biggles. A flying hero with comparable panache was Hal Wilton's Rockfist Rogan, who starred
throughout the war in the Amalgamated Press's weekly adventure paper, *Champion*. In fact this character had been

popular in the '30s when the stories appeared as retrospective
accounts of his dashing adventures in the Great War as a pilot
in the Royal Flying Corps. In September 1939—without any
explanation of the technicalities or the time transposition
involved—Rockfist Rogan was transferred overnight from
RFC to RAF, and from the first world war to the second.
Rockfist, a more bizarre character than W. E. Johns's heroes,
possessed a 'superhuman stamina':

> He could spend the afternoon doing a sweep over Nazi
> territory, shoot up a few enemy aerodromes, smash his way
> out again through a whistling wind of dogfights, and then,
> when an ordinary man would be flat on his back with
> fatigue, go straight into a boxing match, where he would
> slosh and hammer his way to victory against a rough
> heavy-weight.

Rockfist is more dynamic and extroverted even than Biggles:
for him action is obsessive and his spirits flag if he isn't hurling
his spitfire across the sky or indulging in gruelling sessions of
dumb-bells or Indian club manipulation when grounded. On
one occasion he overdoes things and is forced to take some
leave, but cricket and bloodsports soon restore his energy.
Returning to his squadron he 'smacks down' three Messer-
schmitt 109s, mauls two more so badly 'that it was a toss up
whether they would get home'—and sends another four
German pilots fleeing for their lives.

Incessant and improbable action also provided themes for
the five boys' papers issued by the Amalgamated Press's
Scottish rivals, D. C. Thomson & Co. (*Wizard*, *Hotspur*,
Adventure, *Skipper* and *Rover*). The excitement of these stories,
however, was somewhat modified by the sameness of their
style. Editorial policy dictated that the Thomson authors
should remain anonymous, writing in a manner that was easy to
imitate. There was of course sufficient superficial liveliness to
sell the papers to young readers; and the war provided an
abundance of far-fetched, funny or bloodthirsty material. The
onslaught against 'Jerries' and 'Japs' is conducted not only by
British supermen but also by plucky schoolboys—and even
animals like Busty's Brainy Baboon, who helps our troops in the

Far East. The 'natives' too are uniformly loyal to the empire. Their unusual talents are exploited to the full: Chung 'the Squat Himalayan', for instance, stands on a rocky ledge to bat fire-bombs on to German planes refuelling in the secret air base below. The *Wizard*'s off-key but presumably popular wartime covers displayed cartoons of the plate-lipped negro inhabitants of 'Spadger's Isle'. Known as 'the nigs' they speak 'coon' English and wear a weird assortment of civilian and military garments. Possibly Spadger's Isle was intended to be an ironic representation of 'our tight little island'—Bodger's Isle, perhaps? Before the war it had been included in the paper, but only as a minor feature. The racial joke was overplayed, even allowing for the conventions of the time. ' "Well look at de pipers." ' [when the Spadger's Islanders borrow Scottish tam-o'shanters, kilts and bagpipes] ' "Dey's blowin' till dey's black in de face." ' These bizarre covers continued until after the end of the war.

The Wizard's greatest contribution to the war effort was the enlistment of Wilson the Amazing Athlete into the RAF. (The celebrated 'Silver Wings' appealed not only to romantic teenagers but also to the toughest heroes of the boys' weekly papers.) Born on a Yorkshire farm as long ago as 1795, Wilson was endowed with immortality as well as incredible strength— which of course he was able to use to good effect in the service of his country. In the Thomson papers there were also Black Flash Commandos working with the guerrillas in Norway, the Flying Crusher (a bomber with pincer-like grips which could tear up railway lines or lift vessels out of the sea) and a squadron of Nameless Flyers who would take on suicidally perilous assignments without a qualm. When the war finished the stories in these papers moved towards science fiction of a lurid but rather simple nature.

One wartime story 'Army of the Caverns' is memorable because of its Russian background. (Even when the USSR had joined the allies, the media were not always prepared to show solidarity with the Russians. At one time the BBC did not include 'The Red Flag' in its regular programmes of National Anthems of the allies: it compromised with 'The Song of the Volga Boatmen', which, though Russian, was not Red.) 'Army of the Caverns' appeared in the *Wizard* in July 1944

after the opening of the second front so long demanded by
Stalin. The story's action takes place in Nazi-occupied Odessa;
the Russian army of resistance is hiding in caves and cellars
underneath the rubble of the damaged city, venturing out only
for purposes of assassination. The central characters however
are not communists but Celts—'there was nothing of the Slav
in their features. They were in fact British [Scots] youngsters—
Jim and Stanley Goddard.'

Occupied Europe furnished innumerable themes for popular
fiction from tear-jerkers to thrillers. For children's authors it
provided a ready-made setting for tales of escape. In 1942
Kitty Barne turned her attention from evacuees to refugees.
We'll Meet in England opens in Norway: having lived through a
year of German occupation, Heitha Larsen and her brother
Rudy plan to get hold of a boat and cross the North Sea to
England. Surprisingly, they find an English merchant seaman
in a cave—and 'Wapping Bill' takes charge of the operation.
Even the Larsen family's dog is roped in to do its bit. The story
gets duller as it progresses; the prying of the local Quisling
Pieters fails to add the missing quality of excitement. Once
again the Germans have been lumbered with an agent of
singular obtuseness—'We do not ask. We command.... There
is no need . . . to think, only to obey'—who is easily hoodwinked
by two children of average intelligence.

Elinor Brent-Dyer's Chalet School is an early victim of Nazi
persecution. The school's closure and the escape of its pupils is
the subject of *The Chalet School in Exile* and *The Chalet School
Goes to It*. By 1940 when the former was published the series
had been running for fifteen years; the original charm of these
stories of an international, trilingual school in a Tyrolean setting
had begun to fade. At least the Anschluss provided a new
stimulus for the author. As soon as the Nazis make Austria 'a
mere province of the greater Reich' Austrian parents under
orders from the government begin to withdraw their girls
from the Chalet School. Unlike Kitty Barne, Elinor Brent-Dyer
makes the most of every opportunity to stress the destructive
effects of the new régime. Ex-Chalet School pupils, like all
unmarried Austrian girls between the ages of 17 and 25, are
forced to join a women's labour corps; the father of one girl dies
in a concentration camp and former friends and acquaintances

turn out to be Nazi spies. The story's most exciting moment occurs at the end of what must be one of the earliest serious accounts of Nazi Jew-baiting in English children's fiction. (This subject of course occurred more frequently as the war progressed.) Miss Wilson ('Bill'), the Chalet School science mistress, strides in to rescue a party of girls who have got into difficulties while trying to protect an elderly Jew. By fighting her way through the violent mob, Bill leads her pupils to the comparative safety of a nearby church, and here the advantages of a sporty English education are spelt out: 'It was a good thing she was big and muscular, for it took her all her time to do it and when she had reached the church porch her coat was torn off her back, her hat gone, and her magnificent [rich chestnut] hair tumbling in curly masses over her shoulders.' Within seconds, the hair has changed colour. The shock of the experience has been too much for Miss Wilson. Children who had been brought up under constant threats of their mother's hair turning white with worry at their naughtiness—and waiting in vain to see it happen—were thrilled by Bill's transformation. This incident has a more dramatic impact than the violence of the scene that provoked it.

Rather unfortunately as it turns out the Chalet entourage takes refuge in the Channel Islands. These of course were the only portions of British territory to suffer German occupation; and the mobile institution uproots again. A strange conversion occurs while the school is based in Guernsey. Gertrud Beck, a Nazi schoolgirl-spy, is unable to hold out against the grit, glamour and decency of the Chalet girls. She acknowledges the error of her ways: 'I haven't done the School any real harm. . . . You've all been so good to me, I could not. . . .'

An interesting counterbalance to this kind of fantasy is found in *The Diary of Anne Frank*, the authentic record of the effects of Nazi-ism on the life of a Jewish child. Anne was thirteen in July 1942 when she and her family were forced into hiding. For over two years they and another Jewish family were concealed in the secret attic of the Amsterdam building which housed Mr Frank's business. Discovery and arrest took place in August 1944; the family was split up, and Anne and her sister died in Belsen in the following year.

The *Diary* is moving, unsentimental and often funny in its

relating of situations from the quicksilver viewpoint of a resilient adolescent. Her childish excitement over the secret rooms is soon dispelled in the claustrophobic atmosphere, the bickering of people in constant, enforced proximity and the fear of discovery. The presence of office workers in the building below was a constant hazard; during business hours the hidden families had to remain almost silent, unable even to use the lavatory. They could never go out, and in cases of illness could not even call a doctor.

Like most girls of her age Anne needs to assert her independence even while clinging to the security of family relationships. Conflicts between the lively, rapidly maturing girl and her anxious, middle-aged mother are intensified by the unnatural situation. An adolescent's diary, of course, is usually unbalanced and awkward, and rarely of interest to anyone except its writer. Anne's merits publication for its attractive style and perceptiveness, as well as the obvious interest of the events which it records. Although she is a product of the 1930s and 1940s, Anne Frank is direct and unaffected in her references to sex and other bodily functions in a way that wasn't generally accepted in children's books until some time later. She reads with enthusiasm, tries to continue her studies and is generally optimistic: 'Surely the time will come when we are people again, and not just Jews.' The *Diary* was first published in 1947 and it has been produced in many editions and translations. In this sense, one of Anne's expressions of the creative energy common to young people struck a prophetic note: 'I want to go on living after my death! And therefore I am grateful to God for this gift . . . of expressing all that is in me.'

The war ended in 1945, too late to save Anne and thousands of other children. It brought about changes in childhood patterns which have since become consolidated. There was a responsible questioning by young people of the authority of the adult, the state and conventional forms of religion; also a greater acceptance by adults, caught up in the relief of having survived, that life, and childhood especially, should be enjoyed in the present.

XI

THE GAPS BETWEEN THE BOMBS

Today's View of Children in Wartime

His world is a small world of hours and minutes,
Hedgerows shut in the horizons of his thought,
His loves are uncritical and deep,
His anger innocent and sudden like a minnow.

His eyes, acute and quick, are unprotected,
Unsandalled still, his feet run down the lane,
Down to that lingering horror in the brambles,
The limp crashed airman, in the splintered goggles.
Michael Roberts, 'The Child'

AT THE END of the war the bulk of children's fiction was still located in a dream world of boarding school, ponies, the prevention of crime, impossible reversals of fortune and holiday high-jinks. The serious effects of war were not considered suitable for discussion at this level. Only romantic figures like the girl resistance worker in France continued to crop up in stories in the popular girls' papers until well into the '50s. These girls frequently had to take part in the school swimming regatta to retrieve a vital package from a lonely rock; or pose as laundry maids in order to conceal the trained alsatian or the wounded airman beneath a pile of clothing. (In Marghanita Laski's *Little Boy Lost*, 1949, the child is smuggled to safety in a laundry basket: this object became a conventional symbol for courage and quick thinking.) The blustering, blundering members of the Gestapo were pitifully easy to outwit: a clever dog could do it.

The behaviour of the boys' heroes was more straightforward: they could attack the enemy with real weapons instead of having to play-act and use their wits. In recent years there has been a curious proliferation of war comics for boys. These were first brought out by the International Publishing Corporation in 1958, and they make an extremely basic appeal to readers, with vindictive Germans and stalwart British Tommies, respectively furnished with a characteristic expletive, '*Donner und Blitzen*' and 'Cor blimey'.

The heroes of these comics are adults, fighter pilots, commandos, intelligence agents, in all cases effective and indestructible, crudely simplified to pander to the reader's idea of a dashing, formidable quality in grown-ups. In serious children's fiction, on the other hand, the emphasis is on the resistance of the very young; and the first major theme to emerge from the war was the plight of the lost children of Europe, the victims of enemy occupation, extermination camps and post-war chaos. In *The Silver Sword* (Ian Serraillier, 1956) the children are Polish, three members of one family and an urchin, Jan, whose skills at scrounging and thieving help to keep his companions alive. Warsaw is in ruins; in winter the children live in the cellar of a bombed-out house, in summer they take to the woods and fields like gypsies or ragamuffins. They survive; though the boy, Edek, is captured and transported to a German labour camp. At the end of the war begins the long trek to Switzerland where their parents may be.

This is a straightforward story of endurance, the preservation of integrity in trying circumstances, with suitable rewards for courage and perseverance. If the heroine is sentimentalized this is a natural effect of the theme: the author is bound to admire a girl who has gone through so much. In any case there are no subtleties of characterization: the pressure of events has depressed personality, so that only the attributes relevant to survival remain. In terms of the story, the children are less important than what happens to them.

This is a general principle of survival fiction, and it often results in a bland and sentimental tone. The passing kindness of strangers is magnified, the feelings of pathos and horror aroused by the children's sufferings are indulged and the ultimate destination is presented as a kind of promised land. The victims are rarely brutalized or even damaged psychologically by their experiences. They are often representative characters who stand for outraged innocence, the effects of racial persecution concentrated in the most emotive form.

The small, bewildered but sturdy Jewish girl with the degrading yellow star sewn on her coat is a good example. In

Gertie Evenhuis's *What About Me?* (published in Holland in 1970) she is called Hadassa, and her litany of horrors is given in a muted tone that is extremely effective: '. . . I sat in the cupboard for three hours. They stamped through the house. They dragged my brother down the stairs. . . . I saw them all on the lorry, through the gap. My grandfather only had a jar of milk. They pushed him up with their guns.'

The facts of enemy occupation are not evaded but the children's stories are usually hopeful; the little Poles or Jews escape through the intervention of adults motivated by pity, or visiting English or continental children aghast at the depravity of Nazi beliefs. *Storm Warning* (Mara Kay, 1976) is set in Frankfurt in the summer of 1938. The author uses that old standby of children's fiction, the non-fatal accident, to land her heroine in a German household where two Jewish girls are being concealed in the attic. The story is the usual one, with melodramatic overtones that become absurd as the action progresses. The girls' mother is secreted in a convent posing as a nun. English, well-behaved Ann Lindsay is summoned to church, to a clandestine meeting with a Mother Superior: '"Look at your missal. Pretend to be praying,"' she whispers. A Nazi called Gunter has cold eyes, scowls frequently and comes out with remarks like '"All right, Weiss. . . . No more of your games. Where is your wife?"' A spoilt, crippled girl in a wheelchair, a self-sacrificing mother and a mentally retarded woman of 24 who looks like Little Red Riding Hood provide further novelettish touches to hold the reader's attention. The Weiss family escapes of course, driven to the Swiss border in a car with intrepid Ann and her uncle Dick. '". . . Let us hope, at any rate, to meet again one day in a better, saner, freer world."'

This is the conventional sentiment, the expected phrase to end this type of romantic fiction, where ill-treatment may be averted by the actions of kind strangers outside the campaign of terror, and the 'better world' is a clear image, a place where good deeds flourish and there is respect among nations. It is all rather dreamy and idyllic, with some authentic details of persecution added merely to give point to the imagined contrast. Novels like *Storm Warning* don't provide a means of crystallizing the emotions aroused by the facts of Nazi oppression. The moral issue is presented in facile terms, too easily accepted; the form becomes that of a loosely constructed thriller and the seriousness and strength of the theme are consequently eroded.

For English writers the foreign locations are often a disadvantage; the problem of evoking an unfamiliar atmosphere is liable to find resolution in the use of clichéd images or, in the case of war or political strategy, newsreel events. A considerable degree of caution and economy of style are needed to avoid the lush, picture-postcard quality inherent in the conventional idea of continental towns and countryside. In any case, some authors persist in regarding this quality as a valuable short-cut to excitement or romance.

Judith Kerr's *When Hitler Stole Pink Rabbit* (1971) is written in a lower key than *Storm Warning* and it is more successful for this reason. It is simply a family story with embellishments— the effects of certain historical events thrown in for good measure. Its Jewish family on the whole is not badly treated; though Anna and Max and their parents are forced to leave Germany, to move first to Switzerland, then Paris and finally London. For the time being there are no rumours of atrocity; the forms that persecution takes are merely squalid and spiteful, easy to discount. It is the time of the burning of the Reichstag and the rise of the Nazi party, and the children's father is prudent enough to cut his losses and leave Berlin before the holocaust. The adaptable children regard the whole experience as an adventure, both the constant moving and the family's reduced income providing special opportunities to sharpen one's wits. The moral bias is familiar—well-adjusted children turning misfortune to a social gain.

The book is not especially memorable or original, the plight of its characters is after all not severe, the cheerful tone becomes in the end somewhat bland, and the political tensions of pre-war Europe are hardly adumbrated. Of course it takes courage 'to give up everything, . . . to start all over again in a strange country,' as a character in another children's book remarks. In *Journey to America* (Sonia Levitin, 1970) the family is split up, the father makes his escape to America and leaves his wife and daughters to follow. The story has a happy ending, but the narrator, Lisa Platt, is forced to spend some time at a children's refugee camp near Zurich:

'My sister and I are hungry,' Ruth said distinctly. 'We would like something to eat.'

Frau Strom stared at us, and her face turned redder still, as if she could not believe her ears. . . .

'I saw it from the first,' said Frau Strom, her eyes blazing. 'It shows in your face. You are a typical troublemaker. . . . Did you expect the Ritz Hotel? This is a charity camp. *Charity!*' She almost screamed the word, and my hands were trembling.

Christine Nostlinger's reminiscences are sharper and funnier. *Fly Away Home* (first published in England in 1976) is the story of a short period in the life of Cristel Goth, eight years old in 1945 when the Russians come to occupy Vienna. In this defeated society people behave oddly; their nerves give way and their actions become contrary to those usual in the interests of self-preservation. The narrative method of presentation is episodic and this accords with the child's-eye view and the humorous, downright tone.

Certainly Cristel is not indoctrinated with strong ideological views: the ethics of the *Bund Deutscher Madchen* (the Nazi youth organization for girls) appear to have passed her by. Unlike the sillier adults in the story she feels no preconceived terror for the Russian troops; in fact she shows a remarkable capacity to adapt to events as they occur. Among the adults there is continuous grumbling, hysteria about food and a general lowering of standards, not always to the disadvantage of a high-spirited child. Cristel can express her feelings in crude expletives without being seriously reprimanded (' "But everybody says damn and shit!" I shouted back').

With the war about to be lost the Nazi party can be criticized openly, though there is still a feeling that it is dangerous to express a grievance in this respect.

Suddenly she shouted, 'To hell with Hitler! Heil Hitler! To hell with Hitler!'

'Please, please,' said the warden. 'Keep quiet, for heaven's sake! . . .'.

In English children's fiction, of course, there is very little criticism of the conduct of the war or of the government's failure to take the necessary steps to provide adequate relief for the bombed-out and to maintain public services. The English never lost the sense of being morally in the right, and this enabled them to put up fairly cheerfully with a great deal of inconvenience. In fact in some cases morale was not sustained to the extent that newspapers implied; especially after the first raids on London when shock contributed to the defeatist feelings of fury and helplessness. As Londoners became acclimatized to the pattern of the raids there was a resurgence of stamina.

The war in Europe falls implicitly within a romantic tradition, distinct in character from the everyday wartime experiences of people in England. These lend themselves more easily to individual treatment: in this country disaster was not total and reactions were not blunted by the methods of subjugation. Adjustment to wartime conditions was necessary, of course, but spirits were kept up in one way or another. However, it was not until the late 1960s that a new crop of children's writers began to look back to the war in England, to the effects of evacuation and the powerful emotions engendered in school-children by the rescue of 340,000 British soldiers from Dunkirk, to the bombing of London and the fears of invasion, the establishment of new rules of behaviour and special priorities in allegiance.

For some of these writers it was a matter of remembering, for others a matter of concocting a story from fragments of information, using the background to integrate or illuminate the most crucial points of the narrative. Wartime could be treated as a precise historical period with a beginning and an end, all of a piece in a way that the present can never be, but close enough in time to avoid the dangers of quaintness or uninspired guesswork in the author's approach. Many writers find cause for nostalgia in the particulars of wartime, the gas masks and ration books and indoor shelters, the bravery of the bombed-out who put on a cheerful expression for the photographers; but in most cases it is tempered with subtlety or sharpness or realism of execution.

The earliest retrospective English wartime stories, *The Dolphin Crossing* (Jill Paton Walsh, 1967) and Hester Burton's

In Spite of all Terror (1968) deal specifically with evacuation and
with the frustration of schoolboys unable to make a positive
contribution to the fighting until an appeal from the government goes out to the owners and users of small craft. The
British Expeditionary Force was stranded at Dunkirk in the early
summer of 1940, and thousands of small boats sailed across the
Channel to the rescue of the English and French troops. An
'army of freedom queuing up to be taken off by pleasure
boats': the experience was the turning point for Elizabeth
Bowen's traitor Robert Kelway (see Chapter IX), a Dunkirk
wounded man who had been in action then 'on the wrong
side'. For the simpler schoolboy heroes it was still a war of
illusions, a troubadours' war, with Dunkirk a stirring, clear-
cut victory in defeat. Certainly the ensuing spirit of defiance,
courage and solidarity was remarkable—after Dunkirk the war
effort was intensified, though naturally the spurt of enthusiasm
was not prolonged.

The Dolphin Crossing's greatest merits are its clarity, dispassion
and economy of presentation. Its heroes are a couple of resolute,
pleasant schoolboys, one upper middle class, the other evacuated
with his stepmother from the slums of London. The mixing
of social classes is also an important aspect of Hester Burton's
story: her working-class heroine is billeted on a wealthy
professional family with effects that are ultimately beneficial to
all concerned. Liz Hawtin's home life has not been agreeable:
for three years she has lived with an aunt who has taken her in
in a spirit of embittered charity. Evacuation offers a prospect
of nothing but improvement—though naturally to begin with
there are problems of adjustment and organization. The
Brutons, who have three sons, have asked for a boy; they get
Liz instead, and only the grandparents, Sir Rollo and Lady
Bruton, make the girl feel welcome. Liz's lack of table manners
is the first deficiency that has to be corrected: '"Liz," said
Ben, one sunny morning when he was punting her up the
river. "I don't think you ought to blow your nose quite so
obviously on your table-napkin."'

Ben, the middle son, is one of the fictional schoolboys who
get to Dunkirk: he and his grandfather rescue hundreds of
stranded soldiers, though the old man is killed in the process.
Liz, who has hoped to join them, is put ashore at Ramsgate

to wait for news. 'It was terrible being a girl. Terrible to be useless.'

The fear of ridicule and disgrace after an unsuccessful bid to join in the rescue operation is suffered also by the hero of Philip Turner's *Dunkirk Summer* (1973). Andy Birch is a naval cadet who should have known better: '"... You asked if you could come on this trip and I said 'no'. Because I cannot take responsibility for your life, and because if we are going where I think we are going, one extra crew member means one less place for a soldier ...".' He gets no further than Harwich, a stowaway forced to turn cabin boy, but soon he is whistling cheerfully and indulging in introspection: 'He had not stowed away because he had wanted to impress Archie. Or had he? He shrugged. The business of motives was altogether too complicated. Maybe he just wanted to impress Pat? He gave it up and concentrated on corned beef.'

Andrew Birch's unintelligent thoughts are presented in a form that is colloquial, naïve and self-assertive in the typical adolescent way. The uninformed enthusiasm of older children was often a product of impatience, a fear of missing out on important events. In the bulk of wartime fiction the emotion is recognized, applauded and gently redirected: children have a part to play that is relevant to their capacities. The climax of *Dunkirk Summer* is reached when three teenagers save a Norman church from destruction by fire: 'Adolf's policy of frightfulness has come unstuck and he now has a lot fewer fireworks than he had a couple of hours ago. ...'

The predominant tone of this story is inconsequential and glib, with sentimental flourishes contributed by the heroine: '... "We were talking about whether the Germans would invade, and Daddy suddenly said 'Well, whatever happens, at least we've lived to see the country find its soul'. ..."' The necessary but embarrassing phrases give rise to a degree of inarticulacy, as though Patricia Lambert is making an effort to get them out: '... "Andy, have you noticed how happy people are? ... helping one another, and sort of—united."'

In children's fiction it is necessary to stress the unexpected emotional benefits of war and sometimes this can lead to misrepresentation or banality of expression, a mawkish vagueness substituted for the precise spirit of commitment without illusions. In *In Spite of All Terror* the meeting of social classes is sentimentalized and the events of the war are given in a portentous style, usually in separate paragraphs of one line:

A month later the storm broke upon western Europe.
The Germans invaded Holland and Belgium.
It was total war.

This device has a melodramatic effect, but it does help to achieve a suitable distancing of the historical circumstances. The author's concern is with the development of her heroine's personality and in this respect a transformation is effected too smoothly. The security of family life is acquired almost without effort and the complexities inherent in the situation of an evacuee are simplified implausibly. The Brutons' good will extends even to Liz's silly, pregnant cousin Rose, whose mother has put her out on the street at a moment particularly inopportune, the height of the London blitz. Rose is going to lumber the Brutons with a baby (she won't consider adoption) and the narrative implication is that this is the proper course to take: 'Even Rose was blessed by the coming of spring'. Too much is made of 'the bonds of sadness, hope, and love'. The clichés of romantic fiction are fused with those of popular wartime mythology—Liz is aware that out of war has come 'a new quality to life', and her final mood is one of facile optimism: this coincides with the narrative attitude throughout.

The Dolphin Crossing, on the other hand, is remarkably free from sentimentality. The author is perceptive about class difficulties but she does not adopt a reverential tone to describe the ways in which they may be overcome; her characters are simply forthright and practical, and there is no adventitious emotion to get in the way of the story. The boys' achievement is not minimized; to embark for France is a natural course only for those with sufficient stamina to face the risks. The atmosphere, however, is highly charged and this induces a kind of keyed-up courage that gets them across the Channel. When the operation is over one boy is unconscious from exhaustion and the other is missing, unavoidably dead. Until this point he had appeared to have all the qualities necessary for survival: cockney resilience, luck, a carefree outlook, common sense, the will to win. Crazy determination and a power of judgement impaired by tiredness have led him to self-destruction: the logic is impeccable and the issue is not evaded. No platitudes are produced to lull the reader.

For a juvenile audience the right key is struck. The narrative is informative but not solemn, the tone is lively without being irreverent. Perhaps John Aston was exceptionally lucky to find a slum companion who is not a delinquent, not a suitable object for charity and not infested with vermin. Within the context, however, the details are sufficiently realistic. In the opening paragraphs the London boy is being taunted by local bullies:

> 'Look out!' screamed a jeering voice. 'There's a bomb coming!'
> 'Run for a coal-hole, quick,' suggested another.
> 'Go and live in Scotland—no bombs there!' cried another voice.
> 'That's right. We don't want you here, you and your stinking lice!' chorused the rest.

Many evacuees from deprived areas brought with them problems of hygiene and deportment that aggravated the basic issue, the understandable reluctance of householders to accommodate unknown children. The government rates of pay were hardly an inducement: 10/6 a week for the first child, 8/6 each for subsequent boarders. Evacuated mothers with babies paid 5/- for themselves and 3/- for the child.

Many people, not only children, were exposed to unfamiliar conditions and ways of life that shocked or attracted them. Certainly there were long-term benefits to be gained from the inevitable increase in social awareness, and stratification along the most rigid lines was hardly possible once the war was over. At the simplest level, a gloss of privilege must have rubbed off on the luckier evacuees whose billets had been superior in quality to their original homes.

For Noel Streatfeild's slum family (*When the Siren Wailed*, 1974) it was largely a matter of discipline. Laura, Andy and Tim Clark are billeted with an elderly colonel, his ex-batman Elk and Elk's wife. Afterwards, Laura realizes that 'all the months they had lived with Sir and the Elks had taught her a great deal without her knowing it. Not just using a toothbrush and things like that but to be polite, to speak quietly and quite a lot about right and wrong.' But these three children are unnaturally tractable, determined to behave correctly at all costs, and responsive in a wholly encouraging way to the efforts of others on their behalf. The author has kept her characters at a great distance; her object is to tell a pleasant story, give her readers a rudimentary understanding of conditions that existed at the time and affirm without priggishness the value of old-fashioned virtues like order, respect for elders and self control.

When the Siren Wailed has a vantage point in the present; there is no attempt to simulate immediacy in the events related. The story is located firmly and comfortably in the past and this enables it to open on a rather sour and patronizing note: 'The Clark family lived in a house in South London. They thought it was a nice house, for, in the 1930s, when this story happened, people were pleased with a lot less than they are today.' In so far as it indicates a narrative bias, an assumption about today's society and a slightly condescending view of yesterday's, this pronouncement is somewhat disquieting. It establishes an undertow of conservatism; and in a sense the reader is being told what to think. This is against the grain of present-day fiction which is inclined to present character from the inside, to steer clear of moralizing at any level and to acknowledge without admonition the destructive, illogical or anti-social aspects of children's behaviour.

An expected deficiency of retrospective wartime fiction is the failure to convey a sense of apprehension, fears for the future and the more immediate fear of violent death for oneself or one's family and friends. There are exceptions: but on the whole the children's stories generate a feeling that the war and its stresses are safely over, however disruptive and harrowing these may have been. In some cases the historical background is scarcely animated: in Gordon Cooper's *A Certain Courage* (1975) for instance, the whole course of the war is followed, from Chamberlain's annunciatory speech of September 1939 to VJ Day; but the atmosphere of the book is colourless and inert.

Drawing by Marjorie Gill for Noel Streatfeild's *When the Siren Wailed*, 1974

This is the dullest of the children's wartime stories. There is no particular theme to add point or significance to the welter of arbitrary detail. The reader is given, among other things, a great deal of unnecessary information about the tea-drinking habits of an elderly couple. A typical girls' conversation goes something like this:

'Do you get much homework at your school?' . . .
    'Alan gets a lot of homework . . . he has to catch the half-past eight train. He doesn't come home till five o'clock.'
    '. . . What time does Mr Collier go to work?'

The heroine is Hilary Turner, one of those girls unusual in fiction but common in real life, who have no character beyond a certain pleasantness of disposition and a tendency towards industriousness. Hilary is evacuated, with the rest of her school, from London and sent to a town called Norton where she has the good fortune to be billeted on an earlier heroine of Mr Cooper's, Kate Bassett (see Chapter VI), now Mrs Collier and the mother of two unremarkable children, Margaret and Alan.

Hilary's adjustment to her surroundings is effected with extraordinary smoothness. But Norton is a soporific place. People speak kindly to one another; they are pleased to see one another, and whenever these events take place the reader is informed. The author is not interested in the presentation of character. Of Mr Webster the minister we are told 'He was a man of middle age, wearing a dark grey suit'. He opens his mouth to remark that the weather has been very good, that he hopes the evacuees will settle down soon and that he looks forward to getting to know them. The reader is taken through six years of this kind of trivia. Of course the author has handicapped himself by taking such a wide view: only the major events of his characters' lives can be related, but a balance is in no sense achieved by the tedious listing of typical daily occurrences. Everything is generalized to the point of triteness, and presented without implicit irony or even comment. We are told that Mrs Bassett is 'interested' to hear her grand-daughter's opinion of her new school. One cannot imagine why: the information is not interesting. 'It's a lot bigger than Arden Street,' Margaret says. 'And it seems to have a different teacher for each lesson'.

The possibilities for drama are minimized at every turn. There is no question of social conflict: Hilary and the Colliers both belong to a stratum of the lower middle class. Personal conflict too is non-existent: everyone behaves with impeccable decency and politeness. When a bereavement occurs the right gestures are made. A fearful sincerity permeates every emotion and every attitude. Hilary experiences 'a sudden rush of anger' only when the war is over, when she walks with Margaret Collier down the London street that had been her home, now a mess of waste land, piles of rubble overgrown with trails of bindweed and willow-herb 'to soften the desolation'.

Hilary knows what to expect. When the Clark children (in *When the Siren Wailed*) come to London in search of their mother, at the height of the blitz, they turn into the familiar street only to find that it no longer exists. The shock induces normal reactions of fainting, screaming and violent anger: Andy 'picked up some large stones and hurled them at where number 4 might have been'.

Judith Kerr's uncomplicated, agreeable heroine in *The Other Way Round* (1975; a sequel to *When Hitler Stole Pink Rabbit:* see above) 'did not think about what was happening in the war. There was nothing she could do about it. She did not read the papers and she did not listen when the news was on.' But Anna's indifference is not a permanent state of mind; she is temporarily disillusioned because the British government has seen fit to intern her brother. This highlights an anomaly of wartime justice, the fact that many German-born opponents of Hitler were detained in internment camps on suspicion of harbouring anti-English sympathies. ' "We've been fighting Hitler for years," [Anna's mother] shouted. "All the time when the English were saying what a fine gentleman he was. And now that the penny's finally dropped," she finished in tears, "the only thing they can do is to intern Max!" '

Max is released, however, in time to play his part in the war as a true British fighter pilot. Anna and her parents continue to lead a rather seedy, hard-up existence in refugee hotels. Her father, a celebrated German author who can't speak English, is one of those exasperatingly wise, impractical and sentimental gentlemen whose sensibilities must be respected at all costs. The reader's sympathies are with the irritable, tense mother who at least has the gumption to go out and get a job.

Like Gordon Cooper's novel, *The Other Way Round* covers all the years of the war without managing to render the intangible quality of the era: neither author is attuned to the vibrations of the age. (It is not enough simply to write of damaged buildings or of foolhardy or hysterical behaviour during an air raid.) In the second half of the book Judith Kerr comes up against one of the built-in difficulties of children's fiction: when the heroine is 21 or thereabouts, the juvenile mode has become inappropriate.

The wartime writers are usually conscientious about noting the small, significant alterations in everyday behaviour: the way people coming out of a shelter look round to see how much damage has been done in the night; the concern that ordinary, responsible people feel when they see unaccompanied children in the London streets. For the central characters of Jill Paton Walsh's *Fireweed* (1969) the latter reaction is merely officious, a threat to their freedom. Bill and Julie are a couple of runaway evacuees who exist briefly in a kind of dazed, idyllic stupor, evading their own social responsibilities and living for the moment with its physical and emotional risks. The boy has returned illicitly to London from a Welsh mountain farm, the girl has run away from Southampton where she should have boarded the doomed *City of Benares*.

The boy's bravado, the children's crazy indifference to an unexploded bomb, the make-believe sanctuary in a damaged basement, all compound the sense of unreality engendered by an abnormal situation. *Fireweed* has a poetic, ballad-like quality unique in children's fiction of the war. Devastated London emerges with its trails of wreckage, its inhabitants bewildered by the pressure of events and bemused with lack of sleep, its fantastic architectural patterns of broken buildings and slanting beams. It has become an unreal, remote city like Elizabeth Bowen's mysterious Kôr. The allegiances, habits and expectations of normal life are suspended, along with conventional ideas of security and order. People had to cherish what compensations they could find.

The mood of *Fireweed* is such that it cannot end well, in its moral sphere the emotions of guilt and fear of betrayal have arisen to complicate the fantasy of freedom and natural affinity transcending class preconceptions. Julie is really Miss Julia Vernon-Green; Bill is just a grammar-school boy, too ready to resent condescension that may not exist. Like the fireweed of the title their friendship grows on devastated ground. The book is a parable of a mode of surviving, a retreat into an abstract private domain. The imagery has two functions: to indicate how destruction and fear can promote individual escape routes, and to establish a real sense of a city at war. Children's fiction is not the place to look for defeatism or hysteria, of course; the most popular beliefs about wartime resilience (not necessarily ill-founded) are bound to be perpetuated in one form or another. Certainly in terms of representing indomitable spirit, the humour of understatement, repartee and pragmatic wit, which occurs in *Fireweed*, is preferable to the kind of quiet courage posited by Gordon Cooper (see above).

The determination to carry on is not an exclusively British characteristic. In *Fireweed* it is embodied in Marco, a friendly Italian restaurant owner whose premises are bombed. He immediately appears in the street with a handcart and a samovar. In fact Italians in England were in a particularly unfortunate position, especially in the months following the fall of France and the alliance of Italy with the axis powers. All over Britain, fish-and-chip shops and ice-cream parlours were attacked. Many foreigners were interned in camps where conditions were not pleasant. Occasionally there were out-breaks of racial intolerance in the country: in certain areas of the north, the words 'evacuees' and 'Jews' were used inter-changeably as a term of abuse. On this phenomenon a Mass-Observation report noted that 'all those who have run away are thought to be Jews'.

Julie was one of the children whose parents had arranged to send them as far as possible from the scene of war—a mis-judgement in the case of those whose children travelled on the *City of Benares*. '"It is only on the other side of the Atlantic that one can be *certain* of safety,"' remarks Eileen, mother of the heroine of Dorris Heffron's *Crusty Crossed* (1976). Tanis Kane, nicknamed Crusty on the voyage to Canada, is an overgrown eleven-year-old musical prodigy with a somewhat argumentative disposition. She and her sisters Harriet and

Vanessa spend the early war years in Nova Scotia, coping with the emotional discomforts of adolescence, adapting their Oxford airs and graces to fit in with a more primitive community and suffering inevitable psychological stress when they are summoned home. 'Our parents found our talk and tastes shocking and embarrassing.' This was one of the less significant problems caused by war, but it must have involved countless families in agonies of readjustment.

The oddity of living in wartime is expressed most cogently by Jane Gardam, a writer with a special feeling for jaunty, eccentric or wilful behaviour in adolescents. In *A Long Way From Verona* (1971) the energy and flow of the first-person narrative are controlled to exactly the right degree: Jessica Vye's reflections are never allowed to get out of hand, to become tedious, fey, unconvincing or slack. The setting is a northern seaside town; Jessica is a pupil at the local high school where the only evacuee is an unattractive girl named Cissie Comberbach: 'You could tell what a stupid sort of family she must have had to send her to a place like Teeside to get away from air raids.'

Pieces of wartime ephemera are inserted with judicious offhandedness in the narrative. 'When the war is OVER, Hitler will be DEAD,' the small children sing, as an accompaniment to their skipping games. But war functions only as a backdrop until the point when its violence is unleashed on Jessica, at that moment viewing a slum area in the company of a would-be social reformer, handsome Christian Fanshawe-Smithe. A daytime bomb is dropped on Dunedin Street, killing two children and precipitating Jessica into the front room of a house where a huge legless woman is sitting in an armchair, roaring with laughter. The whole episode is extraordinarily grotesque and funny. The author has effectively superimposed a succession of farcical events on a tragic basis, from the moment when intense, self-righteous Christian raises his arms to the sky and begins to shout like an apprentice preacher calling down ruin on the innocent street: '"Hell!" cried Christian, "Hell, hell, hell. I want to get rid of all this. I want to knock it down. Don't you see, it's got to be destroyed?"' With perfect timing, a piece of instant slum clearance is brought about. The subsequent odd behaviour of Jessica is plausibly a result of delayed shock, disillusion ('I thought of Christian sitting in the bus, looking straight forward, not waving as it bowled away') and imminent tonsillitis.

But the raid on Dunedin Street is only a preliminary, a kind of emotional testing ground, necessary to accustom Jessica to the horrible consequences of war. The really profound tragedy in the book is the death of Miss Philemon, senior English mistress at Jessica's school, dotty, intellectual and good-natured, killed when a crashing English plane unloads a bomb on her flat. Jessica's reticence about the event is entirely natural: by omission it puts the emphasis in the right place, given the episodic structure and the faint, persistent self-mockery of the girl's tone. She can describe the effects but not the sensations of shock and misery.

Not all town children in the south of England were evacuated; those whose homes were in the suburbs were considered safe enough, since each family was provided with its own air-raid shelter. The corrugated-iron Anderson shelters could be erected in the garden; the later Morrison was suitable for placing indoors. These contraptions could survive almost anything except a direct hit. In *Dawn of Fear* (Susan Cooper, 1970) a family sleeping in an indoor shelter is wiped out when a bomb falls on the house. This is the climax of the story. The dead boy, Peter, has been one of three friends whose view of the war is not serious; they are young enough to feel nothing but exhilaration when the bombing starts; there is no way for them to imagine that their own lives are at risk. It is not only children who feel a kind of spurious immunity from violent death; but in their case usually there is no rational knowledge to balance the feeling.

It is a commonplace of wartime fiction that Battle-of-Britain losses were presented in the manner of cricket scores, chalked up triumphantly on newsvendors' boards; and *Dawn of Fear* opens with the pure enjoyment of children in a school playground, witnessing the destruction of a German plane as though it were part of a sporting contest. The anger and anxiety of adults are meaningless: ' "You *stupid* boys, come under cover *at once*!" ' the teacher yells; but it is not until he stands looking at the ruin of Peter's house that Derek realizes 'the world was not normal after all'.

Many children in towns and cities made collections of war souvenirs, pieces of shrapnel, spent machine-gun bullets, nose-cones, tail-fins and so on. This habit provides a starting point for Robert Westall's *The Machine-Gunners* (1975), an exuberant re-creation of life on Tyneside in the winter of 1940–1941. School rivalries and natural lawlessness are given a new outlet in the conditions of war, and the book recognizes the obstructive potential of children on the rampage without underlining an implicit authoritarian attitude.

The children cause a great deal of damage, waste the time and energies of the police force and fail to exhibit a proper respect for teachers and parents. They steal a machine gun, in working order, from a wrecked German plane with a dead pilot sitting in the cockpit; they are not squeamish though later the hero Chas McGill is outraged when he finds that the school bully has abstracted the German's helmet. 'Chas broke out in a sweat and felt sick. Boddser had been through the dead man's pockets.'

Chas organizes the removal and concealment of the machine gun; he is helped by an evacuee from Glasgow, a boy named Cemetery Jones, pretty Benjamin Nichol ('Sicky Nicky') and tough Audrey Parton, 'the only girl who always had sticking plasters on her knees'. Finally they succeed in firing the gun from a specially constructed shelter in the garden of Nicky's bombed-out home: they aim at a German plane, miss it by miles but startle the pilot so much that he crashes. Rudi becomes the children's prisoner and this brings another wartime truism into the story: the recognition that Germans are human too.

All the elements of the plot converge at the point when the expected German invasion is thought to have taken place: the moment is one of extraordinary confusion and panic, with the cast finally sorted out into the well-meaning and the weak-kneed. The children are given the credit they deserve:

'I'll not say much for my lad,' said Mr McGill slowly, 'except he thought he was *fighting* the Germans.'

'Oh, hush,' said Mrs McGill, 'Chassy could have killed somebody.'

'I'm not talking about his sense, missus. I'm talking about his guts.'

This is an impressive story of incomprehension bordering on antipathy between the generations, in a world where the children recognize obligations only to one another and where spirit counts for more than caution or common sense. The final phrase, 'Get stuffed,' is a fitting gesture of defiance in the context; it is especially pointed since it is uttered by Nicky, the weakling.

The formidable old ladies of Tyneside have their own view of the enemy, 'the Jarmans': they 'always called Hitler "Hitler" and spoke about him as if he were a personal enemy, a bloody-minded neighbour who did sneaky things like tipping refuse over your garden fence.' There is no mawkishness or false camaraderie in this book: war does not soften the heads or hearts of the ordinary inhabitants of the dockside streets, or cause them to elevate a common objective on to an heroic plane.

The episode of the German prisoner is a small but significant part of the theme.

'What are we going to *do*?' screamed Cem. 'He's a *Nazi*.'

'He's no sae like a proper Nazi,' said Clogger dubiously. And indeed the tattered wretch before them was not much like those black shiny-booted storm-troopers who goose-stepped nightly through their dreams.

In retrospective children's fiction the crashed Germans are never menacing; their function is usually to promote at least a rudimentary tolerance for individual members of the enemy forces, to indicate that the other side is equally vulnerable and pathetic, to show that enmity between nations is not a clear-cut and absolute matter. This approach, of course, is far more refined and admirable than the standard contemporary sacrifice of realism to propaganda, when every German who appeared was a sadistic thug, totally indoctrinated with the ideals of Nazism. But sometimes the children who befriend the wounded Nazis have complex motives, neither purely humanitarian nor dictated solely by a craving for adventure, a natural wish to involve themselves in a clandestine operation. For the young heroine of *Willow's Luck* (Gabriel Alington, 1977), cooped up in the country without friends of her own age, the

I

discovery of an enemy airman is a stroke of good fortune, providing an occupation and a sense of purpose. 'Finding him had been the strangest, the most overwhelming thing that had ever happened to her.'

She acts from instinctive sympathy to begin with; but gradually an ulterior selfishness begins to affect the shaping of Willow's plans. She tries to simplify the relationship, to bring it into line with childish ideas of affection based on an exchange of tokens. Of course in the circumstances it has implications that she cannot fully understand. When she buys cleaning materials to scrub out a caravan in the woods, a new home for 'Von', the whole exercise has entered the realm of make-believe. Willow is deluding herself: her prime concern is not the German's welfare, but her own need for a friend. Her own private war is against the enemies creeping up on Von. Finally she heads for the wood with a demented scheme for 'running away'; but it is too late, a bomb falls, setting the caravan on fire, and Von is shot while trying to escape.

' "You have caused a great deal of worry, Willow," ' her great-uncle remarks; it is a very mild chastisement. But the child's misdemeanour has been slight in moral terms, grounded in her own rather pathetic situation; she merely lets her emotions get out of hand, treating the pleasant friendship as a gift for her amusement, without real thought for the wounded airman.

German soldiers detached from the main body of the army, stranded on alien territory and dependent for their lives on the kindness of children: these indeed are proper subjects for pity, they have no connection with the image of grim ruthlessness evoked by the concept of Hitler's storm-troopers marching victoriously through Europe. In *The Missing German* (David Rees, 1976) the hero Simon thinks of the atrocity stories of Guernica, Warsaw, Rotterdam, London: 'Three thousand dead in one night's raid. . . . He'd been there, huddling in the Anderson out in the garden while the planes roared and the bombs exploded. . . .' But it is no good, these images have receded in his consciousness, they are of less significance than the immediate ethical problem, and the practical problem of finding a hideout for a German sailor—Stefan, the only uncaptured survivor from a wrecked submarine, whom two

English teenagers have discovered on a Devon beach. His helplessness prompts their initial response: and their failure to hand him at once to the proper authorities leads to a situation of hopeless complexity.

'"If you accept that a war is worth fighting, then you mustn't let pity for the enemy affect your actions,"' a character in *Backwater War* (see below) pronounces. But it is not easy for ordinary people to accept so complete a reversal of the humanitarian conditioning of peacetime. It is more difficult, too, when the enemy in question is not incapacitated and therefore liable to return to the sphere of action.

Keith and Simon are paying guests at a Devon farmhouse— devious and open-handed respectively, the scrawny, irritable scholar and the outdoor boy. The types are recognizable in broad outline—that is all the reader is given—and an inevitable conflict of personalities ensues. The issue is complicated by the fact that Keith is half-German—his mother is interned—and it is he who makes the first move to protect Stefan. Simon is childishly affronted by the unfairness of it all: '"I've been . . . dragged into it, haven't I? Completely against my will."' But gradually a complete *volte-face* occurs, with Simon whole- heartedly on the side of the German while Keith holds back. It is Keith who turns to the nearest sensible adult when things get out of hand, while Simon and Stefan embark on a romantic, purposeless flight.

The Missing German is a competent adventure story, but none of its more subtle implications is followed up. The radical concepts of treachery and humanitarianism, and the edges where each shades into the other, are not explored. There is an implicit homosexual element in the attraction between Simon and Stefan but it is hardly acknowledged. None of the technical devices helpful for generating atmosphere, an oblique sense of another era, has been used.

The epigraph, appropriately enough, is taken from Wilfred Owen's 'Strange Meeting': '. . . and one sprang up, and stared/With piteous recognition in fixed eyes'. It is appropriate, that is, to the content if not to its treatment: the latter is altogether inadequate to suggest depth in any of the issues raised. Perhaps the most significant point in the book is made by Keith, at a moment when Simon's patriotism is still in the ascendant: '"You're the real German," said Keith, slowly. "Look at you. Blond, blue-eyed, prancing around in shorts. Hitler youth. They're the type who'd say turn him in, kill him."' Nazism is thereby identified as a state of mind, a disposition towards brutal or evil behaviour, distinct from its use as a classificatory term for the ideological beliefs of Hitler's armies. Keith's pronouncement has a basic irony, of course, in relation to subsequent events; but this is too simple and obvious to be effective, even in the context of a children's story. The theme demands a more thoughtful elaboration.

Serious themes in children's fiction are usually weakened in the long run by the fact that the central characters need not, in the fullest sense, take responsibility for their actions. As a last resort there is always a symbolic adult ready to understand, to make allowances, to protect the children from the consequences of misguided behaviour. Only in the American novel *Summer of My German Soldier* (Bette Greene, 1973) does the twelve-year-old heroine end in a reformatory, sentenced to six months for giving shelter to an escaped prisoner-of-war. Patty Bergen is a Jewish girl of ferocious integrity and resilience, a victim of emotional maltreatment and parental restriction but gifted none the less with a transcending courage and intelligence that enables the novel to end on an optimistic note. For the young heroes and heroines of more conventional fiction, there is usually movement forward in a psychological sense, a re-arrangement of priorities and a broadening of outlook to accommodate the adult values of tolerance, compromise and consideration for every aspect of a problem.

Germans wounded, bewildered and at a loss present a counterpoint to the highly organized and efficient spy networks that featured so prominently in children's stories of the 1940s (see Chapter X). An extraordinarily unrealistic view of spies was propagated, in story after story, when the children's suspicions turn out to be well-founded; and even when they are mistaken a tangible benefit to the country invariably ensues as a side-effect of the initial blunder. In *Wraggle Taggle War* (June Oldham, 1977), children are at it again, reading a dire significance into the use of a foreign phrase, investing the delivery of a parcel with subversive overtones, opting all along the line for mystification instead of elucidation. They get everything wrong:

the young German-speaking evacuee, 'that Madge', is not a spy but a Jewish refugee from Hitler's Germany; Miss Fawkes in spite of her name has no traitorous intentions; there is no plot afoot to free the prisoners from a near-by camp. The local youngsters, including the narrator, Judd, look pretty silly when the facts come out; and in accordance with the spirit of present-day fiction there is no last-page reversal of fortunes, no contrived incident like the apprehension of a prisoner to give a spurious justification to the children's conduct.

The children belong to a group of country lads, lower-class, village-school types who respond with crude antagonism to the arrival of a busload of evacuees. 'Welcome was the last thought in our heads and not a word that was exactly over-used in our conversation. . . . "Numb bums!" Tom jeered, dispelling any notion the party may have been forming that we were country squires.'

For some reason, June Oldham has chosen to lumber herself with a first-person narrative, a form that requires particular discipline and singleness of purpose to bring it off (it works brilliantly in the cases of Jane Gardam and Jill Paton Walsh; see above). In *Wraggle Taggle War* there is obtrusive disjunction between the vernacular and descriptive styles of the assumed persona; the dialogue is lively and colloquial, while the connecting passages are written in a careful, facetious, quasi-pompous manner that does not accord with the boy's supposed personality.

The use of real spies in the genre has fortunately declined, its unwarrantable simplifications going strongly against the grain of all degrees of realism currently in fashion. When foreign agents appear there is an accompanying effect of bathos; paradoxically a feeling of tedium is the most usual response to the idea of a children's thriller. (It needs, to succeed, fast movement combined with a special originality of approach, a quality suited to no other genre, like the fantasy element in Catherine Storr's *The Chinese Egg*.) *Dark River, Dark Mountain* (Sylvia Sherry, 1975) is a spy story that is close in spirit to the obsolete juvenile fiction of the war era. In 1940 Colin North is fourteen, a farm worker evacuated privately from Tyneside to a village west of the Pennines. Fears of invasion and the consequent hysterical rush to identify potential collaborators are the deep preoccupations of the inhabitants of Wenningborough. Soon Colin is invited to join a secret 'auxiunit'—an imaginary offshoot of the home guard, set up by the government 'to make sure there's sabotage after the invasion's completed'. '"This is not a game, feller,"' Colin's informant tells him; '"We have our own way of dealing with blabber-mouths".'

The clichéd, melodramatic language is the book's most serious shortcoming; but it fails also to generate the least sense of excitement or even curiosity for the reader. Its familiar, discredited set pieces are produced without enthusiasm. It is all dull, leaden, expected: the beautiful foreign double agent, the taciturn prime mover of the spy network, a man knee deep in cow dung when he isn't arranging for the reception of enemy parachutists. The narrator is the grown-up Colin, come back to lay a ghost and to see that the wartime episode has a tidy if belated ending.

The ghost is that of French Marthe, the double agent, trapped fiendishly in an underground cave and left to moulder; 'remote, strange and beautiful' Marthe, object of Colin's juvenile affections. '"Oh, you are such a fool. You English— you do not know how to fight!"' she tells him. '"How do you fight a war with no emotions?"'

Her own emotions are expressed in jerks, allusions, broken-off phrases bristling with significance. She behaves throughout in the accepted manner of a foreign adventuress with no sense of humour, defective English and very little verbal control. Colin is another stock figure: the earnest, infatuated, unintelligent but basically sensitive and well-meaning lad at a difficult age. The 'I' of the story, the adult Colin, displays all the vulgarity of a person deluded about his own sensibility: 'Whatever was strange, remote, and outside my normal experience attracted me like a magnet, as did the lonely and isolated.'

The interesting aspect of the 'wounded German' stories is the ethical dilemma in which the authors' protagonists are involved. When the person in need of help is a Nazi victim, on the other hand, there is no question of a conflict of loyalties and the proper mode of action is predetermined. There is nothing at issue but the risk, which no right-minded person will shirk, the practical dangers of detection and reprisal. In Peggy

Woodford's *Backwater War* (1974) a Polish prisoner of war
escapes from a Todt labour camp on Guernsey (located there
for purposes of the story; a foreword explains that the only
prison camps in the Channel Islands were situated on Alderney)
and makes a direct appeal to a family that has remained on the
island throughout the German occupation. They take him in;
though the burden of concealment falls on the daughter Anna
and later on her restless, belligerent companion Fred Ahier.
Three boys, including the Pole, Marek, plan to leave for
England in a small boat in order to join the British army. In the
middle of the preparations Anna naturally complains of a
feeling of uselessness and exclusion and Fred's response is not
tactful:

> 'Why take over someone who could not immediately be used
> to fight the war. Waste of valuable space.'
> 'Damn you, Fred. You really have the knack of making me
> feel small.'
> 'Women can't fight.' Fred looked puzzled by Anna's
> emotion. 'You can only play a secondary part.'

Fred's perceptions are not subtle (a point made subtly by the
author in her choice of name: 'Fred' has unmistakable connotations); he is one of those downright, stolid characters who
believe in speaking one's mind, for whom women have a fixed,
inferior rôle to play when their presence is not actively dis-
tracting. '"Women will always play an unimportant part in
his life,"' Marek observes; but Marek is not altogether
impartial.

An emotional tangle has resulted from the proximity of the
three main characters. It is not a vital part of the plot, merely a
natural complication that could not be avoided. All three
behave well, according to their respective standpoints. Anna's
preference has always been for Fred, although 'you're so much
nicer', she tells Marek in a tone of despair. It is the old in-
explicable working of a sexual force, and its effects are observed
with a fair degree of accuracy, though one might have hoped
for a less traditional predilection in courageous Anna. She
plays her part, her value is acknowledged even by uncouth
Fred, and she is left at home to remain placid and stoical.

'People who get left behind often have the worst of it', according
to Marek; but this trite gesture of sympathy does not provide
much consolation. As a reward, Anna has nothing to look
forward to but a coded telegram, informing her that the boys
have succeeded in joining the British forces.

There is no organized resistance in Guernsey, nothing along
the lines of the French maquis. The Channel Islands had been
demilitarized before the arrival of the Germans and as a consequence the occupation was effected with comparative mildness.
The Gestapo was not sent in.

The resistance in France has provided dramatic material for
fiction at every level from Simone de Beauvoir's *The Blood of
Others* to the weekly children's papers of the Amalgamated
Press. But it has not yet caught the imagination of recent
children's writers in England; here, the home front continues
to exercise a more profound fascination, with intermittent
gestures of recognition for the plight of Jews. One highly
organized children's story of the war in France, however, is
available here in translation: Paul Berna's *They Didn't Come
Back* (1969), a present-day reconstruction of a wartime incident still reverberating to produce discord in a south-eastern
rural community.

On a night in August 1944 100 maquisards have disappeared
without trace in the forest of Chabrières. It is left to a group of
children, 25 years later, to find out what became of them, to
reject the impossible and sift out the distortions in the evidence
of survivors, some of these concocted deliberately from the best
of motives. The children are mostly new arrivals, all connected
with a factory that has been built in the area; they have no
preconceptions and suffer no emotional constraints. An obvious
advantage of the 25-year gap is that it enables them to piece
together the story from opposing sources. From Lieutenant
Richter, a German ex-officer stationed in the district in the
summer of 1944, they learn of a 'dull rumble' followed by an
earth tremor: some time later its cause is identified as an underground explosion and by now the children have gained
complete knowledge of the circumstances in which it came
about.

The theme of historical detection, the clearing-up of a
mystery in the past, is an important one in children's fiction. It

appeals to the imagination, it shows how research can be made palatable, it provides an especially satisfactory means of resolution for parallel strands in the plot, enriching each by reference to its counterpart. It may be treated as a matter of straightforward curiosity (Gillian Avery's *The Warden's Niece*), obsessive interest (K. M. Peyton's *A Pattern of Roses*; Edward Chitham's *Ghost in the Water*) or supernatural compulsion (Nina Beachcroft's *Cold Christmas*). In Paul Berna's story the children's task is made easier by the fact that survivors are still around to be consulted; but it is complicated too by the undiminished tension, suspicions and fears in the surrounding villages that an act of treachery has been committed. In the end the countryside is provided with a valid legend (the French title is *Un Pays Sans Legende*); the lost partisans are discovered inside the mountain, composed like statues in a dramatic group, felicitously preserved by a coating of limestone that has dripped from the roof of the cave on to bodies immobilized by the blast.

An overtly retrospective viewpoint is adopted also in two excellent English novels for children, *Carrie's War* (Nina Bawden, 1973) and *Going Back* (Penelope Lively, 1975). Widowed Carrie has come with her children to revisit the Welsh mining town where she and her brother spent the first year of the war, forlorn evacuees billeted on Mr and Miss Evans, the former a chapel-goer given to displaying notices that state relentlessly 'The Eye of the Lord is Upon You'. But the little girl and her brother Nick are a well-brought-up, adaptable pair. Carrie is anxious and thoughtful, wanting the best for everyone but too intelligent to be a doormat; Nick is a little ingenuous and fickle, a pretty, greedy boy who isn't above emotional blackmail. The children manage to endear themselves to timid, silly Miss Evans and soon cease to miss their own mother, now driving an ambulance in Glasgow to be accessible to her husband, a naval officer on convoy duty in the North Sea.

These details are provided merely to account for the children's stay in Wales: this is the exclusive subject of the fiction. The middle section of the book is given over to Carrie's reminiscences (with the author remaining as narrator), with a little group of pleasantly eccentric characters at the centre of the theme. The war remains firmly in the background; it is used in this case simply as a device to get the parents out of the way, like the ailing relative of earlier fiction. (Actually, a sick grandmother does come into the story at a later point, to explain the circumstances of the children's early departure from Wales.) 'Carrie thought of bombs falling, of the war going on all this year they'd been safe in the valley; going on over

Illustration by Faith Jacques for
Carrie's War, by Nina Bawden, 1973

their heads like grown-up conversation when she'd been too small to listen.'

In Penelope Lively's story the grown-up narrator is continuously present; since the subject is memory there is no need to simulate immediacy or to project the disjointed, evolving personality of a young girl. Unlike Jessica Vye (see above), for example, Penelope Lively's Jane is not concerned with the quirks and distinctions of her own nature. Jessica's moodiness and candour are active ingredients of the plot; married Jane is fundamentally, and in a sense defensively, detached from the child whose experiences she recounts.

The act of memory is sparked off by a visit to Medleycott, the Somerset house where motherless Jane and her brother Edward grew up in the war, a period blighted only by the visits of their soldier father, home on leave to impose his will on the household in a peculiarly insensitive manner. The childhood of Jane and Edward is otherwise idyllic, especially since it has been perfected by distance. The quality of perfection, however, is not absolute in a vapid or sentimental way; the narrator is fully aware of the fusions and distortions of time, the false emphasis and the tricks of memory that can give to a trivial event a delusive significance.

> There was a war on, people said. They said it like a refrain, like 'touchwood' or 'cross-my-heart', so that you stopped hearing it. . . . There was a war on, but the Somerset hills encircled the house and the garden just as they always had done, and the pink lanes tipped up and down between the high hedges full of toadflax and foxgloves.

War brings Pam and Susie, the land girls; a disappointment to well-read children who had confused a land girl with a water nymph, but soon accepted in their own right. It brings evacuees to the village, ill-dressed Stepney urchins who 'bravely claimed for themselves a place in this remote and alien world to which they had been brought by strangers'. It brings twenty-year-old Mike, a student of music turned into a farm worker, a conscientious objector whom the unmilitary children idolize. '"I think Mike's brave," shouted Edward. "I don't think he's a coward at all. Only stupid people think that."'

This isolated act of defiance results in bed for the children, without supper; in a brief banishment to ordinary life, with aunts and cousins and lessons in decorum and scripture; finally in boarding school for Edward, a way of life made unendurable by a sense of loss, the loss of Medleycott, so that he is driven to the frantic expedient of running purposelessly away.

He runs *from* Medleycott rather than go back to school. He and Jane set out for the farm where Mike is working, twenty miles distant; sleeping like fairy-tale children in a ruined cottage, covered in dust and dead leaves; reassuring one another with dwindling conviction; watching a film, with guilty enjoyment, for an hour in the afternoon. Mike sends them home, of course; but the ploy has paid off. They gain a year's respite.

And the war goes on. 'Somewhere else, in London and over there in France, in the world of voices that read the nine o'clock news out of Betty's wireless, other things were happening. The grown-ups used the same words over and over again: Dunkirk, General de Gaulle, the Blitz.' The words are a refrain or an incantation, unconnected with real events. War is part of a pattern of childhood, distant and precise, summoned up in a series of delicate evocations that underline, in Elizabeth Bowen's phrase, 'the eternity of a remembered scene'. Or, as Penelope Lively puts it: 'there is time past, and time to come, and time that is continuous, in the head for ever.'

In children's fiction too there are experiments with time, ways of elaborating a fantasy of continuousness at a level of actuality. Time-travelling is an accepted convention in the genre. At the time of writing, however, only two authors have taken the years of the second world war to provide a suitable time-slip from the present: the era has just become sufficiently distant to justify the intense strangeness of the experience, its supernatural dislocations.

The titles are plainly descriptive: *Time To Go Back* (1972), written by a prolific popular children's author, Mabel Esther Allen, and *Now and Then* (Geraldine Symons, 1977). In a sense they embody opposing literary failings. The former is crammed with incident, it has a trite romantic bias and the technical problems involved in the time-shift structure have simply failed to interest the author (there is none of the scrupulous care that went into the construction of Penelope Farmer's *Charlotte Sometimes*, for instance: see Chapter VI). *Now and Then* is far more literate, restrained and effective; it has a slightly static quality, however, a lack of inner excitement, a sensation of slow movement at both ends of the time span.

Sarah Farrant, heroine of *Time To Go Back*, develops a mild obsession with her dead aunt Lark Ellesmere, poet and school teacher, killed at 21 in one of the German raids on Liverpool. 'That old war!' Sarah muses in chapter one. 'It was always on television in one way or another, but I had always thought of it as just part of history.' A girl with such a silly, complacent view of the war deserves to be made to suffer it, as Sarah is; but the experience doesn't alter the banality of her reflections. 'It was so amazing to be there at all, to be in the thick of it and witnessing such calm courage.'

Sarah's position is rather peculiar: '*Could* I be killed before I was born?' she wonders, making nonsense of the whole theme. In the past she wears her own clothes and behaves as though she were on an excursion. She is not provided with a gas mask and this should have made her conspicuous, but in fact the deficiency is not mentioned until the penultimate chapter:

'You should always wear your gas mask. You never do.'
'I—I forgot it,' I muttered.

The pseudo-poetic name of Sarah's aunt is a warning: the book is written in the bland, heart-felt style of teenage magazine fiction. 'I think war is worse in May. It seems so unnatural when the world is beautiful. More beautiful than usual, I mean.' Of present-day Liverpool Sarah remarks that it 'had a raw vitality that was rather exciting. No wonder it gave birth to the Beatles and to so many others who understood rhythm.' But bathos is a natural effect of the would-be sensitive tone.

The moments of convergence of different times or unnatural propulsion from one decade to another should properly be rendered as moments of special intensity, hallucination or sheer panic and bewilderment. In the case of Jassy (heroine of *Now and Then*), however, the transition is effected with ease; she has only to walk down the garden to find herself chronologically dislocated, back in wartime England with its unfamiliar restrictions and emergencies. Like Willow Stubbs (see above) Jassy is isolated, slightly at a loose end until a young man appears to give purpose and interest to her days. He is no wounded German, however, but an English aristocrat about to leave for Europe on a dangerous wartime mission. The theme is unnecessarily complicated by the inclusion of a twin brother; naturally Jassy is disconcerted, though not repelled, by Piers's apparent changes of character.

Jassy behaves with decorum and courage throughout. When two dogs are killed by a blast from a German bomb she overcomes her natural squeamishness and helps to bury them. She doesn't panic when she finds an enemy pilot asleep in a wood. She crawls through a horrid pipe underneath a stream when the irresponsible twin dares her to. But the supernatural strand is underplayed; in Jassy's real world these people have been dead for 30 years, the house is unoccupied, the cucumber frames unused and the lawn divested of its croquet hoops. Jassy's matter-of-fact acceptance of her ability to skip backwards and forwards is slightly off-key and unconvincing. Again, as in *Willow's Luck*, the lack of other children seems strange— *would* there have been country places not overrun with evacuees? The mood of one era is not noticeably distinct from that of the other; at a naturalistic level, however, the mild damp pleasant atmosphere of rivers and meadows is unchanging, and it is palpably conveyed.

In the majority of the stories discussed above, the lives of children in wartime have been subjected to imaginative and conscientious scrutiny. War meant in one way or another an ending of security, a disruption of family life and easy hopes for the future. In some cases there is withdrawal from the historical events into private worlds but this is a natural consequence of childhood in any case. In real life, there was an increase in political awareness, at least in broad outline: for once every child in the country must have known the name of the prime minister and had a rough idea of his home and foreign policies. Every child knew how he or she could contribute to the national effort: largely it was a matter of carrying on, of adopting the right attitudes in relation to the major priority and putting up willingly with deprivations and inconveniences.

In present-day fiction there is no need for endings to be invariably happy: missing relatives are not always alive and well off-stage; father does not have to appear on the last page to restore the family's fortunes. In wartime, even children can be killed and this is freely acknowledged in fiction for all age groups. Of course the authors' general conclusions must still be positive and optimistic, but currently the emphasis in this respect is on psychological adjustment or degrees of comprehension. Real emotions are recognized and placed in context— for example, the real desire of adolescent boys to achieve a sense of personal worth by joining in the actual fighting.

Certain images have become so strongly connected with the war era that it is possible to use them in fiction to conjure up a whole set of related ideas. Poor children at a railway station, for instance, tearful or defiant, clutching their belongings in pillow-cases or paper bags, name-tags pinned on their coats and cumbersome gas masks on straps draped horizontally across their chests: this is the typical view of evacuees. Less mundane, perhaps, but more easily adapted to various dramatic purposes is the crashed airman, a symbolic figure whose implications are subtler than those associated with earlier invincible heroes like Captain W. E. Johns's Biggles (see Chapter IV). In fact the crass, inflated hero is completely out of fashion, surviving only in the war comics which need not be considered seriously. The serious stories are all attempts, in various ways, to record the realities of the period.

XII

IN THE SOMBRE SEASON

Recent Adult Fiction of the Second World War

Old jaundiced knights jog listlessly to town
To fight for love in some unreal war.
                                    Alun Lewis, 'Autumn 1939'

SINCE THE WORLD wars have passed out of the sphere of immediate history a natural tendency has developed to regard them as providing material suitable for historical fiction, a genre that still retains connotations of the sub-literary. However, in certain cases important contemporary novelists have turned to the theme of war from the standpoint of the present day, adopting an historical approach to investigate the societies in which war was possible, reconstructing and examining general attitudes through the medium of a particular sensibility, pointing the contrast between current social values and those which may have existed at a given time in the past.

Mass-Observation reports have charted the difference between on-the-spot impressions of air raids, to take that as an example, and subsequent recollections of the same events. In the latter there is a tendency to minimize the remembered sensations of fear and confusion; naturally heroic defiance, high spirits and resilience are brought to the fore. It is not a matter of falsification, merely a shift of emphasis; and this is true also of most retrospective fiction, though in an opposing sense. In the case of subjective memories the distance in time has a mellowing effect; for the novelist looking back for the purpose of recreation, on the other hand, distance often means productive disenchantment. When a period has been completed, of course, it can be viewed with a kind of objectivity; its stresses and effects are accorded varying degrees of prominence in relation to an overall scheme. As we have seen, a number of critics believed that a national crisis produced pressures inimical to art; and certainly in a time of war there is a new outlet for emotional writing. For the serious novelist, however, the ability to observe and assess is hardly likely to be submerged in an onrush of feeling, patriotic or otherwise. It is only the weaker novelists and the propaganda writers whose work will be radically affected by popular sentiments.

Retrospective fiction of the wars has an obvious advantage in the fact that its authors are enabled to add a layer of implicit social comment in relation to present-day beliefs. In some cases the author's stand-point is overtly in the present time: the objective is to trace the long-term effects of a wartime experience (Nina Bawden's *Anna Apparent*, for example). Usually, however, there is complete apparent identification with the historical modes of feeling and behaviour.

The second world war is 25 years or so closer to the present climate of realism, disabusement and irony in the novel. It is less remote than the first war, more accessible to memory—and these are factors that make it an easier subject for treatment in modern terms. At the same time, the period has acquired a technical interest, partly derived from the pressures of nostalgia, partly sociological in bias. In one sense, public and private events fall into a new kind of order in retrospection, even when it is the novelist's imagination and not the memory that is being exercised. In Anthony Powell's major sequence of novels *A Dance to the Music of Time* the natural patterns of convergence and dissolution are formalized, though the structure retains a necessary flexibility to accommodate the vast scale of the narrator's experience. The single unchanging quality is the self-effacement of the narrator, Nick Jenkins. (The method is almost precisely the opposite to that of Dorothy Richardson in a similar sequence of twelve volumes entitled *Pilgrimage*; in her case it is the inner consciousness of the central character that acts as a filter for the experience. Nick is the observer and recorder of other people's behaviour.)

In the wartime volumes of *A Dance to the Music of Time* the emphasis is naturally enough on army life; but there are some illuminating civilian intermissions. At the Café Royal, 'the large tasteless room looked unfamiliar occupied by figures in uniform'. This observation is the prelude to an evening of spectacular abnormality, in which two of Nick Jenkins's dining companions, husband and wife, are killed in separate bomb attacks. Restless, indiscreet Priscilla Tolland—Nick's sister-in-law—is wiped out 'at Lady Molly's'. The whole episode is rendered with telling detachment; though naturally in this case and others the impact of the violent deaths is felt most strongly by readers addicted to Anthony Powell's narrative.

One of the least accountable figures of the later volumes appears in wartime, in *The Military Philosophers* (1968): Pamela Flitton, at this point an ATS driver, already exercising a notable capacity to project around her a sense of discord and violence, 'a cosmic rage with life'. Pamela is continually cross, abrupt, wilful and virulent. Too relentless for an *enfant terrible*, she is none the less given to uttering proclamations of a disconcerting rudeness or perversity. To cause the maximum inconvenience at social occasions she brings up her lunch in fonts and urns. Marriage to insufferable Widmerpool and ultimate involvement in a necrophilic relationship are in store for Pamela Flitton, a girl of startling appearance and dark inclinations, whose presentation is never weakened by a softening in the narrative view.

She is so loath to conform to ideas of ordinary behaviour that she strolls out in London in the middle of an air raid, like any tedious silly girl avid for notice. But Pamela Flitton is altogether on a more rarefied plane than this. Equally farouche in war or peace, destructive of personal relations, arrogant in the most formidable and uncompromising way, she is isolated in a state of superb waywardness, beyond moral assessment. At the moment—surely one of the most effective in modern literature—when Nick Jenkins is told of the manner in which she has met her death, dramatic irony is at work and also a sharply concentrated feeling for the importance of the felicitous conclusion. Pamela Flitton's exit is conducted with powerful reference to the black undercurrents in her nature.

Other characters in wartime make 'violent readjustments' in their personal and public demeanour. Several peripheral women put on inelegant garments to drive ambulances or work at service canteens. In some cases change is for the better: 'Her manner . . . so out of place in ordinary social relations, had . . . come into its own.' The usual complaints about women's behaviour are voiced by the appropriate characters: '"If there's one thing I hate, it's a woman who lowers herself in that sort of way. I'm afraid there are quite a few of them about in wartime."' And, at the other extreme, at once crass and pathetic: '"I've never had a free poke in my life," he said. "Subject doesn't seem to arise when you're talking to a respectable woman."' In the army as elsewhere the most important quality in a woman is her degree of physical attractiveness. A pretty girl in uniform 'was something rather different from, more exciting than, the intermittent pretty secretary or waitress of peacetime, perhaps more subtly captivating from a sense that you and she belonged to the same complicated organism, in this case the army.'

In Brian Moore's *The Emperor of Ice-Cream* (1965) war comes to Belfast, and the issue is complicated by the Catholic/ Protestant divisions in the city. Seventeen-year-old Gavin Burke is the central character who joins the ARP in opposition to his family's wishes. '"Gracious God," Aunt Liz said. "Did I ever think I'd live to see the day when my own nephew would stand in this room dressed up like a Black and Tan."' Gavin's troubles proliferate on all fronts: his uniform trousers are too big and he trips over them, he fails his exams and upsets his father, his girl-friend is a good Catholic who refuses to sleep with him, an opportunity for sexual experiment is bungled when he is sick down the front of his jacket—and the author makes an amusing story of all this. Gavin's loss of faith is treated with rueful humour: this isn't one of those intense Irish novels of painful apostasy. But its theme at more than one level is serious none the less.

Gavin is regarded with contempt by his relatives who affect to believe that Hitler will never bother to attack an outpost like Northern Ireland. At the same time, Catholic nationalists make a point of ignoring the blackout regulations, hoping that German bombers will be guided by the lights that they show illegally. Of course they get more than they bargained for. When the bombing starts the Falls Road is hit as well as the Shankill, there is a sudden exodus of Catholics who head for the neutral south, and a great deal of venom on the part of working-class Protestants who hold the IRA directly respon- sible for the blitz.

Gavin is young enough to react with suppressed glee to the declaration of war, though this attitude is slightly defensive: his own failures will be of no account in a world that is devastated anyway. Then, he sees the war as a vindication of the poets' prophecies:

> We shall go down like paleolithic man
> Before some new ice age or Genghiz Khan

MacNeice wrote. But Gavin keeps his anarchic feelings to himself. 'How could you tell him [his brother Owen] that for you, the war was an event which had produced in you a shameful secret excitement, a vision of the grown-ups' world in ruins?' And, when the bombers finally come, he is conscious of nothing but elation: 'History had conferred the drama of war on this dull, dead town in which he had been born.' Still, he acquits himself well, working with courage and efficiency to get the wounded to hospital, and volunteering to help put the dead in coffins, 'a nasty job'.

Gavin's dominant characteristic is a wry good-natured self-assertiveness and this is matured effectively in the course of the story. The boy 'grows up'; the war acts as a kind of initiatory rite, or at least it provides the conditions in which his natural integrity can find a tangible outlet.

There has been little interest in recent fiction in the type of woman suited to army life. There is something depressing and unglamorous about the women's services in peacetime, an overwhelming idea of drabness and regimentation, and this is carried backwards to apply even at the period when conscription was in force. In the rare case of a woman who would have come into her own in uniform there is often a reason why she has failed to acquire one:

> When Wanda walked into this headquarters or that, and demanded her right to help her country, there would be so much shifting of weights and pressures behind closed doors that even Wanda could not persevere. Why? Because she carried a Party card and named her child after the blood of martyrs? How could that be? Was not Russia our ally? Nevertheless, there it was. She, who would have looked so good in Air Force glory, or Wren gloss, or even A.T.S. norm, had to do without.

Down Among the Women (1971), Fay Weldon's episodic, coy and bitter novel of female life, is set mainly in the early 1950s but moves forward and backward in time. The women are all misguided, often through no fault of their own, victims of circumstances and social conditioning, making gestures of protest that are largely futile and sordid. They marry, if at all, for the wrong reasons. They whine and rage and behave deviously and badly. They get what they want, but remain unhappy. Their intelligence, or ability to foresee the outcome of a move, stops short exactly at the point where it is about to become of practical use. They are all duped in one respect or another.

Characters and incidents are naturally selected to suit the author's purpose, in this case to emphasize the muddle and emotional havoc that can result from the pursuit of a false ideal or a lack of control in social life. But the novel has a sentimental aspect in its implication of a general state of debasement or disaffection and the more-or-less instinctively passive behaviour of its cast. The *use* of women is a valid cause for resentment but these women are certainly not blameless, or only when they can be reduced to complete anonymity:

Let us praise, for example, truckloads of young Cairo girls, ferried in for the use of the troops, crammed into catacombs beneath the desert floor.... Where are their post-war treats; their grants, their demob suits, their cheering crowds? Come re-union day, where have they gone? Lost to syphilis, death or drudgery. Those girls, other girls, scooped up from all the great cities of East and West, Cairo, Saigon, Berlin, Rome. Where are their memorials? Where are they remembered, prayed for, honoured? Didn't they do their bit?

A more enigmatic and stylish group of characters is found in Muriel Spark's *The Girl of Slender Means* (1963). The end of the war is still some months away; and in the garden of the May of Teck hostel in Kensington lies an unexploded bomb. Naturally it will go up at a crucial point in the narrative, to provide a moment of dénouement. In the meantime the residents, girls of good family but deficient income, pool their resources to create an effect of aplomb. In the prevailing conditions of scarcity, rationing of food and clothes, an apparent spirit of communism exists at the May of Teck where a solitary evening dress is shared out among the self-possessed inhabitants of the top floor.

The underlying tone is sharp and mocking: as usual Muriel Spark has arranged an elaborate joke for her readers, in this case based on an incident that is given more significance than it can well sustain. The bomb goes up, fire breaks out and the girls on the top floor are trapped; slim Selina, who has escaped through a tiny window, goes back to rescue the Schiaparelli dress and this event has a profound effect on her lover Nicholas Farringdon, whose conversion to Catholicism perhaps dates from the moment when he saw Selina on the roof with the dress in her arms.

The trick is to present the serious or metaphysical matter in light or humorous terms, to comment on obvious absurdities by appearing to go along with them. In *The Hothouse by the East River* (1973) Muriel Spark's fantasy moves on to a supernatural plane, like that of *The Comforters* and *Memento Mori*, and the basic postulation has an enriching ambiguity that adds greatly to the macabre effect of the humour. In the last war, a V2 bomb demolishes the rear end of a train pulling out of St Pancras Station, killing a number of passengers who had been engaged in specialized war work at the Compound, 'a small outpost of British Intelligence in the heart of the countryside'.

. . . In the summer of 1944, [Paul] is telling his son, life was more vivid than it is now. Everything was more distinct. The hours of the day lasted longer. One lived excitedly and dangerously. There was a war on. . . .

'We really lived our life,' says Paul.

Paul Hazlett, his future wife Elsa, Princess Xavier, Colonel Tylden and Miles Bunting are travelling in the compartment that receives the direct hit. Yet all these people are regrouped in New York at the present time. Paul and Elsa have managed to conceive a son and daughter. Naturally in the circumstances none of the characters is quite normal. ('The norm in the air about Elsa and Paul is the war with Germany.') Elsa's shadow falls the wrong way and this causes her analyst to remark that she has externalized her problem. Poppy Xavier breeds silk-worms that crawl over her bosom to create, as a visual pun, an image of decay.

Elsa is the most important person in this highly charged little parable of delusion and alienation, with its complicated structure in which every statement is either literal or symbolic. ' "Her shadow falls the way it wants to," ' her son declares; and certainly she is most aware of all the possibilities in each *trompe d'oeil* situation.

On one level, the story is simply a rationalization of the statement 'We really lived our life'—a dig at nostalgists who idealize their own past. Naturally in retrospect the last war may be considered as a time of excitement and fulfilment, when all experience was memorable and people's most admirable qualities could be displayed. ' "Oh, the war was a godsend for her. She always liked taking risks. Whatever else, she wasn't cosy," ' a character in Elaine Feinstein's *Children of the Rose* (1975) says of her mother, a French Resistance heroine shot by the Gestapo. To be credited with heroism, resilience or cheerful-ness in the face of danger, in any situation, was naturally stimulating. But in many lives the predominant quality was an unalterable drabness. In *The Dressmaker* (Beryl Bainbridge, 1973) seventeen-year-old Rita is 'so put down, so without passion, living all her life with the old women down the road. As a child she had never played out in the street, never put her dolls to sleep on the step, never hung around the chip shop on Priory Road. In the air-raid shelter she wore a hat belonging to Auntie Nellie as if she was in church.'

Rita is a natural subject for the kind of infatuation that cannot prosper, that remains dismally on one side. In love, she is ineffectual; 'joyless', the young American soldier calls her, a girl with no instinct for amusement. She has had no chance, brought up by two aunts: Nellie, the dressmaker, respectable and cantankerous; and Margo, who would be brassy and flirtatious in the right circumstances.

Ira, the soldier, is illiterate and inarticulate, but that makes no difference to Rita, a girl whose best subject at school was English. She displays all the messy hopelessness of her age: the tears, the exaggerations, ' "Oh, Auntie, I wish I was dead" '. She has no inner resources but a fear, derived from her Aunt

Nellie, of behaving badly, and even this is not strong enough to withstand the pressure of emotional desire: 'She was begging and she knew it.' Begging for notice from a dunce, a boy with a sure instinct only in relation to his own erotic needs. Auntie Margo is more to Ira's taste, 'a woman of the world' or what passes for one in the neighbourhood of Bingley Road in Liverpool. Nellie catches them in bed, loses her temper and stabs the young man in the neck with her dressmaking scissors, causing him to meet his death in a fall downstairs. Ira's grubby little association with Rita, which began in a wardrobe at Valerie Mander's party, ends when the boy is sewn into a chenille curtain by Nellie who remains impassive, 'very capable, a dressmaker to her bones'.

Valerie Mander is the alluring girl who lives near by, successful in her pursuit of an American soldier where Rita has failed. All over England, hopeful, pushing, red-lipped girls are converging on the American army bases, avid for promises, for enjoyment, for amatory prestige. In Ladies' Rooms they stand in rows, combing their hair and rubbing sand into bare legs to create an impression of silk. 'The war had made everyone lax, openly immodest. It wasn't only the Yanks. There were all the jokes she heard at work about girls in the Land Army getting in the hay with the Italian prisoners of war, and Up with the Lark, and To Bed with a Wren.'

An assumption of moral deterioration is constant in some strata of society; if it cannot be ascribed to war, then it is the pressures of modern life. In *The Dressmaker*, Uncle Jack the butcher is outspoken about the behaviour of girls who run after soldiers: '"They're wicked women."' Rita knows better, but it is only her youth and a kind of muted goodwill that make her more tolerant: 'The women looked common enough with their bleached hair and their mouths pouting as they put on lipstick, but they weren't wicked.'

The death of Ira is the extreme event that illuminates the force of the tensions underlying these ordinary lives. This is its function on the plane of social comment; but it also infuses the narrative with a sense of ironic absurdity and takes it beyond the idiom of the merely factual. However, Beryl Bainbridge, like Henry Green, knows how to present the trite or commonplace from an unexpected angle that gives it an edge of complexity.

It is the retrospective view that enables her to give exactly the right emphasis to the condition of being at war. This is not an overwhelming state, as it would have been in a contemporary novel; it has faded to the point where it functions without drama, as a background atmosphere. There is no war action, even as it affected the civilian population. The bombing has taken place off-stage and its effect is merely to add to the city's dejection and disorder:

> When the roof split open, the prams and bedding spilled from the top floor to the next, mingling with Auntie Nellie's rolls of dress material, snaking out wantonly into the burning night, flying outwards higgledy piggledy, with the smart hats hurled from their stands, the frail gauze veils spotted with sequins shrivelling like cobwebs, tumbling down through the air to be buried under the bricks and the iron girders—covered now by the grass and the great clumps of weed that sprouted flowers, rusty red and purple, their heads swinging like fox-gloves as the tram lurched round the corner and began the steep ascent to Everton Brow.

The débris of wartime—the corrugated iron shelters, barbed wire, pill boxes, Nissen huts, unexploded shells and stretches of concrete—is absorbed into the natural landscape of Beryl Bainbridge's stories. In *A Quiet Life* (1976), unruly fifteen-year-old Madge is 'cavorting' with a German prisoner, shortly to be repatriated, while her brother Alan becomes increasingly anxious about her welfare. 'He wouldn't put it past Madge to be hanging about the Camp, though God knows what she hoped to attract, wearing her mac and knee socks.' Some time earlier the depraved girl has been caught showing her bottom to the evacuees across the railway line. In *Harriet Said* (1973) it is Italian prisoners who provide for the precocious central characters an opportunity for sexual misbehaviour. In the society evoked by Beryl Bainbridge the sexual instinct is repressed in accordance with ideas of respectability; but girls like Madge have a natural style and gaiety, an ability to deride convention. Madge goes her own way, upsetting her brother and causing trouble at home, adopting an awkward or an affectionate stance as it suits her, being silly about the German

soldier and extravagant in her pronouncements. It is a remarkably sparing, delicate portrait; especially since the girl is seen
all the time from the point of view of her inhibited brother.

The war is over, but its effects still linger. When Martha, in
Doris Lessing's *The Four-Gated City* (1972) asks for a dozen boxes
of matches at a London kiosk, she is told sourly:

> 'There's been a war on, you know.'
>   'I'm sorry, I was forgetting.'
>   'I suppose some people can.'

It is 1950: London is still full of bomb craters and people talk
incessantly about the blitz.

> Now the place where the bomb had fallen. That was how
> they spoke of it: 'the Bomb'. Their bomb, out of the thousands
> that had fallen on London. About three acres lay flat, bared
> of building. Almost—it was a half-job; the place had neither
> been cleared, nor left. . . . The ground floor of a house stood,
> shacked over with iron, in the middle, and a single wall
> reared high up from it, intact, with fire-places one above
> another.

Jacky Gillott and Nina Bawden have both written about the
long-term effects of evacuation on a central character, in each
case an illegitimate girl whose mother is soon removed from the
scene of action. One mother falls under a train at Aldgate
East Station, the other is killed in the blitz. In Jacky Gillott's
War Baby (1971) the child goes from London to stay with her
father's relatives, the Pendletons; her name is Beryl but her
cousins quickly assess her worth and call her Garbie. The
horrible child accepts this gratefully because it is 'a family
name'. She is the garbage girl who drives around with her Aunt
Cissy collecting rubbish for the war effort. Garbie is snobbish,
clumsy and graceless, an embarrassment to her relatives who
are all awful themselves in various ways. The girl can amuse her
cousins only by concocting gruesome stories of the blitz in
London. As she grows older, Garbie's aptitude for the inappropriate gesture increases. A need to be grateful has eroded
her sense of self-esteem; she is not even aware of this.

The fact that Garbie is unfortunate in her manner and circumstances will not affect the reader's disinclination to take her seriously as a character or to see in her portrait the inexorable working of cause and effect. The narrative attitude veers from sympathy to ironic exposure; but the irony is laborious, people behave selfishly or outrageously in the most obvious way and this diminishes the effect of grotesque comedy. The natural sense of selection that occurs, for instance, in Beryl Bainbridge, is missing. Rita, in *The Dressmaker*, is a bleak little girl but every detail of her personality is relevant to the author's design; she is a wholly impressive creation because she is recognizable in the sharpest sense.

In Nina Bawden's *Anna Apparent* (1972) the most horrifying possibilities in the idea of evacuation are realized: the child Annie-May is landed in a family of brutes, an imbecile woman and her degenerate half-brother, Welsh hill farmers whose cruelty is perhaps a result of ignorance—but the seven-year-old is subjected none the less to the worst excesses of ill-treatment. Because she wets the bed, she is put to sleep in an outhouse with a bundle of sacks, fed on scraps from a tin bowl and reduced to a state of inarticulate terror. The ordeal is cut short when she is rescued by Crystal Golightly, a privileged woman whose husband has just left her for an ATS worker. 'Crystal's motives were not obscure. She had lost her rôle in life and seized on a new one. The more exacting the task, the better it would compensate for her sense of outrage and failure.'

Annie-May is transformed into Anna, 'Crystal's good girl'. Sometimes, however, it frightens her to think 'she had not really changed at all but was only pretending to be someone nicer and better. . . . She was afraid of being found out.' This is the novel's principal theme, the rôles forced on Anna and the extent to which these are assumed, the confusion of 'natural' tendencies with those developed for reasons of expediency and the consequent distortion in her sense of identity. She grows up to become the second wife of Crystal's son Giles, a man with a strong feeling for the casualties of war. Earlier, Giles has married a Jewish survivor of a concentration camp—Tottie, whose wartime experiences make everyone else's seem trivial. Yet Tottie is an ordinary intelligent girl who does not want to be regarded as a victim. From the point of view of

Anna, the horrors of Auschwitz and Belsen should provide a means for getting her own experience of cruelty into perspective: she knows this. But horror is subjective, it cannot be graded in an absolute way. In Anna, the will to please is a constricting tendency, not natural. It has come about as a result of the wartime period when she was treated like an animal. She is a victim of ignorance, not organized brutality, but the effects remain.

There is no dramatic central incident in Francis King's *A Game of Patience* (1974). 'Waiting for the end' might have been an alternative title: the characters are brought together because of the war, for no other reason. Two are farm workers, seventeen-year-old Valerie Garth Merrall and an ex-undergraduate conscientious objector named Roy. Their employer is Marion Thurloe whose husband is believed to be a prisoner of the Japanese. Marion is stoical, Roy is prickly and often ill-humoured, and Valerie is a sensible but slightly disturbed teenager who has had to leave London when her home is damaged by a bomb. '. . . There, seemingly hanging without support, was the room where she had slept with her koala bear. And next door—but that was in the slice that had been spirited away—had been the room of Nanny, who had been spirited away with it.'

Valerie's sense of disorientation promotes an extreme fear of the new German weapon, the V1: a pilotless bomber that descended with terrifying randomness whenever its fuel gave out. '"You know, it's no good getting yourself into a tiz about things like that. If you've had it, you've had it,"' she is told. 'It was the popular philosophy of the day. She wished, oh how she wished, that she could share it.'

'If it's got your name on it . . .' is the catchphrase expression of this philosophy, the rendering of a kind of resolute fatalism in palatable terms. It was one way to cope with the idea of death: to accept it beforehand in a spirit of wryness or pragmatism. Generally, however, it requires a degree of insensitivity to use a popular expression without irony, and the man who so glibly reassures Valerie is indeed a person of limited discernment, a member of a balloon-barrage crew that barges into the Thurloes' sheltered Surrey village.

A village in Norfolk is the setting for Sarah Patterson's *The*

Distant Summer (1976), a first novel of remarkable competence considering that its author was only fourteen when she wrote it. Beyond this, it is a work of noticeable self-indulgence and sentimentality. Its popular romantic theme is love, requited and unrequited, and the peculiar difficulties encountered when its professors have to contend also with the stresses of war. Sixteen-year-old Katherine's love for Johnny is chaste, deep and unalterable: he is a young rear gunner with bleak indifference in his empty eyes, a dauntless, reckless lad who is sometimes filled with incommunicable pain and anger at the futility of war, 'the waste'.

The brave young men conceal their inner feelings behind a façade of indifference or light-heartedness but they don't fool Kate, a girl whose heart lifts when she hears the opening chords of 'Jerusalem'. Johnny is a pianist:

> ... I stood behind the Bechstein and put a hand on it. 'There's still this.'
> 'How long for?' he said gravely.
> 'Does it matter? All we ever have is a day at a time.'

Johnny is cheered by Kate's wisdom, but soon he has relapsed into a state of moroseness: '"Find someone with a future, Kate, and forget me. I'm already dead."' But in fact it is another pilot who has to die, the American Richie whose feelings for Kate are chivalrously repressed. Johnny survives to become older and a little stiffer with the years. 'Some stories do have happy endings, even in real life. . . .' Poor Richie, dear Richie who finds Kate irresistible is an object for romantic pity, handsome and dashing and awfully noble in the way that he is able to renounce both love and life in a carefree manner. Only at one point do his emotions overwhelm him: 'He turned my hand over and kissed the palm fiercely.'

It is interesting to compare this novel with romantic fiction written during the second world war: it is simpler, more straightforward and apparently more realistic, at least in its avoidance of patriotic guff. The patriotic motive for fighting is entirely discounted; but this has come about because motivations of a complex nature are outside the author's area of concern. Her young men are heroic and sensitive because these are basic qualities attractive to the narrator. In fact the wartime setting merely provides an opportunity to show spectacular courage and comradeship in action. It also enables the author to add the ingredient of poignancy to an ordinary adolescent tangle of emotions. In these respects the book resembles the currently popular children's battle comics which use the war situation to present a rationalization of legitimate aggression at a very low level.

POSTSCRIPT

'Happiness was a mug of tea, a cigarette, and a
record of Bunny Berrigan playing "Let's do it".
Sharing it with a friend . . . rounded off the occasion. What's happened to us all since then? . . .'
Spike Milligan, *Adolf Hitler: My Part in His Downfall*

REFERENCE TO BOTH the wars has persisted in literature
throughout the twentieth century, providing a complex of
traditional imagery, all kinds of ironic connections and
transpositions; and a major thread of continuity.

At the most obvious level the first world war has been invoked
in terms of horror, revulsion and confusion; or regarded as a
time of strengthened resolve and heroism. Not surprisingly, after
four years of mass slaughter, novelists writing retrospectively
about the war often sought to justify the sacrifice of so many
young men's lives. We have seen the backwards-and-forwards
shift of attitudes: chauvinism gave way to realism, and that was
followed by cynical repudiation. At the same time, backward-
looking novelists like Ernest Raymond began to romanticize the
concept of war when it was safely in the past.

The effects of the first world war on women and children
were seldom given serious consideration in fiction. Stories
appeared, of course, in which they were cast in the expected
rôles of widows or fatherless children. There was, however, no
vital reflection of the new independence that the war had
brought to many women who had then earned their livelihood
for the first time; or of their increased capacity to undertake
family and community responsibilities during the prolonged
absence of their husbands, sons and fathers. The view of
women's behaviour in wartime was still largely traditional,
coloured by a moralistic or an idealistic preconception. When
the change in women's situation *was* alluded to, it was often in
an extremely biased way—for instance, a prurient fascination
with the effects of the sexual freedom that is endemic in a time
of crisis.

There was little credit in adult fiction for the women who drove ambulances and underwent dangers comparable with those of the trenches, a deficiency noted by Vera Brittain who attempted to rectify it in her own novels in the 1930s. At the time, in fact, women's patriotic spirit was usually acknowledged only in a context where it was presented with a lack of light and shade that made it appear ridiculous: in the stories, for example, of children's writers like Angela Brazil and Bessie Marchant whose heroines were always fearfully eager to get off to the front with no regard for the consequences. (In this way the first world war at least *did* provide a bonus for real-life children of both sexes; there was a profusion of lively, if unrealistic, adventure fiction.) In these stories, as in many topical and romantic novels for adults, there is guarded praise for women's efforts so long as these do not clash with the conventional attributes of femininity.

None of the leading writers of the Modern Movement had direct experience of the trenches, and few were concerned with the kind of direct transcription that war writing appeared to demand. Nevertheless the war had unavoidable repercussions in their work. In criticism of T. S. Eliot, for example, it has become statutory to remark that *The Waste Land* is composed of images of disintegration that have a particular relevance to the immediate past: the four years of the Great War. In *Jacob's Room* (Virginia Woolf, 1920) the central character is killed in Flanders; the war is used therefore to furnish an appropriate conclusion to the life of a typically well-meaning but innocent young man; and the innocence of the whole pre-war era is thereby illuminated.

This loss of personal and collective innocence is a recurrent theme in the fiction and popular culture of both the wars. Each of them marked the schism between the accepted way of life that preceded it, and a challenging new social structure that grew up in its aftermath. When the second world war began, the memory of the first was still extremely potent for many young adults who had been children in 1914–1918. Long before the pernicious effects of Nazi policies became widely known, they had grown up regarding Germany as the traditional enemy. This view was supported, at various levels of seriousness, by the propaganda of the first world war and its retrospective

fiction and films; also by the occasional, rueful remarks of their
ex-soldier fathers about the only good Germans being dead ones.

Before it began, the developments of the second world war
were often of course envisaged in terms of the first, or at the
end of the '30s, of the Spanish Civil War. (It was feared, for
instance, that women and children streaming out of the cities
would block the roads and provide targets for bombers, like
panic-stricken refugees killed at Malaga in 1937.)

In one recent novel (David Martin's *The Ceremony of Innocence*,
1977) there is a symbolic lunatic figure, Shellshock Sam. He
wanders through the streets with the delusion that he is still in
the trenches: 'waiting, Lieutenant Sam, for a future that is
already history, weary, counting out the weeks, months, years,
of a past that is yet to come—*Mon Dieu, que la guerre est longue!*'
The ironic point of this old soldier's confusion is that the wheel
has come full circle: there *is* a war, though it is not the one he
imagines. In fact his demented roving is extended right up to
the present time, when he finds himself standing once again in a
bombed-out ruin (the novel is set in Ulster).

Shellshock Sam is an obvious linking device, but there are
other ways in which the literature and the myths of each war
impinge upon each other, and upon the present, in the provision of images, modes of response or significant moments of
displacement. For example, Vernon Scannell, who fought in
the second world war, finds none the less 'Whenever war is
spoken of / . . . The war that was called Great invades the
mind.'

Naturally many women after 1918 experienced an acute
sense of futility and disorientation. For some, normal family life
would not be possible because of the large scale extermination
of so many of the potential husbands of the same generation;
and as a result of the post-war economic depression women
were often no longer welcomed in jobs which they had come to
take for granted during the war.

The 'war to end wars' is today remembered largely in terms
of slaughter and sacrifice. However when the war of 1939–1945
is recapitulated, its home front activities are frequently evoked.
The heightened intensity of the period remains an extraordinary attraction for writers of fiction (as well as producers
of the television programmes and films that are avidly watched

K

even by people who never experienced the war). Equally fascinating to the popular imagination are the songs and printed ephemera of the war, and its fashions—square-shouldered, skimpy, drab, and yet in retrospect strangely appealing. The authentic atmosphere is to some extent still accessible in records which were kept at the time by the official photographers and war artists, who conscientiously illustrated bomb damage, fire fighting, food queues and life in the improvised tube-station air-raid shelters. Less formalized but more compelling reflections of ways in which the war involved women and children are available in recorded radio programmes and illustrated magazines of the time.

During the war the national appetite for poetry and most kinds of fiction increased. An obvious reason was the limitation of available entertainment. Theatres and cinemas reopened soon after the war began, but were often inaccessible because of blackout travel difficulties. Children in the air-raid danger zones were particularly restricted in this way. Their lives tended to focus only on school and the home; even street games began to wane in popularity as worried mothers endeavoured to keep their children safely indoors—or in the shelters. During these long, cooped-up hours many children started to read more widely. There was often not much else for them to do, except to listen to the wireless.

It is significant that a book greatly in demand by adult readers was Tolstoy's *War and Peace*. Its title of course had a special relevance. In war, peacetime is seen as an idyllic period just as war, in peacetime, can take on the symbolic qualities necessary to make a coherent pattern of the experience. (There was another reason for the popularity of *War and Peace*. Members of the BBC Brains Trust panel had been asked to select the world's finest novels, and nearly all of them included *War and Peace* in their choice. A tremendously popular—and long—radio serialization soon followed and the novel was sold from bookstalls throughout the country.) There was too a newly awakened interest in everything that came out of Russia. Her people had suddenly and surprisingly been forced into the war on the same side as Britain, and they were resisting the previously invincible German armies with astounding ferocity and courage.

The development of suitable literary forms for fiction and poetry during the second world war did not follow a pattern of progression comparable with that of the first. There was no need: sophisticated modes for rendering the experience of war already existed. In poetry, there was nothing to match the outpourings of Rupert Brooke and others in 1914. Romantic fiction, of course, continued to present its patriotism in emotional or elevated terms; but literature at this level, though it responds quickly to alterations in fashion or idiom, is usually slow to adapt itself to fundamental change. In the second world war there were many resolutely bright and topical stories of the women's services, Land army and girls in government employment. Most of these had the standard happy ending. At the same time, in keeping with the mood of uncertainty—for no one could be sure of having any future—even light fiction writers produced some books that ended on a note of unresolved challenge.

In children's fiction, another genre that was slow to develop before the 1960s, the last war provided a stimulus for writers like Richmal Crompton and Noel Streatfeild who turned out some of their best work then. Children were making their own contribution to the war effort and their increasing consciousness of social responsibilities led to the beginning of the vogue for 'teenage' stories in this country. (They were of course already popular in America.) Fiction of this nature was featured in wartime issues of magazines like the *Girl's Own Paper* and *Boy's Own Paper*; it was an extension of the school stories that had been standard fare in the 1920s and 1930s. Fictional boys and girls started to function in a broader society than the school community. Such stories were still distinct from adult romance novels. The emphasis was on doing one's bit for the war effort and, in this context, careers as a theme assumed a special significance in children's fiction. After the war there was a proliferation of career books, especially for girls. Like record and fashion manufacturers, publishers discovered the new and profitable adolescent market. ('Teenager' of course is largely a post-war term. Between 1939 and 1945, one recognized expression for girls who were 'too old for toys and too young for boys' was 'in-betweens', after a song popularized by the young Judy Garland.)

Present-day children's writers have found a rich source of material in the wartime era; the current fascination with the years between 1939 and 1945 is derived partly from a wish to look back at the areas that were completely ignored in fiction written at the time. Children's writers of the '40s were hedged in by many restrictions that no longer operate; the most obvious of these was the necessity for euphemism in relation to the effects of aerial bombardment. In adult fiction, the impulse to re-create wartime experience is usually more subtle; there is a general tendency to make the implicit point of a connection between the stresses of war and the various inadequacies in the structure of modern life.

As far as women and their rôle in war is concerned, the conventional images have been identified and to an extent repudiated. At any rate, they have been re-examined with suitable reference to the social requirements that led to their development. Anachronistic ideas of self-sacrifice and un-principled seductiveness were treated with ridicule almost as soon as they were postulated; but between these laughable extremes there is a whole range of stereotypes whose embodiments appear more or less reasonable in fiction of the wars. Of course it is impossible to avoid the use of stereotypes in any real sense; every character naturally can be classified in one way or another. But in modern fiction there is more knowledge of the distortions inherent in rigid forms of classification. There is more scope for humour and ambiguity. From a feminist point of view, in sociological terms, the wars provide the most obvious contradictions of certain assumptions about women's innate incapacities. There is still room for a great deal of fiction on this subject.

It is of course not only certain writers who are preoccupied with looking back to the second world war. Amongst people who remember the period, and many who do not, there is a desire to recapture or evaluate the extraordinary amalgam of insecurity and exhilaration, boredom and heightened aware-ness, solidarity and bloody-mindedness that was then prevalent. There was, for many people in the 1920s and 1930s a similar retrospective attraction about the first world war. That war began with idealism and ended in varying degrees of disillusion. At the beginning of the second world war the mood was more subdued, but in 1945 there was a buoyant anticipation that the better society promised after the *first* world war would at last come into being. Women, of course, expected to play a significant part in the creation of this. Also—although concepts of 'pupil power' were far away in the future—children and adolescents began to demand a voice in the organization of their society.

SELECT BIBLIOGRAPHY

Anderson, Rachel, *The Purple Heart Throbs*, Hodder & Stoughton, London, 1974

Bato, Joseph, *Defiant City*, Gollancz, London, 1942

Brittain, Vera, *Lady into Woman*, Andrew Dakers, London, 1953

—— *Testament of Youth*, Gollancz, London, 1933

Bigland, Eileen, *The Story of the W.R.N.S.*, Nicholson & Watson, London, 1946

Burton, Elaine F., *What of the Women*, Muller, London, 1941

Calder, Angus, *The People's War*, Cape, London, 1969

Chase, Edna Woolman, and Ilka, *Always in Vogue*, Gollancz, London, 1954

Cockburn, Claud, *Bestseller*, Sidgwick & Jackson, London, 1972

Fayne, Eric and Jenkins, Roger, *A History of the Gem & Magnet*, Museum Press, Maidstone, 1972

FitzGibbon, Constantine, *The Blitz*, Allan Wingate, London, 1957

Fussell, Paul, *The Great War and Modern Memory*, OUP, London, 1975

Goldsmith, Margaret, *Women at War*, Drummond, London, 1943

Johnson, B. S. (ed.), *The Evacuees*, Gollancz, London, 1968

Johnston, John H., *English Poetry of the First World War*, OUP, London, 1964

Klemmer, Harvey, *They'll Never Quit*, Right Book Club, London, 1942.

Marwick, Arthur, *The Home Front*, Thames & Hudson, London, 1976

—— *Women at War, 1914–1918*, Fontana, London, 1977

Priestley, J. B., *British Women Go to War*, 1945

—— *Out of the People*, Collins, in association with Heinemann, London, 1941

—— *The Edwardians*, Heinemann, London, 1970

Stafford, Ann, *An Army Without Banners*, Collins, London, 1942

Spender, Stephen, *Citizens in War—And After*, Harrap, London, 1945

Usborne, Richard, *Clubland Heroes* (revised edition), Barrie & Jenkins, London, 1974

—— *Jane at War*, Wolfe Publishing Ltd., London, 1976

—— *King and Country: Selections from British War Speeches*, Chatto & Windus, London, 1940

INDEX